Equality, Discrimination and the Law

When Mr and Mrs James – each aged 61 – went swimming, Mr James was charged for entry, while Mrs James was admitted free. The reason was that the local authority offered free swimming to those of 'pensionable age' (at the time, 65 for men and 60 for women). The House of Lords found that Mr James had suffered direct sex discrimination. This majority plurality decision indicated that sometimes a given set of facts does not neatly accord to traditional definitions of discrimination. This in turn encourages the judiciary to shape the law to fit the facts, which results in an inconsistent body of law full of 'fuzzy borders'. Starting with the James case, this book investigates a number of 'fuzzy border' cases in the EU and UK based on nationality discrimination, notions of indirect discrimination, pregnancy and sex discrimination, marriage and sexual orientation discrimination, perceived discrimination, and victimisation. The argument concludes that fixed notions such as 'direct and indirect discrimination are mutually exclusive' do not stand up to scrutiny and that it must be recognised that the traditional concepts of discrimination and victimisation do not reflect the reality of practice.

This work is essential reading for students, scholars and practitioners in all EU and English-speaking jurisdictions, particularly post-graduates, Policy/Lawmakers, and those on dedicated equality undergraduate courses.

Michael Connolly is a Reader in Law at the University of Portsmouth, UK, who specialises in Equality Law. He also serves on the Equality, Diversity and Inclusion Committee of the Society of Legal Scholars, and the London Management Committee of the Commonwealth Legal Education Association.

Equality, Discrimination and the Law

Michael Connolly

Routledge
Taylor & Francis Group
LONDON AND NEW YORK

First published 2022
by Routledge
4 Park Square, Milton Park, Abingdon, Oxon OX14 4RN

and by Routledge
605 Third Avenue, New York, NY 10158

Routledge is an imprint of the Taylor & Francis Group, an informa business

British Library Cataloguing-in-Publication Data
A catalogue record for this book is available from the British Library

Library of Congress Cataloging-in-Publication Data
A catalog record has been requested for this book

ISBN: 978-0-367-85709-7 (hbk)
ISBN: 978-1-032-03486-7 (pbk)
ISBN: 978-1-003-18754-7 (ebk)

DOI: 10.4324/9781003187547

Typeset in Bembo
by Taylor & Francis Books

Contents

Table of Cases

Australia

Canada

European Court of Human Rights

European Union

Ireland

United Kingdom

United States

Table of Legislation

Belgium

Canada

Council of Europe

European Union

Treaties

Regulations

Directives

United Kingdom

Statutes

Statutory Instruments

United States

About the author

Michael Connolly is a Reader in Law at the University of Portsmouth, UK, who specialises in Equality Law. His academic legal education began at Ealing College of Higher Education (LLB) (nowadays, University of West London), and progressed to the University of Warwick (LLM), and University College London (PhD).

His principal research interest is in Discrimination and Equality Law, especially the employment discrimination laws of the United Kingdom, the European Union, the United States, South Africa, Canada, and Australasia. He speaks regularly on this subject in the UK, the Commonwealth, and the United States. He has published many papers on domestic and comparative discrimination law, and four books on the subject.

Michael also serves on the Equality, Diversity and Inclusion Committee of the Society of Legal Scholars, and the London Management Committee of the Commonwealth Legal Education Association.

1 Introduction

Suppose a local authority had a concern for retired persons, who as a group, live in isolation and lack physical activity. It resolved to offer free swimming to those of a pensionable age, at a time when the state pension age was 60 for women and 65 for men. When Mr and Mrs James, each aged 61, approached the turnstile, he was charged for entry, while she was admitted free. Mr James sued for direct sex discrimination. Whether the authority is liable could turn on a number of factors, including the motivation of the authority (socialisation and fitness of a particularly vulnerable group), the 'foreground' reason (facially neutral pension ages), or the 'background' reason (discriminatory pension ages). In the mix as well could be variations of the comparison. These could range from a one-to-one (a 60-year-old man compared with a 60-year-old woman), a limited group (all those aged 60–65), or men and women generally. The first two comparisons would produce an exclusive advantage/disadvantage for women and men respectively, pointing to direct discrimination. The third itself is packed with variations, ranging from those who attend the swimming pool, or in addition those who *would* attend but for the charge, or those in the catchment area, or men and women more generally. Any of these *might* demonstrate a disproportionate impact on men, and will point to indirect discrimination.

The point is, this could be direct or indirect discrimination, depending upon the doctrinal view taken. It matters, because only indirect discrimination would provide the local authority with a defence, which is likely to succeed in a case such as this. To the layperson, what matters is whether the ingredient of sex discrimination against men outweighs the benign motive of the local authority. This could play a role in any litigation as a 'policy matter'. Beyond those concerns, one could venture quite reasonably that this was both directly and indirectly discriminatory.

A good starting place to discuss these questions is Lady Hale's assertion that 'Direct and indirect discrimination are mutually exclusive'.[1] Of course, any

1 *R (E) v Governing Body of JFS* [2010] 2 AC 728 (SC) [57] (Baroness Hale). See also: *R (Elias) v Secretary of State for Defence* [2006] 1 WLR 3213 (CA) [114] and [119] (Mummery LJ).

DOI: 10.4324/9781003187547-1

such assertion is a risky one, inviting just a single undreamt-of case to undermine it. As this book illustrates, there were already many such instances. Indeed, at about the same time Lady Hale wrote her opinion, at the European Court of Justice Advocate General Sharpston opined that 'the distinction between direct and indirect discrimination lacks precision'.[2] This may not be an overly helpful observation, but the admission of uncertainty is at least faithful to the reality of the case law. Sometime earlier, again in the Court of Justice, Advocate General Jacobs advised that it was not always necessary to distinguish between direct and indirect discrimination on grounds of sex. He was alluding to the equal pay regimes, which for historic reasons, have a different evidential basis which tends to blur the boundary.[3] Nonetheless, the Canadian Supreme Court took a more sweeping view and abolished the distinction altogether.[4] It is not the purpose of this book to enter into the debate as to whether or not the distinction should be abolished.[5] It is merely to highlight that there are many fuzzy borders in the doctrinal structure of existing discrimination law, and that strident statements such as Lady Hale's do not always hold true.

The first two chapters examine the case law in the context of Lady Hale's assertion. The book then examines a number of areas of discrimination law, where again hard and fast borders cannot be guaranteed, returning occasionally to Lady Hale's theme.

Chapter 2 examines the difficulties of 'incorporated' and 'cumulative' cases. The first is where a facially neutral policy incorporates a facially discriminatory factor, such as the swimming pool example above, played out in *James v Eastleigh BC*,[6] which, as if to emphasise the confusion, produced a plurality majority decision reversing all below. 'Cumulative' cases involve multiple and alternative factors for qualification, where just one is discriminatory. Here, the ECJ has analysed the factors as a single bundle, a suspiciously general approach, suggesting a policy-led agenda and seemingly at odds with the decision in *James*.

The doctrinal origins of that debate lay in the attempts to reconcile pregnancy discrimination as sex discrimination. This reasoning is examined in Chapter 3, which highlights a long-standing difference of thinking, this time, between the common and civil law jurisdictions. Common law thinking, deferential to literary interpretation, centres on the reality that as not all women

2 C-73/08 *Bressol* [2010] 3 CMLR 20, para AG46.
3 C-79/99 *Schnorbus v Land Hessen* [2000] ECR I-10997, para AG30.
4 *British Columbia (Public Service Employee Relations Commission) v BCGEU ('Meiorin')* [1999] 3 SCR 3 at paras 27–29, 50–53; extended beyond employment to all areas by *British Columbia (Superintendent of Motor Vehicles) v British Columbia (Council of Human Rights) ('Grismer')* [1999] 3 SCR 868, at para 19.
5 See e.g. Hugh Collins & Tarunabh Khaitan, *Foundations of Indirect Discrimination Law* (Oxford: Hart Publishing, 2018); Andy Yu, 'Direct and Indirect Discrimination, a Distinction with a Difference' (2019) 9(2) *Western Journal of Legal Studies*https://ojs.lib.uwo.ca/index.php/uwojls/article/view/8072 accessed 30 December 2020.
6 [1990] 2 AC 751 (HL).

are or become pregnant, any discrimination could only be indirect, opening the anti-policy possibility of employers justifying pregnancy discrimination for cold-eyed but legitimate business reasons. This necessitated dedicated legislation for pregnancy discrimination, which does not resemble discrimination law in any doctrinal sense. By contrast, the Court of Justice asserted baldly that as only women become pregnant, pregnancy discrimination amounts the direct sex discrimination. Subsequent attempts to rationalise this have explained that pregnancy is 'necessarily linked' to gender, or 'indissociable' from it (AG Jacobs),[7] or that there was an 'exact coincidence' between the challenged practice and its impact on men and women (AG Sharpston).[8] The matter became even more fuzzy when, after the ECJ ignored these rationalisations, the UK Supreme Court took them up as explanations for *James* as well as their own cumulative cases. Within this, there was disagreement as to their meaning, and an apparent unfamiliarity with AG Jacobs' qualification that *legal* links were excluded from his indissociable rubric (something discredited in turn as the ECJ linked sex discrimination with maternity leave). A fairly obvious problem here is a willingness of lawyers all too quickly to create rubrics of general principle that do not stand up and certainly do not survive migration to other legal species.

Chapter 4 moves away from the direct/indirect debate, with a focus on the fuzzy borders around the notion of indirect discrimination. Rather than a focus on the border between direct and indirect discrimination, this chapter looks at scenarios where there is either indirect discrimination or no discrimination. The problem is highlighted in cases that policy suggests should be held to be discriminatory. These are the mistreatment of vulnerable migrant workers. Again, we see there is no clear border here.

Chapter 5 continues with an examination of the objective justification defence deployed for indirect discrimination. There is a concealed difference of opinion again between civil law and common law jurisdictions of the EU and the UK, with the EU imposing its strict proportionality formula and the UK covertly drifting towards the notion of reasonableness, invoking notions of *Wednesbury*.[9] The UK approach is mired in rather duplicitous language, creating another fuzzy border.

Chapter 6 explores the notion of 'perceived discrimination', whereby a person treats unfavourably another because of a mistaken belief that the other possesses a protected characteristic. The archetypal example is a shopkeeper refusing to serve a turbaned Sikh man misperceiving him as a Muslim (and in the wake of the 9/11 attacks on New York, associating him with the Islamic

7 C-79/99 *Schnorbus v Land Hessen* [2000] ECR I-10997*Schnorbus v Land Hessen*, para AG56.

8 C-73/08 *Bressol v Gouvernement De La Communauté Française* [2010] 3 CMLR 20, paras AG33 and AG36-AG41.

9 *Associated Provincial Picture Houses Ltd v Wednesbury Corporation* [1948] 1 KB 223 (CA) provided the common law standard for judicial review, before its shift towards proportionality.

terrorist Osama bin Laden). Policy expressly dictates there should be liability for perceived discrimination, yet the statutory formula presented to the judiciary does not lend itself to this. This is either because of the absence of a comparator with a different protected characteristic (the claimant in the example is not a Muslim) or, for disability, because it is unlikely the defendant would assume somebody has all the technical characteristics required to satisfy the legal definition of disability. There is a tendency here to disregard the comparison where the reason for the treatment is obvious. The problem with this is that it places an undue focus on the reason for the treatment, and brings the law back to a problem highlighted in *James*, that is whether the meaning of direct discrimination should turn on the motive of the defendant.

Chapter 7 picks up on the theme of comparisons, this time in the context of a requirement to be married as a proxy for sexual orientation discrimination. England's senior courts cannot agree on whether such a proxy was directly or indirectly discriminatory. In two cases, one decided in the Court of Appeal, and the other running to the Supreme Court, the judges were divided six-five in holding that hoteliers barring unmarried couples amounted to direct sexual orientation discrimination. Unlike *James*, the focus in these cases was on the comparison rather than the reason for the treatment. At the time before same-sex marriage, the technical difficulty stemmed from the statutory requirement that marriage (uniquely opposite-sex) and civil partnerships (uniquely same-sex) were to be treated as the same thing. Among other things, this caused problems for same-sex couples not in a civil partnership but suffering the same treatment. Otherwise, the matter has largely been ameliorated by the introduction of same-sex marriage and opposite-sex civil partnerships, thus removing the major anomalies. But the problem remains, notably, for those facing a requirement to be 'married according to the Holy Bible', another facially neutral requirement incorporating a facially discriminatory factor.

Chapter 8 addresses not so much a fuzzy border, but a gulf, between expressed state policy and judicial practice regarding compulsory retirement and age discrimination. Unusually, direct age discrimination is provided with an objective justification defence, albeit defined in stricter terms than that for indirect discrimination. The arrival of the Coalition Government in 2010 produced a U-turn in government policy towards this issue. State policy from then on expressed the wish that older workers continue to work past any notional retirement age and that stereotypes regarding fitness and performance should be disregarded, as they would be for any other protected characteristics. In the meantime, the ECJ directed that the justification defence should turn on each state's social policy. However, the UK courts have entirely ignored this and followed ECJ decisions based on other state social policies, which, unlike the UK's, have been extremely generous towards employers.

Finally, Chapter 9 examines the problem of victimisation provisions containing no defence. The provisions are included in the principal anti-discrimination legislation in the United States, EU, as well as the United Kingdom. These are to protect those who complain about discrimination, or bring proceedings, or merely give evidence in such proceedings. The difficulty arises when a defendant defends a case with the normal vigour associated with litigation. Any such move is likely to be unfavourable to the claimant and as such results in victimisation. This chapter examines the courts' attempts to provide a 'reasonable' defence when none exists in the statutory provisions. These attempts are somewhat clumsy and have created yet another fuzzy border: the basis of any defence is not at all clear. This chapter argues that there is no easy solution for statutory interpretation, and suggests legislative amendments to resolve the problem.

Within all the various doctrines and approaches documented here and throughout the book, there are more subdivisions and subtleties. For example, for direct discrimination, a form-based requirement for facially discriminatory conduct would exclude incorporated and cumulative cases, while a requirement for discriminatory intent would *include* the cumulative cases, but not an incorporated one such as *James* (because of the benign motive). In the meantime, such cases could turn instead on the comparison taken. This is especially so in the case of *James*, but extends to pregnancy, sexual orientation, and perceived discrimination. And while pregnancy discrimination can amount to *sex* discrimination under the indissociable rubric, it can only do so under the exact coincidence rubric if one assumes that only women can become pregnant, rather than acknowledging that not all women actually become pregnant and are not pregnant all of the time. A similar factual analysis is required for cumulative cases to amount to direct discrimination. The requirement here is to isolate the challenged factor, rather than rolling up into a single bundle with all the compensatory non-discriminatory factors, a suspiciously general analysis suggesting a policy-led agenda.

The UK courts are also capable of driving the proverbial coach and horses through the statutory formula to fulfil a policy aim. This is the case with perceived discrimination, but not for the mistreatment of vulnerable migrant workers or the forced retirement of older workers. The UK courts here have decided these cases, respectively, on an apparently literal interpretation of the statutory formulas or a misplaced deference to ECJ authority.

Another rather obvious policy, and one expressed by the ECJ, is that the victimisation provisions are there, among other things, to prevent employers acting in a way to deter persons from making complaints of discrimination. Yet, this policy imperative, and ECJ authority, has played no part in the UK's victimisation cases. Instead, the doctrinal approach has been tainted with a barely disguised sympathy for the employer.

For discrimination, the permutations are therefore many and varied, and probably far too many to assemble into the comprehensible matrix. The judicial approaches are not the only cause of the fuzzy borders. It must be acknowledged that the direct/indirect statutory model (which itself varies between the EU, the UK, and the United States) does not neatly encapsulate human behaviour. The same could be said, but to a much lesser degree, of the statutory definitions of direct and indirect discrimination, and victimisation.

This is especially so with the United States' requirement for a discriminatory intent and little focus on a comparison, which is in contrast to the form-based approach generally taken in the EU and the UK. But within that, the judiciary has many options and it is here that fuzzy borders again are created.

Lady Hale's assertion that direct and indirect discrimination are mutually exclusive can hold up only as long as the law forces that analysis of any set of facts. Judging where the border is between the two, and between other areas of discrimination law remains a matter of discretion for the judiciary, and one of mystery or luck for the litigant.

2 Incorporated and cumulative cases

Direct or indirect?

Introduction

The importance of the distinction between direct and indirect discrimination lies in the much more general defence of objective justification available for indirect discrimination. Direct discrimination remains very difficult to defend. Lady Hale's assertion that 'Direct and indirect discrimination are mutually exclusive'[1] appears highly relevant to this distinction. It assumes that any set of facts cannot be both at the same time. This of course relies on the clear and widely understood borderline between the two. But, as Advocate General Sharpston observed at about the same time as Lady Hale's assertion, 'the distinction between direct and indirect discrimination lacks precision'.[2] This is true. There are many cases where the distinction lies either in policy, the particular judge, and/or the tools used to discover the type of discrimination. Rather than an agreed definition of direct and indirect discrimination, these factors can dictate whether a given set of facts could be designated as direct or indirect discrimination. Indeed, as we shall see below, the highest courts repeatedly divide over whether any given set of facts amounts to direct or indirect discrimination, leaving the matter somewhat uncertain. It may be that all of these opinions do not breach Lady Hale's assertion as they eventually plumped for one or the other. But for this assertion is to have more than this limited utility, one must be able to recognise direct from indirect discrimination. Given this uncertain case law, such recognition is not always possible.

There are two particular classes of case where the border is particularly fuzzy. According to this case law, any given set of facts could amount to either direct or indirect discrimination. These arise where a facially neutral factor incorporates a facially discriminatory one, or where a cumulative 'bundle' of rules includes just a facially discriminatory one. Each is discussed in turn below.

1 *R (E) v Governing Body of JFS* [2010] 2 AC 728 (SC) [57] (Baroness Hale). See also: *R (Elias) v Secretary of State for Defence* [2006] 1 WLR 3213 (CA) [114] and [119] (Mummery LJ).

2 C-73/08 *Bressol v Gouvernement De La Communauté Française* [2010] 3 CMLR 20, para AG46.

DOI: 10.4324/9781003187547-2

'Incorporated' cases

The varying importance of the incorporated rule

These 'incorporated' cases occur where a facially neutral policy incorporates a facially discriminatory rule. Three cases illustrate the difficulties arising if this is not recognised. The simplest involve just two causes of the treatment, *a* policy and *a* rule. In *James v Eastleigh BC*,[3] the Council's municipal swimming baths admitted free-of-charge persons 'of pensionable age'. In the United Kingdom at the time, the state pension age was 65 for men and 60 for women.[4] So when Mr and Mrs James, each aged 61, visited the baths, Mrs James was admitted free whilst Mr James was required to pay. Mr James invoked the Sex Discrimination Act 1975 and complained that he had been treated less favourably on the ground of his sex. The Council's policy was to 'give benefits to those whose resources would be likely to have been reduced by retirement' to 'aid the needy'; it was not motivated not by sex.[5] The county court found for the Council. The Court of Appeal upheld the decision, expressly agreeing with the Council's reasoning, but as we, a bare majority of the House of Lords reversed, finding that the Council directly discriminated against Mr James.[6]

R (E) v Governing Body of JFS[7] was a slightly more complex case. Again, there was a division of opinion. In the Supreme Court, eight speeches and a five-four split on the direct/indirect question. The case centred on the admissions policy of an Orthodox Jewish school. It gave preference to children recognised as Orthodox Jewish by the Office of the Chief Rabbi (OCR), which required that the child's mother be Jewish either by matrilineal descent or by conversion under the OCR doctrine. The child, 'M', was refused admission because he did not meet these requirements. His Italian (previously Roman Catholic) mother was a Masorti Jew convert, a denomination not recognised by the OCR. His father brought claims of direct and indirect *racial* discrimination under the Education provisions of the Race Relations Act 1976, as 'faith schools' enjoyed an exemption from *religious* discrimination in their admissions.[8]

The High Court rejected claim. The Court of Appeal reversed, holding that the admissions policy amounted to direct discrimination. The Supreme Court,

3 [1990] 2 AC 751 (HL).
4 Under the Pensions Act 2009, Sch 4 (as amended), women's State Pension age will increase to 65 between April 2016 and November 2018. From December 2018, the State Pension age for both men and women will start to increase is due to reach 68 in 2046.
5 See [1990] 1 QB 61 (CA) 73.
6 [1990] 2 AC 751, 774 (Lord Goff) 765 (Lord Bridge). Lord Ackner agreed with both Lord Goff and Lord Bridge (769).
7 [2010] 2 AC 728 (SC).
8 At the time, EA 2006, s 50. See now EA 2010, Sch 11, para 5, exempting liability from s 85(1) and (2) (a)–(d) (discrimination in school admissions and provision of education).

by five-four majority (Lord Phillips PSC, Lady Hale, Lords Kerr, Clarke and Mance, JJSC) affirmed, although of the minority (Lord Hope DPSC, Lords Rodger, Walker, and Brown JJSC), two (Lords Hope and Walker) found the policy indirectly discriminated, and so a seven-two majority found in favour of M. (Lords Rodger and Brown found that any prima facie indirect discrimination was objectively justified.) Eight of the Justices gave reasoned speeches, with Lord Walker agreeing with Lord Hope.

The principal difficulty in this case is that being Jewish is both a religious and a racial matter. The principal issues were whether the admissions policy was religious and/or racial; and even if it were facially racial, whether the religious motive behind it rendered the ground of the treatment solely religious. The default position seemed to be that if it were not directly discriminatory, the policy would be analysed as indirect discrimination. This is unlike *James*, which was argued solely on direct discrimination.

The *JFS* majority finding of direct discrimination was rooted in two bases. First, a challenged policy need not discriminate against everyone sharing the claimant's protected characteristic. Second, the admissions policy contained a racial or ethnic element. This second base resembles the decision *James*, which brought the incorporated rule to the fore. That said, the reasoning as a whole overlooked the (incorporated) similarity with *James*. There was a facially neutral ('religious') policy incorporating a facially discriminatory rule ('racially Jewish') from an independent source (the OCR's interpretation of Jewish Law).

The challenged policy in *R (Mormoroc) v Ministry of Justice*,[9] was that where a foreign prisoner had been notified of liability to deportation but no decision to deport had been made, the prisoner should be deemed unsuitable to be considered for release on home detention curfew unless there were exceptional circumstances. This apparently neutral rule incorporated (fairly obviously) the patently discriminatory one that only foreign nationals were liable for deportation. Here though, a unanimous Court of Appeal (agreeing with the High Court below) found that the practice was *not* directly discriminatory. Instead, it should be analysed as indirect discrimination (that was justified).

There are two interesting features to the judgments. First, as a whole, the judiciary was undecided on whether such cases should be analysed as direct or indirect discrimination. At all levels in the litigation, in *James,* just three from nine found direct discrimination. In *JFS* it was eight from thirteen, and although there was unanimity in *Mormoroc*, this was out of step with the majorities in *James* and *JFS*. The disparity of views might be because, under the orthodox form-based formula, each case could readily be analysed either way.

If *James* were subjected to a conventional form-based formula, there would be two questions to ask. First, was there less favourable treatment? Here, the relevant circumstances for the comparison (requiring everything to be the same, but for sex), could be either:

9 [2017] EWCA Civ 989.

1 A one-to-one comparison between Mr James and a woman of the same age (e.g. Mrs James).
2 A one-to-one comparison between Mr James and the woman similarly four years below her retirement age.
3 A comparison between men aged 60–65 and women aged 60–65.
4 A comparison between men and women generally.

It is immediately obvious that there are at least four plausible comparisons based on a simple form-based formula. Comparisons 1 and 3 would suggest less favourable treatment, while 2 and 4 suggest that men were being treated no less favourably than women. These possibilities are discussed in more detail below.[10] For the time being, assume that Comparison 1 is the correct approach (as the majority had), then the second question asks, what was the ground of that treatment? Here, again, the matter becomes contentious. There are three arguable responses, two of which led the way in the House of Lords. On the one hand, as the minority found, the ground was the council's desire to help pensioners. On this basis, it could only be analysed as indirect discrimination. On the other, it was the claimant's sex. A third, and perhaps more obvious, answer is that it was the claimant's age. After all, that was on the face of the challenged requirement. Moreover, it does not carry the flavour of a benign, or 'alternative' motive. Nonetheless, the majority, as we know, chose the second answer (sex) and found that the age requirement amounted to direct discrimination. To add to the uncertainty, this was a somewhat pluralist decision, with Lord Goff leading with a but-for approach,[11] Lord Bridge labelling the age criterion 'convenient shorthand' for sex,[12] while Lord Ackner considered of that sex was inherent in the policy.[13] A perhaps unifying feature was an underlying purpose of the decision to bar benign motive defences.

For a prima facia case of indirect discrimination, at the time, there had to be a requirement that applied to both men and women, but the proportion of one sex who could comply was considerably smaller than the other.[14] The pensionable age policy was a requirement with which a considerably smaller proportion of men could comply, given the extra five-year wait.[15] Indeed, during the passage of the Sex Discrimination Bill, the Government informed Parliament that concessions for pensioners should be objectively justified on the basis that they were indirectly, rather than directly, discriminatory.[16]

10 See text et al. to n 62.
11 [1990] 2 AC 751, 774 (Lord Goff) 765 (Lord Bridge). Lord Ackner agreed with both Lord Goff and Lord Bridge (769).
12 Ibid., 764.
13 Ibid., 769.
14 SDA 1975 s 1(1)(b).
15 If the pool for comparison comprised persons in the catchment area of all ages, then the difference might be sufficiently small but persistent (Case C-167/97 *Seymour-Smith* [1999] ICR 447).
16 HL Deb 14 July 1975, vol 362, cols 1016–1017 (Lord Harris).

Much the same could be said about the *JFS* case, although given the alternative admission route via conversion, the precise treatment could be characterised in several ways. The key here is the claim, which was one of *racial*, and not religious, discrimination. Upon this, the challenged rule is the one that states if you are not racially Jewish you must pass the 'convert' test. With the challenged rule in mind, the comparison should be between the treatment given to a racially Jewish child and that to a non-racially Jewish child. One gains automatic admission, the other faces a further test. Again, identifying the ground of the treatment is more contentious: was it religion or race? In this case, the comparison points to it being race, as the majority found.

For a prima facie case of indirect discrimination, the requirement to be racially Jewish for *automatic* qualification would be one with which a considerably smaller proportion on non-Jews could comply. In fact, the proportion would be none, but such extreme effects that should not matter.[17] If one supposed the school's practice were defined more broadly, to include the 'convert rule' there would remain a sufficient disparity in racial terms, as a considerably fewer proportion of non-Jews could comply with these combined limbs of the admissions policy.

In *Mormoroc*, the finding was that the difference in treatment was due to the liability to be deported, and not nationality.[18] One could just as easily follow *James* bring to the fore the 'background' element of nationality, which dictates the *liability* to deportation (not deportation itself) and the consequent less favourable treatment of being deemed unsuitable for release on home detention. Just as in *James*, 'but-for' his nationality, Mormoroc would not have been treated less favourably, while 'liability to deportation' was convenient shorthand for nationality, and that nationality was inherent in the policy. It was notable that the claimant relied on *R (Johnson) v Secretary of State for the Home Department*.[19] Here, the claimant's Jamaican mother never married his British father with the consequence he was not a British national. As an adult he became liable for deportation as a 'foreign criminal'. The Supreme Court, reversing the Court of Appeal, held (unanimously) that the claimant had been directly discriminated against under the European Convention on Human Rights on the ground of birth status,[20] again, a somewhat background element the treatment.

On the other hand, Mormoroc's liability to deportation was not itself a protected characteristic. Upon this, an indirect discrimination analysis could be applied. Quite clearly, a higher proportion of non-nationals will be put at a particular disadvantage by the liability to deportation. (Of course, no British nationals would be subjected to such an order.)

17 *Greencroft Social Club v Mullen* [1985] ICR 796 (EAT). See also Case 34/79 *Henn and Darby* [1979] ECR 3795, para 12, holding that 'quantitative restrictions' include a complete ban as the 'most extreme form of restriction'.

18 [2017] EWCA Civ 989 [58]–[59].

19 [2016] UKSC56.

20 Ibid. [29]–[30], combining Articles 8 and 14.

The second talking point is that, in these cases, it appears that the closer that the challenged criterion could be aligned with the protected characteristic, the *less* likely it is that the treatment would amount to direct discrimination. In *James* the council had no control over the content of the incorporated rule and would apply it even if it were not discriminatory. Indeed, since *James*, the state pension ages are gradually being equalised. The link was closer in *JFS*. It was the avowed policy of the school to recruit non-practicing Jews in the hope and expectation that they would learn the Jewish faith and come to practice. This incorporated the racial aspect of the policy. Following the Court of Appeal ruling, the school introduced a 'religious practice test' for admissions, thus squeezing out the racial component from its admissions procedure.[21] And so, even though the admissions policy and OCR definition were closely tied, it was still possible to run the school somewhat detached from the OCR definition and its racial element. Despite recognising some distance between the criterion and protected characteristic, the majorities in these two cases still held that the discrimination was direct. However, short of reintroducing transportation to the colonies, it is quite impossible to detach liability for deportation from nationality.[22] Yet, in *Mormoroc*, there was unanimity that they were distinct. This could not be direct discrimination.

The comparison

One might expect that the comparative process is both straightforward and so rigid as not to allow any discretion. After all, the circumstances of the comparator must be exactly the same save for the relevant protected characteristic. But it is not so straightforward with incorporated cases, as we saw above with *James*, where four alternative comparisons could readily be reeled off. Even the rigid statutory formula can be the source of fuzzy borders.

We know that the direct discrimination formula demands *less* favourable treatment, and this supposes a comparison between how the claimant was treated and how a person without the protected characteristic, in the same circumstances, was, or would have been, treated. The phrase 'or would treat', in the statutory definition (section 13) enables the utilisation of a hypothetical comparator. In full, the Equality Act 2010 provides,

> 23 Comparison by reference to circumstances
>
> (1) On a comparison of cases for the purposes of … [direct and indirect discrimination] there must be no material difference between the circumstances relating to each case.

21 [2010] 2 AC 728 [253] (Lord Brown); United Synagogue (intervening) [2010] 2 AC 728, 735.

22 Some might argue that the stripping of nationality of your citizens amounts to the same thing. But those with single nationality (the vast majority) could easily be classed as a subgroup.

This means, in other words, the comparison must be 'like with like', the only difference between the two being the protected characteristic, such as sex, race, etc.

EU legislation also requires a comparison for direct discrimination as a matter of substantive law. Its 'comparable situation' rubric is embedded in its formula for direct discrimination:

> direct discrimination shall be taken to occur where one person is treated less favourably than another is, has been or would be treated in a comparable situation on grounds of racial or ethnic origin.[23]

It is arguable that this EU formula affords some discretion in fashioning a 'comparable situation'. But, as will be seen below, this leeway was apparently closed down by the ECJ iterating that the 'situation' should be comparable or *identical.* No discretion, it would seem, is afforded by the UK legislation, requiring 'no material difference between the circumstances relating to each case'. This informs the comparison required to fulfil the 'less favourable' element. That said, UK case law has offered mixed messages. On the one hand, the comparison is 'compulsory',[24] while on the other, some judges have suggested that where the discriminatory 'reason why' (or 'ground') is established, then a tribunal can 'avoid arid and confusing disputes about the identification of the appropriate comparator'.[25] Nonetheless, when employed, orthodox comparisons help distinguish the protected characteristic in question, and thus isolate direct discrimination from unfair, or equally bad, treatment (the latter suggesting an indirect discrimination analysis is due). However, for incorporated cases, the relevant, or comparable, circumstances become difficult to define with the extra rule lurking.

Bearing in mind that ordinarily the comparator is a person with a different protected characteristic from the claimant, and the relevant circumstances should comprise everything but the claimant's relevant protected characteristic, it comes to this. For the relevant circumstances, the inclusion or exclusion of the background rule can dictate the identity of both claimant and comparator, and thus affect the outcome of the comparison. For example, in *James*, it was excluded. Lord Bridge found that the discriminatory state retirement age was incorporated into the facially neutral policy, it being 'convenient shorthand' for (sex) discrimination. It thus played no part in identifying the claimant and comparator. Upon this, Lord Bridge concluded, 'On a proper application of [what is now s 23(1)] the relevant circumstance which was the same here for the purpose of comparing the treatment of the plaintiff and his wife was that

23 Race Directive 2000/43/EC, art 2(2)(a). See also Recast Directive 2006/54/EC, art 1(2)(a), and Framework Directive 2000/78/EC, art 2(2)(a).

24 *Glasgow CC v Zafar* [1998] ICR 120 (HL).

25 *Shamoon v Chief Constable of the RUC* [2003] ICR 337 (HL) [11] (Lord Nicholls), applied, *Chief Constable of Norfolk v Coffey* [2019] EWCA Civ 1061 [76] where Underhill LJ considered this approach 'very well established'.

they were both aged 61'.[26] In other words, the comparator was exactly the same as the claimant except for the claimant's sex.

On the other hand, had the state pension age been kept separate from the treatment, it would have been included in the relevant circumstances. Here, the comparator would have been a woman in the same position as Mr James, that is a woman *not* of pensionable age, say aged 56. Here, comparator is exactly the same as the claimant except for the claimant's sex *and* actual age. The age is changed to comply with the circumstances which dictate that both claimant and comparator are not of a pensionable age. Such a comparison would reveal that there was no direct sex discrimination.

The purpose of the test is to discover how the defendant would have treated the person of a different protected characteristic in the same circumstances. If this reveals the claimant was treated less favourably, it can also suggest the reason for the treatment was the same protected characteristic. The difficulty with these incorporated cases is that a prior finding that the treatment includes a facially discriminatory factor neuters the comparison of any purpose to detect discrimination. In *James,* Lord Bridge excluded from the circumstances the state pensionable age because, in his opinion, it included sex discrimination. That rather dictates the answer to the question. This suggests that in these incorporated cases, a compulsory comparison can give you the answer you desire, or at best, depends upon the rather fuzzy question of whether the background rule is part of the treatment or merely a consequence of it.

There are two ECJ cases, strikingly similar to *James*, where this latter approach was taken. In *Birds Eye Walls v Roberts*,[27] when workers took early retirement (say for ill-health) the employer gave them a bridging pension, which was reduced when the worker became entitled to a state pension. This meant that women, but not men, aged 60–65, would have their bridging pensions reduced. Again, the question was whether this scheme amounted to direct sex discrimination. So far, the case closely resembles *James*. There was a benign motive, this time to help early retirees bridge the gap between their retirement and entitlement to a state pension. But the policy incorporated the different state pension ages. Indeed, the employer recognized the scenario, pointing out that the state pension age was something beyond its control.[28] Meanwhile, the EC Commission (as amicus curiae) highlighted the policy aim of the practice, which was to achieve substantive (as opposed to formal) equality. Indeed, the Court noted if the scheme were abandoned because it was found to be, it 'would give rise to unequal treatment … of men who do not receive the state pension until the age of 65'.[29] In other words, a finding of discrimination would lead to discrimination against the allegedly favoured

26 [1990] 2 AC 751, 766.
27 Case C-132/92, [1994] IRLR 29.
28 Ibid., para 16.
29 Ibid., para 21.

group (men). This again could be said to resemble *James*, but in more precise terms.

The Court resolved the case on the comparison, noting that the principle of discrimination 'presupposes that men and women to whom it applies are in identical situations'.[30] Upon this, the Court reasoned:

> Accordingly, although until the age of 60 the financial position of a woman taking early retirement on grounds of ill health is comparable to that of a man in the same situation, neither of them as yet entitled to payment of the State pension, that is no longer the case between the ages of 60 and 65 since that is when women, unlike men, start drawing that pension.[31]

In other words, the background rule (different state pension ages for men and women) was part of the relevant circumstances or 'situations'. For the ECJ, this shows that men and women were not in comparable situations and therefore there was no direct sex discrimination. The ECJ (along with the Strasbourg Court) tends to conclude a matter upon the impossibility of a comparable situation, rather than go the extra step and compare the situations to demonstrate that there was no direct discrimination. If the Court had gone onto make a comparison, it would have compared women aged 60–65 with men aged over 65. Of course, such a comparison would demonstrate that men and women were being treated equally. On very similar facts and policy concerns, the Court effectively utilised a comparison opposite to that used in *James*.

It was notable also that this comparison was made on a group basis, rather than an individual one,[32] such as the more familiar one-to-one model deployed Lord Bridge in *James*. Ms Roberts's particular circumstances were not compared with that of a particular male worker. Instead, the position of male and female employees in general was compared. This was important because upon the facts of this particular case Ms Roberts was not in fact entitled to a state pension because she had chosen to pay lower National Insurance contributions. This was the impetus behind her claim. She received a reduced bridging pension with no compensatory state pension, while a comparative man received a full bridging pension. The Court addressed this point by noting the omission to make National Insurance payments was her choice, and a decision otherwise would confer an unfair advantage of women who had chosen to do the same.[33] This again, is taking the matter in general rather than addressing the particular claim using a one-to-one comparison

30 Ibid., para 17.
31 Ibid., para 20.
32 This distinction was made by Advocate General Kokott in the *Hlozek* when advising the individual comparison is the correct one (AG54–56).
33 Ibid., para 29.

usually associated with direct discrimination, especially for equal pay claims, which include occupational pensions.[34]

The Court followed this logic in *Hlozek*,[35] where dismissed older workers were awarded a 'bridging allowance' intended to compensate for the higher risk of unemployment in the years preceding the state retirement age, which was 65 for men and 60 for women. Accordingly, the award was made to women who had reached the age of 50 and to men who had reached 55. This meant that a 54-year-old man did not get the award while a 54-year-old woman did so. The ECJ dutifully declared that the man and his comparator should be in identical or comparative situations.[36] It consequently ruled:

> Male workers … who were in the 50 to 54 years age group at the time of their dismissal were further away from the statutory age for early retirement and, accordingly, were not in a situation identical to that of female workers in the same age group in terms of the likelihood of unemployment to which they were exposed.[37]

It might be argued that these ECJ cases can be distinguished from the directives' formula on the basis that they were heard under the equal pay regime of Article 157 TFEU (previously 141 EC), which provides no formulas for direct and indirect discrimination.[38] However, it is clear that the Court adopted the legislative formulas when stating that the claimant and comparator had to be in comparable or identical situations.

Thus, the comparisons in all these UK and EU cases were made under substantively the same formula, either that the relevant circumstances *must* not be materially different, or should be comparable, or even 'identical'. These ECJ equal pay comparisons differed from *James* into particular ways. First, there was a group comparison, rather than the conventional (especially for equal pay claims) one-to-one comparison. Second, the background rule was included as a relevant circumstance. This meant that the comparators age different group was dictated by the background rule. In *James,* it seems, the majority made a one-to-one comparison between Mr James (aged 61) and Mrs James (age 61), with no account of their relative relationships with the state pensionable age. Under rigid formulas for the comparison, with similar facts and policy considerations, there is little consensus as to how to treat the external incorporated element.

34 Ibid., para 10.
35 C19/02 *Hlozek v Roche Austria Gesellschaft mbH,* [2004] ECR I-11491.
36 Ibid., para 44.
37 Ibid., para of 48.
38 It was notable here that in *Hlozek,* after advising that there was direct discrimination, Advocate General Kokott went on to consider whether discrimination was justified (ibid., AG79-AG87).

The comparison, justification, and positive action

Each of these three cases, *James, Roberts, Hlozek,* presented strong policy features. The various approaches to the comparison smacks of manipulation. In *James*, there was a conflict between a genuine policy to help pensioners and the expressed fear that endorsing this would also endorse less benign motives, such as customer preference. The majority set itself against such 'benign motive defences', with Lord Bridge in particular finding that the state retirement age was not a relevant circumstance for the comparison.

The minority judgments completely bypassed the comparison when coming to their dissents. But there is a hint in Lord Griffiths' speech of how this may have played out. Unlike Lord Bridge, he distinguished the state pension age as an 'earlier act of discrimination', and thus treated it as quite separate from the challenged policy. Upon this, Lord Griffiths could have made a straightforward comparison which *included* the state pension age as a relevant circumstance. Instead, he reasoned:

> But what I do not accept is that an attempt to redress the result of that unfair act of discrimination by offering free facilities to those disadvantaged by the earlier act of discrimination is, itself, necessarily discriminatory, 'on the grounds of sex'.[39]

In effect, the characterisation of the policy as a matter of 'redress' endorses positive discrimination, and in doing so, drove the proverbial coach and four horses through the form-based symmetrical statutory definition of direct discrimination.[40] This fuzzy logic has little relationship with the statutory framework. However, it does show that had Lord Griffiths made a comparison, it would have included the 'background' state pension age as a relevant circumstance. This would have given him the result he clearly desired, which was to endorse a policy that, in his eyes, redressed a previous act of discrimination.

A similar, underlying, feature of redress was apparent in the Roberts Judgment. Although the Court's reasoning centred on a comparison, it was no doubt driven by a concern for substantive equality, which was to redress the disadvantage suffered by men who would have to wait five years longer for their state pension. Despite the Court's reliance on a comparison, the Judgment fuelled fears that the Court was covertly entertaining a justification defence for direct discrimination.[41] This was not least because of the Commission's view that some instances of direct discrimination should be justifiable, a view

39 [1990] 2 AC 751 (HL) 768.

40 An observation made by Lady Hale, *JFS* [2010] 2 AC 728 (SC) [60].

41 See. e.g. David L Hosking, 'Great expectations: protection from discrimination because of disability in Community law' (2006) 31 (5) EL Rev 672, 674; M Rubinstein, IRLR Highlights January 1994. Cf J Bowers, E Moran, 'Justification in direct sex discrimination law: breaking the taboo' (2002) 31 (4) *ILJ* 307, 308 and n 8.

apparently supported in the Advocate General's Opinion,[42] but not disavowed in the Judgment. It could be argued then, that the Court incorporated a justification defence into its comparison; this was by including, as a comparable circumstance, the justifiable (or 'substantive equality') feature of the scheme.

This argument is supported by the Court's Judgment a few years later in *Hlozek*. Immediately preceding its conclusions on the comparison, the Court noted that the new arrangement: was agreed between employer and worker representatives, was made before data was available on the risk of unemployment between men and women, was temporary, and not intended to cause sex discrimination.[43] These factors, which one would ordinarily associate with the justification defence, should be irrelevant to the comparison. Indeed, given did not consider indirect discrimination and a consequent objective justification defence, they were not relevant to any discussion of direct discrimination.

This acceptance of a form of 'redress' explaining otherwise direct discrimination is all the more surprising given that in the past the Court has rejected such an argument. In *Gravier v City of Liege*,[44] a fee for vocational training courses was imposed on non-Belgians. As fewer Belgium students studied abroad (than foreign students educated in Belgium), it was argued that this was not discriminatory because the requirement restored the (budgetary) balance and would thus 'place foreign students on an equal footing with Belgian nationals'. The Court rejected this argument, effectively that a degree of 'redress' could somehow neutralise the direct discrimination.[45]

More concrete evidence of the influence of the benign motive lays in the choice of an unusual *group* comparison. Ordinarily, direct discrimination involves a one-to-one comparison, whereas group comparisons are normally associated with *indirect* discrimination. This is particularly so with equal pay claims, where an individual claimant may choose her comparator.[46] Indeed, in both *Roberts* and *Hlozek*, the claims were characterised in that way, with each claimant choosing an individual comparator of the opposite sex and the same age. Moreover, the Court ignored Ms Roberts' individual circumstance of not being entitled to the state pension. Instead of an individual comparison, the Court adopted the employers' policy of dividing employees into age groups. This inherently imported a flavour of the employers' benign motive, as the age divisions were at the heart of the disparity in pay designed to redress other

42 Case C-132/92, Opinion of Advocate General Walter Van Gerven, at para 14 and n 23. It must be presumed that this was following the equal pay regime.

43 C19/02, paras 46–48.

44 Case 293/83 *Gravier v City of Liege* [1985] 3 CMLR 1. Discussed below, text to n 86.

45 Ibid., para 12.

46 Case C-381/99 *Brunnhofer v Bank der Ústerreichischen Postsparkasse* [2001] ECR I-496, [2001] IRLR 571, paras 58 and 62. For the UK, see *Pickstone v Freemans* [1988] ICR 697 (HL).

shortfalls. This is also consistent with legitimate positive action, which tends to rely on group disadvantage or needs.[47]

The type and detail of the comparison also plays a role in the next section, considering the rubrics used to identify proxies for direct discrimination.

The 'indissociable' and 'exact coincidence' rubrics

These rubrics have been advanced as a method of identifying whether a factor neutral on its face is in fact a proxy for direct discrimination. The indissociable rubric is relatively straightforward. The exact coincidence rubric is less so; it works like this: if those of a protected characteristic directly correspond to those disadvantaged and vice versa, that is those not of the protected characteristic directly correspond to those advantaged, then the factor is a proxy for direct discrimination. However, the rubric is not entirely watertight, nor understood by all, and has led to divisions as to where to place the border between direct and indirect discrimination.

These rubrics have origins in the case of *Dekker*, where the ECJ ruled that pregnancy discrimination amounted to direct sex discrimination.[48] The technical curiosity here is that the relevant legislation expressly prohibiting *sex* discrimination did not mention discrimination because of pregnancy. It was made all the more difficult by the facts. While a pregnant woman was rejected for a job, another woman was appointed. Thus, the rejection was not because of sex, but because of pregnancy. Nonetheless, the Court's reasoning amounted to this: 'only women can be refused employment on the ground of pregnancy and such a refusal therefore constitutes direct discrimination on the ground of sex'. This does more to serve policy aims than provide a clear doctrinal explanation.[49] The policy here would be to avoid a finding of indirect discrimination and the consequent objective justification defence, which may well succeed for organisational and economic reasons given by any employer. In *Dekker,* for example, the employer's decision was dictated by its insurance policy. In terms of statutory interpretation, this is an extraordinary decision. As seen in Chapter 3, the UK courts have struggled because of the want of a suitable comparator, while the US Supreme Court has roundly rejected such an approach, not for want of the comparator, but more simply because a failure to hire because of pregnancy is not necessarily a failure to hire because of sex.[50]

One interpretation of pregnancy discrimination cases is that the treatment favours all men and disfavours some women. As such, when other similarly structured cases arrive at the ECJ, a more logical explanation would be required to either follow, or to distinguish, *Dekker*. This occurred first in *Schnorbus v*

47 *Z v Hackney LBC* [2020] UKSC 40 [78]–[82] citing in support Equality Act 2010, Explanatory Note 158.

48 C-177/88 *Dekker v Stichting Vormingscentrum voor Jonge Volwassenen Plus* [1990] ECR I-3941.

49 The relationship between pregnancy and sex discrimination is discussed in Chapter 3.

50 *General Electric v Gilbert* 429 US 125 (1976), 134–135.

Land Hessen.[51] Here, a priority for vocational training was provided to those who had completed national service, where only men were eligible for national service. Here, although all men were *obliged* to complete national service, the priority was given only upon completion.[52] As such, this was the inverse of *Dekker,* favouring some men and disfavouring all women. Advocate General Jacobs explained *Dekker* with the reasoning that pregnancy was a proxy for sex discrimination because it was *indissociable* from sex. He then distinguished this physical nexus from the legal one in *Schnorbus.* In accordance with this, he advised that unless the incorporated measure was 'indissociable' from sex (e.g. pregnancy) the case should be addressed as indirect discrimination.[53] The Court of Justice agreed with the outcome, but gave its reasoning in more bland terms: 'only provisions which apply differently according to the sex of the persons concerned can be regarded as constituting discrimination directly based on sex'.[54] This proverbial statement of the obvious has encouraged those interested in understanding the jurisprudence to revert to the Advocate General's Opinion.[55]

But the matter did not rest there. In *Bressol v Gouvernement De La Communauté Française,*[56] Advocate General Sharpston developed the indissociable rubric by equating it with a notion of 'exact coincidence'. AG Sharpston reasoned:

> I take there to be direct discrimination when the category of those receiving a certain advantage and the category of those suffering a correlative disadvantage coincide exactly with the respective categories of persons distinguished only by applying a prohibited classification'[57]

On the one hand, it would seem this was quite a logical interpretation, given AG Jacobs' bilateral reasoning. On the other, it ignores the limitation which confined the indissociable principle to a physical nexus.

In the case itself, priority in medical training was given to those with the right to remain permanently in Belgium, where only Belgian nationals had an *automatic* right of residence. Once again, this is something facially neutral loaded with something facially discriminatory. Applying her rubric, the Advocate General advised that this was direct (nationality) discrimination. The Court rejected AG Sharpston's Opinion and treated this as *indirect* discrimination

51 C-79/99 *Schnorbus v Land Hessen* [2000] ECR I-10997.
52 Ibid., Opinion of AG Jacobs, paras A38 and 41.
53 Ibid., paras AG33 and AG36–AG41.
54 Ibid., paras 33.
55 See e.g. *Onu v Akwiwu, Taiwo v Olaigbe* [2016] UKSC 31 [28] (Lady Hale, giving judgment for the Court); *Patmalniece v Secretary of State for Work and Pensions* [2011] UKSC 11 [66]–[68], [79] (Lord Walker).
56 Case C-73/08 *Bressol v Gouvernement De La Communauté Française* [2010] 3 CMLR 20.
57 Ibid., para AG56.

(which could be justified). However, the Court failed to explain this decision, and offered no opinion on AG Sharpston's advice and the exact coincidence rubric. One suggestion is that the Court considered her Opinion 'too analytical'.[58]

Given that the exact coincidence rubric seems to have been roundly rejected by the ECJ, it is quite surprising it has developed a life of its own in the UK courts, although there is no consensus as to its meaning. The confusion was played out in the Supreme Court case of *Patmalniece v Secretary of State for Work and Pensions*.[59] The Justices were faced with the task of reconciling *Bressol* with established UK discrimination law, notably *James v Eastleigh BC* (where free swimming for pensioners incorporate a d the discriminatory state pension ages).[60] These attempts generally failed, exposing again that there is no agreed border between direct and indirect discrimination. The facts of *Patmalniece* are presented in more detail below,[61] but in essence, this was another 'right of residence' requirement, something automatically acquired by British citizens, but not those of other EU member states.

First, Lord Hope (with whom Lords Rodger and Brown agreed) cited the 'pensionable age' requirement from *James v Eastleigh*[62] and its 'exact coincidence' with the disadvantaged group (men), which 'was true of every male, not just some or even most of them'.[63] This relies on a 'group' comparison where the respective groups were qualified (see 'The comparison' above). Rather than all men and women, this group is reduced to those aged 60–65. As Lord Walker noted (see below) one could just as readily attribute the 'pensionable age' requirement as favouring just *some* women whilst disfavouring *some* men. If anything, this is a scenario suggesting an enquiry for *indirect* discrimination. Nevertheless, Lord Hope used this logic to sidestep *James*, as in the present case there was 'no such exact match'.[64] In case this logic was not convincing, Lord Hope observed that *James* (and all English precedents) could be sidestepped as the Court was 'not required in this case to say whether this amounts to direct discrimination in domestic law'.[65] This is a fairly bald admission that different definitions of direct discrimination exist within what *should* have been consistent regimes.

The two remaining speeches, those of Lady Hale (with whom Lord Brown also agreed, suggesting more ambiguity) and Lord Walker, adopted the *Bressol* Court's approach, but with Lord Walker notably uncomfortable in doing so, apparently lacking faith in the integrity of its logic.

58 *Patmalniece v Secretary of State for Work and Pensions* [2011] UKSC 11 [33] (Lord Hope).
59 [2011] UKSC 11.
60 [1990] 2 AC 751 (HL), see further, above text to n 3.
61 See text to n 123.
62 See above, text to n 3.
63 [2011] UKSC 11 [29].
64 Ibid.
65 Ibid.

Lady Hale made three observations relating to both rubrics. First, in a seemingly approving manner she cited the Advocate General's 'exact coincidence' rubric.[66] Lady Hale reasoned that this rubric could just as easily explain the decision in *James*.[67] In this sense, *Schnorbus* and *James* are identical. The starting point for this is a replication of Lord Hope's 'group' comparison to explain *James*. Such a comparison departs from Lady Hale's view, expressed elsewhere, that *James* is explained on a one-to-one comparison.[68] This does not mean that the rubric and *James* are irreconcilable, but it puts a particular gloss on *James* to demonstrate the consistency with *Schnorbus*. Lady Hale makes a similar omission regarding *Schnorbus*, this time the men eligible for national service, but yet to complete it.[69] These men would also be disadvantaged by the requirement to have completed national service.

However, Lady Hale was cautious over the Advocate General's conclusion that this meant *Bressol* was a case of direct discrimination. This is her second observation. For Lady Hale, this was 'certainly a development' of her exact coincidence rubric.[70] Lady Hale felt that this went beyond the rubric's requirement of absolute symmetry between those advantaged and disadvantaged by the challenged treatment:

> It suggests that there can be direct discrimination even when some members of the disadvantaged group do fulfil the requirement in question even though others do not. The equivalent in the Schnorbus case would have been if all men were eligible to do national service but only some women were eligible to do so.[71]

This analysis brought Lady Hale to agreement with the Court in *Bressol*, because the residence requirement did not disfavour all non-Belgian nationals, as it was possible for *some* to achieve the status of permanent residence. Her first two observations show that Lady Hale is committed to the 'exact coincidence' rubric, but only so far as it produces a precise symmetrical result.

Fully explaining the difference between AG Sharpston's original rubric and the 'developed' one applied to *Bressol,* risks becoming terribly convoluted.

66 Lady Hale has since deployed it on several occasions: *Lee v Ashers Baking* [2018] UKSC 49 [25] (giving judgment for the Court); *Bull (Preddy) v Hall* [2013] UKSC 73 [19]; *Taiwo v Olaigbe, Onu v Akwiwu* [2016] UKSC 31 [28] (giving judgment for the Court).

67 [2011] UKSC 11 [91].

68 See e.g. *Col v Secretary of State for Justice* [2017] UKSC 40 [29] (Lady Hale). In fact, this 'group' comparison was used in *James*: [1990] 2 AC 751 (HL), 767 (Lord Bridge), 772 (Lord Goff), 782 (Order of the Court).

69 Conscientious objectors were compelled to give civilian service, and were included in the exemption for those having completed national service (C-79/99 [2000] ECR I-10997, para 20). There was some ambiguity as to whether the exemption applied to all men, or the 'overwhelming majority' of men (ibid., AG38).

70 [2011] UKSC 11 [91].

71 Ibid.

Some clarity comes if the rubric and the choice of challenged factor to which it is applied are considered separately. AG Sharpston applied her rubric to the incorporated factor of automatic right of residence: Belgians had it, non-Belgians did not. Lady Hale applied it to the more generalised factor of the right to remain permanently in Belgium. Thus, AG Sharpston had not developed her rubric as suggested by Lady Hale, but merely applied her original (undeveloped) one to a different factor, which produced a different result. (It was the equivalent of including the 'automatic' factor in the relevant circumstances for the comparison. This produced two groups, one with an automatic right of residence and the other without such a right. This coincides exactly with Belgians/non-Belgians, and so indicates direct discrimination. By contrast, *excluding* the 'automatic' factor would produce a group with a right of permanent residence in Belgium and a group without that right. As some with the right of permanent residence could be non-Belgians, then there is no exact coincidence with Belgians/non-Belgians, as Lady Hale found.)

Lady Hale's third observation relates to AG Jacobs' distinction between *Schnorbus* and *Dekker*, which was, it may be recalled, between a legal and (for pregnancy) a physical nexus. For Lady Hale,

> [T]his … might come as something of a surprise, for example, to readers of *James v Eastleigh Borough Council* … where the discrimination between male and female swimmers was linked to a legal requirement, the statutory retirement age, which was indissociable from sex.[72]

Here, Lady Hale concedes that AG Jacobs' narrow view on the meaning of indissociable presents a more than nuanced difference between *James* and *Schnorbus*.[73] Although not repeated by the ECJ, its decisions in *Schnorbus* and *Bressol* are consistent with it, suggesting a fundamental difference between EU and UK notions of the indissociable rubric and by extension the meaning of discrimination.

In fact, rather than for any jurisdictional reasons, AG Jacobs' indissociable rubric could be disregarded simply for not being watertight. The Court of Justice continued its *Dekker* logic when it came to a pregnancy-related illness, *but only* where it fell inside the standard maternity period,[74] something dictated by a legal, rather than physical, nexus. For less favourable treatment because of a pregnancy-related illness falling outside of the maternity period, the 'sick man' comparison *should* be made: 'the sole question is whether a female worker's absences, following maternity leave, caused by her incapacity for work

72 Ibid., [90].

73 Lady Hale glossed over this difference in *Bull (Preddy) v Hall* [2013] UKSC 73 [20], suggesting that at a time predating same-sex marriage, a requirement to be married was indissociable from sexual orientation, because heterosexual persons could marry and homosexual persons could not. The connection between marriage and sexual orientation was of course a legal one.

74 Case C-399/96 *Brown v Rentokil* [1998] ICR 790.

brought on by such disorders, are treated in the same way as a male worker's absences'.[75] And on the matter of maternity *pay*, lower-than-normal pay was not discriminatory because *no* comparison was possible: women on maternity leave were 'in a special position which requires them to be afforded special protection, but which is not comparable either with that of a man or with that of a woman actually at work'.[76] This in turn was sidestepped where maternity pay is *related* to the worker's salary.[77] Thus, maternity pay failing to reflect a general pay rise during the maternity period can amount to sex discrimination under the equal pay provisions even though there is no comparator.[78] Again, the ECJ has made a distinction based on something other than a physical nexus. These distinctions demonstrate that the ECJ has not followed AG Jacobs' physical nexus limitation, and so it need not be followed in any UK cases whether or not they fall within EU jurisdiction.

The third speech given in *Patmalniece* was by Lord Walker. He was more sceptical of the ECJ's decision in *Bressol*, although not AG Sharpston's ultimate advice pointing to direct discrimination. Lord Walker argued that there could be direct discrimination where a practice favoured 100 per cent of one group, and disfavoured just *some* of another. Building on AG Sharpston's 'exact coincidence' rubric, he cited *James v Eastleigh*[79] to show that the rubric only worked if the 'cohorts' were limited to those aged 60–65, as Lord Hope and Lady Hale had maintained. He drove home the point with this example: 'an organisation which admitted all men but only women graduates would be engaged in direct discrimination on the grounds of sex'.[80] Hence, the 'exact coincidence' formula was 'too narrow'[81] and Lord Walker's preferred analysis of the case before him was that the right to reside requirement remained directly discriminatory even though it was possible for other EU nationals to acquire this right.

On the face of it, attacking the 'exact coincidence' rubric using the 'women graduates' example is flawed. The example is discriminatory on its face, which, as Lady Hale has subsequently ruled, renders the rubric's utility limited to test if

75 Ibid., [26].

76 Case C-342/93 *Gillespie v Northern Health and Social Services Board* [1996] ICR 498 [17].

77 Case C-147/02 *Alabaster v Woolwich plc* [2004] ECR I-3103, paras 47–50. Upon its return, the Court of Appeal implemented this ruling through the Equal Pay Act 1970, by disapplying the Act's requirement for a comparator: *Alabaster v Barclays Bank (No 2)* [2005] EWCA 508. See now Equality Act 2010, ss 73–74.

78 Upon its return, the Court of Appeal in *Alabaster*, ibid., implemented this ruling through the Equal Pay Act 1970, by disapplying the Act's requirement for a comparator: *Alabaster v Barclays Bank (No 2)* [2005] EWCA 508. See now Equality Act 2010, ss 73–74.

79 [1990] 2 AC 751 (HL).

80 [2011] UKSC 11 [64], citing *R (E) v Governing Body of JFS (United Synagogue intervening)* [2010] 2 AC 728 [89] (Lord Mance, adopting the example provided by counsel, Dinah Rose QC).

81 Ibid., [64].

a facially *neutral* factor is a proxy for a facially discriminatory one.[82] In fairness to Lord Walker, AG Sharpston made no such limitation, stating that this was a general definition that 'accurately reflects' all cases of direct discrimination on any protected characteristic.[83] This included the pregnancy case of *Dekker*. Again, this turned more on the application of the rubric, rather than its meaning. AG Sharpston reconciled her rubric with *Dekker* by deploying it, respectively, to 'people who can under no circumstances get pregnant, i.e. men' and 'people who can get pregnant i.e. women'.[84] It is *this*, rather than her application to *Bressol*, that goes too far. As the facts of *Dekker* demonstrated, not all women are disadvantaged by pregnancy discrimination, and so, there cannot be an 'exact coincidence' of the factor (non-pregnant/pregnant) and sex (men/women). Likewise, there is no exact coincidence in Lord Walker's example, as some women (graduates) are not disadvantaged. This shows the wisdom of Lady Hale's ruling that the rubric is not appropriate for facially discriminatory factors, as facially discriminatory factors that disadvantage just some of the protected group would not be identified by the rubric.

In sum, both Lord Hope and Lady Hale could only reconcile the rubric with *James* by utilising a particular comparison, with Lord Hope rather undermining his conviction with an 'in any case' deference to EU jurisdiction. Lord Walker identified this flaw and diluted the 'exact coincidence' rubric for a non- proxy case disadvantage in just some of the group, and in turn applied this diluted version to the proxy case (as he saw it) before him. This was an approach ruled inappropriate some years later by Lady Hale. Meanwhile, Lady Hale conceded that the origin of the rubric, the notion of indissociability put forward by Advocate General Jacobs was incompatible with *James*. Thus, any proxy governed by law, rather than Nature, that meets the 'exact coincidence' rubric can only amount to direct discrimination if it is beyond EU jurisdiction. Given that the 'exact coincidence' rubric can explain neither asymmetrical proxy cases (such as pregnancy discrimination) nor asymmetrical non-proxy cases (such as 'all men, only women graduates'), and that the indissociable principle was confined to proxy cases with a physical nexus, one must wonder if the symmetrical 'exact coincidence' rubric has any utility at all. This might explain why it has not been taken up by the ECJ Judgments, and renders its apparent endorsement within the English judiciary all the more curious. There is no doubt that Lady Hale's endorsement of the rubric was more committed than Lord Hope's tentative approval. The concurrences added to the ambiguity here, with Lord Brown concurring with both Lady Hale and Lord Hope and Lord Rodger confining his agreement to Lord Hope's speech.

82 *Lee v Ashes Baking* [2018] UKSC 49 [25], citing *Bull v Hall* [2013] UKSC 73, and *James v Eastleigh BC* [1990] 2 AC 751 (HL). See also *Col v Secretary of State for Justice* [2017] UKSC 40 [29].

83 Case C-73/*08 Bressol v Gouvernement De La Communauté Française* [2010] 3 CMLR 20, AG56.

84 Ibid., AG57.

This indulgence is even more surprising when one considers the rubric's lucidity, fidelity and utility. First, its apparently attractive symmetry disguises its opacity, as the author herself, and some of the Justices of the UK Supreme Court demonstrated, quite often inadvertently. It is in fact a linguistic puzzle, with uncertainties and qualifications, that takes some time and effort to deconstruct and apply. As such, it is hardly likely to endear itself to the many lay parties who need to understand the concepts of discrimination.

Of course, as noted above, extended beyond the 'physical nexus', the rubric has no fidelity with AG Jacobs' principle of indissociability. Indeed, it would undermine claims of pregnancy discrimination as sex discrimination, as not all women become, or are, pregnant. It has been applied with little fidelity to the principles and purpose of discrimination law. The confused explanations suggest that claims against barely disguised intentional discrimination, such as those in *Bressol* and *Patmalniece*, should fail the test (thus facilitating a justification defence), while claims against a genuine benign motive, such as *James*, pass the test and cut off any opportunity to justify the measure.

Neither is the rubric convincing in a practical sense. One presumes it is trying to replicate 'ordinary' direct discrimination. That is, discrimination where there is no proxy. There are two problems here. First, the rubric seems designed to supplant the ordinary practice of evidence and inferences. For example, an employer dismisses a black Jamaican worker saying, 'You have an attitude typical of people in your estate'. As a rule, the tribunal would make inferences from this and surrounding evidence suggesting the reason for the dismissal, which could be the worker's race or something else, such as his place of residence. If the 'exact coincidence' rubric were to gain too much purchase on the thinking of tribunals, the employer's comment could be regarded as a proxy for racial discrimination. At present, no tribunal would think of deploying the 'exact coincidence' rubric in such a case. Yet, when the proxy in *Bressol* and other such cases is so much more tangible, and its purpose is so much more obvious, why did the courts not simply draw inferences?

The second problem is that not all cases of 'ordinary' direct discrimination follow the binary rule. These could be labelled, 'individual discrimination' cases. And where these could be characterised as 'proxy' cases, the substantive law is not interested in group effect, only that the individual suffered discrimination. The employer dismissing the woman for being 'a typical airhead' or a black Jamaican for being 'typically lazy' may not treat all of its female or black Jamaican employees as such. But that in itself would not prevent the individual victim's claim of direct discrimination.

The 'exact coincidence' rubric is flawed, impractical, and not universally understood. And yet UK courts still treat it as good law, deploying it in their legal reasoning.[85] Moreover, it demonstrates that there is no consensus over the

85 See e.g. *Banks v The Commissioners for Her Majesty's Revenue & Customs* [2020] UKUT 0101 (TCC); *Lee v MacArthur* [2016] NICA 55 and [2016] NICA 39; *Bull (Preddy) v Hall* [2013] UKSC 73; *Taiwo v Olaigbe, Onu v Akwiwu* [2016] UKSC 31.

boundary between direct and indirect discrimination. As noted above, it originated in *Bressol,* and the Supreme Court wrestled with it in *Patmalniece*. The feature of these cases is their multi-layered criteria. They are often dubbed 'cumulative' cases. These are discussed next.

The cumulative cases

Cumulative cases are so-called because they comprise two or more criteria assembled to implement a single policy. *Bressol* (above) is an example. An acknowledged purpose of these policies is to deter 'benefit tourism' and the drafting is intended to represent the policy as indirectly, rather than directly, discriminatory. This, of course, carries the opportunity of objective justification. At least one of the criteria will be a proxy for discrimination. The question for the courts is whether such a criterion could be isolated and treated as directly discriminatory.

The history begins in 1985, with *Gravier v City of Liege,*[86] a case noted for establishing that access to vocational training came within the reach of the Treaty of Rome, and hence its bar on nationality discrimination. Its brief rationale for its finding of discrimination made far fewer headlines. In this case, a fee for vocational training courses was imposed on non-Belgians, although there were some exceptions, the main ones being:

- The person has Belgian nationality or resides in Belgium or carries out his or her principal professional activities there and is liable for Belgian tax;
- Children of a Belgian national, or someone residing and working (being liable for tax) in Belgium;
- Students who themselves reside in Belgium, carrying out their principal professional activities there and being liable for Belgian tax;
- Students residing and working (being liable for tax) in Belgium;
- Luxembourg nationals;
- Those who are given discretionary dispensation such as nationals of particular developing countries.

These cumulative requirements favoured 100 per cent of the advantaged group (Belgian nationals) and *dis*favoured most (but not all) of the disadvantaged group. It was held that the exceptions were irrelevant to the principal challenged factor:

> The inequality of treatment therefore is based on nationality and that finding is not affected by the mere the fact that certain exceptions are made to the discrimination as between Belgian and foreign students.[87]

86 Case 293/83 *Gravier v City of Liege* [1985] 3 CMLR 1.
87 Ibid., para 14.

Two conclusions follow, one concrete, one tentative. First, it is clear that the Court did not consider a cumulative approach. Second, it could be inferred from the Court's blunt appraisal (along with the absence of any consideration of objective justification), that this was treated as direct discrimination.[88] But given that the Belgium defendant offered no defence in such terms, instead arguing simply that it was not discriminatory at all,[89] *and* that the Court of Justice was yet to formulate a concrete direct/indirect formula,[90] this might be reading too much into the judgment. Nonetheless, a retrospective analysis would conclude that once the cumulative approach was disregarded, charging fees only to foreign students amounted to direct (nationality) discrimination.

Of course, civil law jurisprudence relies more on what the Court said, rather than what was done, or, if you prefer, it relies on statements of general principle rather than a ratio decidendi narrowly tailored for the facts of the case. The *Gravier* Judgment said very little on the definition of discrimination. It did not express its finding in terms of direct or indirect discrimination, and given that the defence was not shaped in terms of objective justification, it had no need to do so.

The matter rested there for some 20 years. Then, in two cases decided in 2004, the Court took baby steps towards identifying the related concepts of direct and indirect discrimination in the context of these 'cumulative' cases. *Commission v Belgium*[91] was clearly one of indirect, or 'covert' discrimination, but the language used in the Judgment betrays a somewhat loose appreciation of the concepts. In this case, Belgium faced an influx of French students in (para)medical studies, who came to study in the Belgian French Community (there being no language barrier). They did so because places in France were capped (*numerus clausus*). In response, Belgium barred automatic access to those schooled in another country (except for Luxembourg) and who did not have access to the same courses in the country of that schooling. Instead, such applicants had to pass an aptitude test, not applicable to those schooled in Belgium.

88 That was the view of AG Sharpston in Case C-73/08 *Bressol v Gouvernement De La Communauté Française* [2010] 3 CMLR 20, para AG128 and n 94.

89 As fewer Belgium students studied abroad (than foreign students educated in Belgium), the requirement restored the (budgetary) balance and would thus 'place foreign students on an equal footing with Belgian nationals'. This was rejected. Case 293/83, para 12.

90 See, for instance, the Court's rather ambiguous definition(s) in Case 96/80 *Jenkins v Kingsgate* [1981] 1 WLR 972, paras 9–15 (noted by Browne-Wilkinson J [1981] 1 WLR 1485 (EAT) 1493–1494), only clarified in Case 170/84 *Bilka-Kaufhaus* [1986] ECR 1607, para 37, sometime after *Gravier* was decided. Earlier cases suggested a 'justification' defence to apparent, but unclassified, direct discrimination: Case 118/75 *The State v Lynne Watson* [1976] 2 CMLR 552, para 16; Cases 198–202/81 *Micheli v EC Commission* [1982] ECR 4145, paras 5–6.

91 Case C-65/03, [2004] ECR I-6427 (1 July 2004).

The Court found that this was 'covert'[92] discrimination (which Belgium did not justify), as it was possible (theoretically anyway) that some non-Belgians were schooled in Belgium, while some Belgians were schooled in another Member State. For the present discussion, the case is notable only because that on two occasions in a short judgment the Court framed the Belgian response as if applying to 'nationals' of another state.[93] As such, that would be direct discrimination. This might explain why Advocate General Sharpston subsequently considered the terms 'covert' and 'overt' vague and 'not helpful'.[94]

In the meantime, Austria faced very similar problem. In *Commission v Austria,*[95] German students were studying medicine in Austria because of a German *numerus clausus*. The Austrian response was rather convoluted. Holders of secondary education diplomas acquired in other Member States had to meet the entry conditions of the relevant (or parallel) course in the Member State where the secondary education diploma was acquired. This was held more explicitly to be indirect discrimination. This time, in a lengthier Judgment (aided by an Opinion), the Court displayed a better grasp of the definition of indirect discrimination,[96] assuming, it seemed, that 'covert discrimination' was just another expression of indirect discrimination.[97] However, the Court lapsed again into looser thinking when addressing Austria's first objective justification defence. This was based on 'safeguarding the homogeneity' of the Austrian education system, which, Advocate General Jacobs interpreted as 'tantamount to "privileged access for Austrian citizens"'.[98] The Court rejected the defence, but only because Austria had failed to show that in 'each individual case that their rules are necessary and proportionate to attain the aim pursued'.[99] The Advocate General's strong hint that the aim itself was rooted in nationality was not mentioned by the Court,[100] seemingly forgetful of the principle that the defence cannot based on the protected characteristic in question.[101]

92 Ibid., para 28. In Case C-147/03 *Commission of the European Communities v Republic of Austria* [2006] ECR I-5969, Advocate General Jacobs merged 'covert' with 'indirect' (AG20); the Judgment seemingly did so (at paras 41 and 47).
93 Ibid., paras 13 and 16. The Judgment was circa 2,400 words, or 32 paragraphs. The Court proceeded without an Opinion.
94 Case C-73/08 *Bressol v Gouvernement de la Communauté Française* [2010] 3 CMLR 559, Opinion of AG Sharpston AG47-AG50.
95 Case C-147/03 *Commission of the European Communities v Republic of Austria* [2006] ECR I-5969 (7 July 2004).
96 Ibid., paras 47 and 60.
97 Ibid., para 21, and Opinion of AG Jacobs, para AG20.
98 Case C-147/03, para AG30.
99 Ibid., para 63.
100 See especially ibid., para 63.
101 See e.g. Case 96/80 *Jenkins v Kingsgate* [1981] ICR 592, [11], stating that 'factors used as a defence should be objectively justified and be in no way related to any discrimination based on sex'. See also *Allonby v Accrington and Rosendale College* [2001] ICR 1189 (CA), [29] (Sedley LJ): 'In particular there is no recognition [by the tribunal] that if the aim of the dismissal was itself discriminatory ... it could never afford justification'.

The Belgian and Austrian cases triggered a political backlash from nations whose public finances were being upset by policy choices in neighbouring countries.[102] Subsequent cases involved the consequent redrafted prohibitions. The first of these, *Bidar*,[103] was technically muddled and did little to clarify matters.

Bidar could be dubbed a *mini*-cumulative case. It was entertained on the premise[104] that (non-UK) EU students studying in a University in England or Wales were subject to a two-fold requirement in order to qualify for a maintenance loan. The first was a 'settlement' criterion. To be an 'eligible student', the person had to be 'settled' in the UK. This meant 'being ordinarily resident there without being subject under the immigration laws to any restriction on the period for which he may remain'.[105] The second 'integration' limb referred specifically to eligibility for maintenance loans. This required that 'the person has been ordinarily resident throughout the three-year period preceding the first day of the first academic year of the course' not being in full-time education during that time.[106] Typically, that would preclude a school pupil from going straight to university, which was the case in *Bidar*.

Without much explanation, the ECJ treated this as indirect discrimination, although still using the terms 'overt' and 'covert':

> It must be recalled here that the principle of equal treatment prohibits not only overt discrimination based on nationality but also all covert forms of discrimination which, by applying other distinguishing criteria, lead in fact to the same result.[107]

Advocate General Geelhoad attempted a broader rationalisation:

> I would only remark in this regard that where the eligibility conditions are more cumbersome for EU citizens who are lawfully resident in the UK than for British nationals, it is quite clear that this amounts to an indirect discrimination on grounds of nationality.[108]

102 For an excellent summary of the political background, see, S Garben, 'Case Comment on *Bressol*' (2010) 47(5) *CMLR* 1493, 1496–1498.

103 Case C-209/03 *R (Bidar) v Ealing LBC* [2005] ECR I-2119 (15 March 2005).

104 The precise (somewhat convoluted) legislative sources were not explained fully. See also, [2001] EWHC Admin 1177.

105 The 'trail' would seem to be thus: SI 2001/951, reg 4, Sch 1, para, 1, and the Immigration Act 1971, 'Interpretation', s 33(2A).

106 Education (Student Support) Regulations 2001, SI 2001/951, reg 19(2) – sch 1, para 8 (b) and (c).

107 Case C-209/03, [51].

108 Ibid., Opinion of AG Geelhoad, AG55.

Bearing in mind that non-UK students could never achieve settlement status,[109] a finding of indirect discrimination requires further explanation.[110] The 'settlement' criterion here meant that 100 per cent of (non-UK) EU students cannot meet the requirement by comparison with all UK citizens, to whom it did not apply.[111] As such, this has all the hallmarks of direct discrimination (and would satisfy the yet-to-be devised 'exact coincidence' rubric).[112] It was surprising that neither the claimant nor the Advocate General raised this contention. The matter became more confused when the Court discussed the objective justification defence. It found that the 'settled' element could not be objectively justified, because,

> [T]he rules at issue ... preclude any possibility of a national of another Member State obtaining settled status as a student. They thus make it impossible for such a national, whatever his actual degree of integration into the society of the host Member State, to satisfy that condition and hence to enjoy the right to assistance to cover his maintenance costs.[113]

This factual observation that 100 per cent of non-UK nationals could not meet the criterion suggests that this was in fact a case of *direct* discrimination. But given the indication that it saw this as indirect ('covert') discrimination, a better explanation is that the Court took 'the two layers as a single bundle',[114] which we shall see became the more formalised approach to these cumulative cases.

Amid this technical confusion, there can be found a more convincing explanation of why this was treated as indirect discrimination, even though in the instant case the defence failed. This relates to the political backlash to the earlier decisions. Bearing in mind that the defence failed on the 'settlement' requirement, the Court announced,

109 They would not be given permission to remain indefinitely. See *Patmalniece v Secretary of State for Work and Pensions* [2009] EWCA Civ 621 [25] (Moses LJ).

110 In *Patmalniece v Secretary of State for Work and Pensions* [2009] EWCA Civ 621, the Court of Appeal suggested that *Bidar* should have been the case of direct discrimination ([25]) and that the decision 'was for reasons that remain unexplained' ([20]).

111 Case C-209/03 *R (Bidar) v Ealing LBC* [2005] ECR I-2119, para AG55.

112 Case C-73/*08 Bressol v Gouvernement De La Communauté Française* [2010] 3 CMLR 20, Opinion of AG Sharpston, para 56. 'I take there to be direct discrimination when the category of those receiving a certain advantage and the category of those suffering a correlative disadvantage coincide exactly with the respective categories of persons distinguished only by applying a prohibited classification'. Discussed above, text to n 56.

113 Case C-209/03, para 61.

114 S Currie, '"Free" movers? The post-accession experience of accession-8 migrant workers in the UK' (2006) 31(2) *EL Rev* 207, 221.

> [I]t is permissible for a Member State to ensure that the grant of assistance to cover the maintenance costs of students from other Member States does not become an unreasonable burden which could have consequences for the overall level of assistance which may be granted by that State.[115]

It was permissible also to achieve this aim with a 'residence' requirement: 'it is thus legitimate for a Member State to grant such assistance only to students who have demonstrated a certain degree of integration into the society of that State'.[116] One could infer that the Court is signalling that various residence requirements taken by Member States are potentially justifiable. This positive reaction to the political backlash could only be made with the demonstration that residence requirements will be analysed merely as indirectly discriminatory. The only problem with the defence in *Bidar* is that the impact, being 100 per cent, was not proportionate.[117] This also could explain why the 'settlement' requirement was treated as indirect discrimination, and yet treated in the justification stage as if it were direct. The Judgment suggests that such absolutist requirements will never be permissible, but advises Member States (and their legal drafters) that residence requirements could be wrapped up in a 'single bundle' with other criteria and be regarded as only indirect discrimination, with the potential for justification. But from the point of view of providing a clear dividing line between direct and indirect discrimination, this Judgment was a complete failure.

A less-muddled attempt to reconcile the definitions of discrimination with these policy considerations was made in *Bressol*.[118] This was a multi-layered cumulative case. Belgium (again) adopted a policy that non-resident students on certain (medical) courses should not exceed a 30 per cent threshold. To qualify, an applicant had to prove that 'his principal residence is in Belgium' *and* fulfil one of eight further conditions, which included 'the right to remain permanently in Belgium', or other factors related to refugee status, parental residence, scholarships, a six-month work and residence record, and so on.[119]

115 Case C-209/03, and para 56. See also para 61.

116 Ibid., para 57.

117 Although, see *Patmalniece* (below), where proportionality was not an issue.

118 Case C-73/08 *Bressol v Gouvernement De La Communauté Française* [2010] 3 CMLR 20.

119 Art. 1 of the decree: 'A resident student for the purposes of this decree is a student who, at the time of his registration in an institution of higher education, proves that his principal residence is in Belgium and that he fulfils one of the following conditions: 1 he has the right to remain permanently in Belgium; 2 he has had his principal residence in Belgium for at least six months prior to his registration in an institution of higher education, at the same time carrying on a remunerated or unremunerated professional activity or benefiting from a replacement income granted by a Belgian public service; 3 he has permission to remain for an unlimited period [in Belgium] on the basis of [the relevant Belgian legislation]; 4 he has permission to remain in Belgium because he enjoys refugee status [as defined by Belgian legislation] or has submitted a request to be recognised as a refugee; 5 he

Belgian nationals enjoyed an automatic right of residence, and so on the face of it, non-nationals were treated less favourably, as they had the extra burden of showing their 'non-automatic' right of residence. The Opinion of Advocate General Sharpston took this line. She considered the 'exact coincidence' between the automatic right of residence and nationality qualified this as direct (nationality) discrimination.[120]

However, the Court seemed to prefer its advice from *Bidar* (although without repeating the apparently contradictory reasoning), ruling *08 Bressol v Gouvernement De La Communauté Française* that for (EU) nationality discrimination, a 'residency' requirement for certain benefits incorporating an automatic right to residence for Belgian nationals, amounted to *indirect* discrimination. The Court gave no reason for dismissing the Advocate's General's Opinion on this issue.[121] As with *Bidar,* the most plausible explanation is that the Court rolled up the multiple layers into a single bundle. (In the spirit of *Bidar*, it then issued guidelines on the objective justification issue, without ruling categorically one way or another, but providing enough leeway for the referring court to permit the requirements.)[122]

The UK Supreme Court came to the matter for the first time in *Patmalniece v Secretary of State for Work and Pensions.*[123] Patmalniece was a Latvian national living in the UK. She claimed that Britain's refusal to give her state pension credit discriminated on the ground of nationality, contrary to EU law.[124] To qualify a person had to be 'in Great Britain'.[125] This in turn was defined with a *Bidar*-style two-fold formula, which was drafted in the negative. First, a person was treated as *not* in Great Britain if she was not 'habitually resident' in the

has the right to reside in Belgium because he benefits from temporary protection on the basis of [the relevant Belgian legislation]; 6 he has a mother, father, legal guardian, or spouse who fulfils one of the above conditions; 7 he has had his principal residence in Belgium for at least three years at the time of his registration in an institution of higher education; 8 he has been granted a scholarship for his studies within the framework of development cooperation for the academic year and for the studies for which the request for registration was introduced'.

120 Case C-73/08, AG43-AG58.

121 As noted above, Lord Hope suggested that the Court considered the Opinion 'too analytical': *Patmalniece v Secretary of State for Work and Pensions* [2011] UKSC 11 [33].

122 The Belgian Constitutional Court was reported to have validated some, while invalidating other, programmes. See L Burgorgue-Larsen 'The Constitutional Dialogue in Europe: A "political" dialogue' (2015) 21(1) *European Journal of Current Legal Issues*, Part 3. http://webjcli.org/article/view/412 accessed 27 December 2020.

123 [2011] UKSC 11. In *Bidar* (QBD, 18 December, 2001) [31], the High Court did not discuss the discrimination point. Instead, it found that the local authority did not have the power to issue the benefit claimed.

124 Council Regulation (EEC) No 1408/71 (social security) art 3(1). See now (from 1 May, 2010), Regulation (EC) No 883/2004.

125 State Pension Credit Act 2002, s 1(2)(a).

UK's 'Common Travel Area', comprising the UK, the Channel Islands, the Isle of Man and the Republic of Ireland.[126] And second, a person was not to be treated as habitually resident in the Common Travel Area unless she had a right to reside there.[127]

It is this second limb that causes the doubts. It could be directly discriminatory, as it favoured 100 per cent of nationals of the Common Travel Area, and disfavoured most (but not all) of other EU nationals. It is distinguishable from *Bidar* in the sense that it does not disfavour 100 per cent of the 'victim group', as some other EU non-nationals could obtain the right to reside in the Common Travel Area.[128] Such a nicety did not inform the Supreme Court's *decision*, although some doubts were expressed along the way. The Supreme Court upheld be Court of Appeal's finding that the 'cumulative' formula amounted to indirect discrimination, and (Lord Walker dissenting) was objectively justified.[129]

There was a 'hard to avoid' suspicion that the strategy behind this drafting was to prevent 'benefit tourism',[130] with a formula designed to preserve the potential for objective justification by not directly discriminating.[131] The Supreme Court ultimately followed the *Bressol* approach of treating the two limbs as a single measure. Thus, as some British citizens may not be habitually resident (the first limb), while some other EU citizens could obtain the right to reside (the second limb), the combined rules should be analysed as indirect discrimination. This might be the correct application of *Bressol,* but there was some varying logic en route.

Given the complex drafting of the challenged regulations, Lord Hope thought it was 'necessary to look more closely at their effect'.[132] A feature of this approach – a departure from the traditional 'less favourable' and 'reason-why' questions, which focus on the *treatment* rather than its effect – is that it cannot distinguish between direct and indirect discrimination (thus sharing the same failing as the improperly expressed *but for* test[133]).

126 State Pension Credit Regulations 2002, SI 2002/1792, reg 2(1). This common travel area comprised the UK, the Channel Islands, the Isle of Man and the Republic of Ireland. This itself carried a number of qualifications: those 'habitually resident' *included,* (a) EU workers, (b) refugees, (c) persons granted exceptional leave to enter the UK, (d) deportees to the UK and not subject to immigration control, (e) persons who left Montserrat because of the volcanic eruption. Patmalniece, although from the EU, was not a worker.

127 Ibid., reg 2(2).

128 A point made in the Court of Appeal [2009] EWCA Civ 621 [25].

129 [2009] EWCA Civ 621; [2011] UKSC 11 [31] (Lord Hope), [63] (Lord Walker).

130 [2011] UKSC 11, [72], [76] (Lord Walker), [38], [51]–[52] (Lord Hope), [97] (Lady Hale).

131 Ibid., [25] (Lord Hope), [72] (Lord Walker), [96] (Lady Hale).

132 Ibid., [25].

133 It is normally expressed as, 'would the claimant have received the treatment but for his or her protected characteristic?' See either M Connolly, *Discrimination Law* (2011, Sweet and Maxwell) pp. 93–94; or *The English Judiciary, Discrimination Law and Statutory Interpretation* (2018, Routledge) pp. 91–101.

Lord Hope then seemingly cited with approval the case of *James v Eastleigh,*[134] which he suggested tentatively was at odds with *Bressol.* Save he was correct, he would defer to *Bressol,* as he was not deciding the position in domestic law.[135] As already noted in this chapter, this is a concession that the different jurisdictions have different definitions of discrimination.[136]

Lady Hale departed from AG Sharpston's application of her 'exact coincidence' rubric to this case, because of the absence of exact symmetry between the measure and the advantaged and disadvantaged. This effectively rolled up the two roles into one bundle. Lord Walker was more sceptical of *Bressol,* preferring to isolate the 'right of residence' criterion and its *automatic* characteristic, which distinguished it from any *discretionary* right for nationals outside of the Common Travel Area. This then accorded with AG Sharpston's 'exact coincidence' rubric. Lord Walker's preference was for a diluted version of the 'exact coincidence' rubric (although, as noted above, this may have been a misunderstanding of the rubric[137]). This would have applied, even if some from outside the Common Travel Area could obtain a right of residence. In the result though, Lord Walker deferred, like his colleagues, to the superior authority of *Bressol.*

There are several layers of inconsistency here. First, the ECJ will treat these cumulative cases only as indirect discrimination. Second, there is AG Sharpston's Opinion that 'proxy' cases can amount to direct discrimination if they meet the 'exact coincidence' test. Third, Lord Hope's emphasis on the *effects* of any treatment loses focus on the distinction between direct and indirect discrimination. Fourth, Lord Walker would have preferred a diluted version of the 'exact coincidence' test for 'proxy' cases. Fifth, Lady Hale endorsed the 'exact coincidence' rubric, even though in no way is it in endorsed by the ECJ. Sixth, to varying degrees, all accepted that the domestic definitions of direct and indirect discrimination (represented by *James*) differ from that understood by the ECJ, which itself differs from that of Advocate General Sharpston.

There is then, no settled view on whether these cumulative cases should be analysed as direct or indirect discrimination, only that the ECJ rather bluntly dictates the latter, almost certainly for policy reasons driven by the political backlash. Within that binary disagreement, somewhat imaginative notions of a comparison were formulated by AG Jacobs and AG Sharpston, although it is notable that these were not repeated in the respective ECJ Judgments. The UK Supreme Court wrestled with these, producing different interpretations, while attempting in vain to reconcile them with *James.* A common feature though, was a tendency to analyse the facts for *group* disadvantage. This is something

134 See above, text to n 3.
135 [2011] UKSC 11 [29].
136 See above, text to n 73.
137 See above, text to n 82.

usually associated with indirect discrimination (and a trigger for positive action), which somewhat loads the conclusion against a finding of direct discrimination.

An interesting footnote to this discussion is the Supreme Court's approach to the objective justification defence. Lord Walker's opinion (see below) was particularly relevant to the boundary between direct and indirect discrimination.

The difficulty of labelling the challenged practice in this case as indirectly discriminatory is exposed also when considering the justification defence, which as everybody agrees should be for reasons independent of the protected characteristic in question, in these cases nationality.[138] Lady Hale dutifully focussed on Court of Justice case law[139] that indicated that states could limit means-tested social security payments to those with a right to reside under EU or domestic law.[140] But of interest in the context of this discussion was whether the practice was 'independent of nationality', given the proximity of 'right to reside' to nationality. Lord Hope held that it was:

> The Secretary of State's purpose was to protect the resources of the United Kingdom against resort to benefit or social tourism by persons who are not economically or socially integrated with this country. This is not because of their nationality or because of where they have come from.[141]

This rather binary conclusion evades the reality that things are often done for many reasons. Here it was quite obviously for both financial and nationality reasons, with nationality discrimination serving the financial policy (assuming there is no xenophobic element). A host country can choose to save money in many ways. In this case, it chose to do so by withholding benefits from certain EU nationals. Lord Walker dissented, and did so by iterating his views on direct discrimination:

> In my opinion the provisions of regulation 2(2) are probably aimed at discriminating against economically inactive foreign nationals on the grounds of nationality. Whether or not that was the intention of those who framed them, they have that effect.[142]

He 'simply demonstrated' this by comparing the claimant with a British national who had returned after 50 years in Latvia, with 'no family, friends or other human or financial resources here'. Thus, 'Even though classified as indirect discrimination, it is not capable of justification because the proposed justification, once examined, is founded on nationality'.[143] Here, Lord Walker

138 Citing Case C-209/03 *R (Bidar) v Ealing LBC* [2005] ECR I-2119, para 54.
139 Case C-456/02 *Trojani v Centre public d'aide sociale de Bruxelles* [2004] ECR I-7573.
140 [2011] UKSC 11, [102]–[106].
141 Ibid., [52].
142 Ibid., [79].
143 Ibid.

has reverted to a technique apt for direct discrimination. Not only that, he has made a conventional one-to-one comparison. Although apparently barred by ECJ authority from holding that this is direct discrimination, Lord Walker transferred his view of events and the law to the justification defence and achieved his desired result. For Lord Walker, this prima facie case of indirect discrimination cannot be justified because it is direct discrimination (although he cannot call it that). Lord Hope and Lord Walker took equally binary views on a factual situation more realistically understood as comprising at least two reasons. But Lord Walker's logic extends to recognising that the challenged practice was at least tainted by nationality. The remorseless logic is that if something tainted by a protected characteristic is not direct discrimination, it cannot be justified as indirect discrimination. One could suggest this is the result of tidy statutory drafting. However, one could say with a good deal more certainty that the demarcation between direct and indirect discrimination is somewhat fuzzy.

Conclusion

The 'incorporated' cases exposed that the judiciary at all levels, including the ECJ, cannot agree on whether a certain set of facts amounts to direct or indirect discrimination. In the meantime, the 'cumulative' cases presented just as many inconsistencies. The early ECJ cases finding a facially discriminatory element rendered the policy directly discriminatory, until a political backlash coincided with a U-turn, the departure not only from its own case law, but that of the UK, notably espoused in *James*.

From a more technical perspective, the apparently strict comparative element of direct discrimination could have been afforded four interpretations in *James* alone. These permutations comprise two decisions. First, whether to make a one-to-one or group comparison, and second whether to incorporate the background rule.

1 A one-to-one comparison ignoring any background rules (the majority).
2 A one-to-one comparison incorporating background rules.
3 A group comparison ignoring any background rules (Lord Lowry, Lord Griffiths, dissenting,[144] Lady Hale's and Lord Hope's retrospective in *Patmalniece*).
4 A group comparison incorporating any background rules (Lord Walker, retrospective, *Patmalniece*).

The ECJ equal pay Judgments in *Roberts* and *Hlozek* were consistent with option 4, utilising group comparisons defined by the background factor.

144 [1990] 2 AC 751 (HL) 780 (Lord Lowry), 769 (Lord Griffiths, agreeing with Lord Lowry), although the dissent turned on the cause of the treatment, which in their view was to help pensioners rather than discriminate against men.

A similarly varied, but less concrete, range of attempts were made in the cumulative cases. AG Jacobs confined his indissociable rubric to a physical nexus (pregnancy). AG Sharpston's 'exact coincidence' variety did not do so, and was expressed to cover pregnancy as only women *can* become pregnant. AG Jacobs' virtually redundant indissociable rubric was given new life *in the UK* by Lady Hale's refined interpretation of AG Sharpston's 'exact coincidence' rubric, or indeed, by Lord Walker's more concordant interpretation. Amongst all of this, the taciturn ECJ in the more recent cumulative cases made decisions *consistent* with the physical nexus restriction of AG Jacobs' rubric, but no more than that. Its credibility was crushed when any physical nexus pregnancy-related illnesses was ignored. In the meantime, Lord Walker in *Patmalniece* escaped any stricture confining cumulative cases to indirect discrimination with the simple expedient of finding that there was no objective justification because of the discriminatory nature of a criterion. Rather than deploying a particular comparative model, the minority in *James* brought the objective justification into play via the 'reason why' element, endowing it with a degree of subjectivity.

Behind these expressed technical niceties, or in the case of the ECJ, unexpressed reasoning, one can detect policy considerations dictating the decisions, rather than principles of discrimination law. Even here there is a lack of consistency. While barely disguised intentional discrimination (e.g. *Bressol*) is approved seemingly in deference to political and economic considerations, genuine benign motives (as in *James*) are discounted in a broad-brush principled stand against motive being used as a defence in more pernicious circumstances, such as customer preference.

Even given these technical and/or policy inconsistencies, each and every judgment and Opinion was at least clear in finding that the challenged practice was either direct or indirect discrimination. This gives some credence to Lady Hale's 'mutually exclusive' assertion, albeit limited to this binary choice. However, it cannot disguise that the distinction between the two is somewhat fuzzy, or in AG Sharpton's words, 'the distinction between direct and indirect discrimination lacks precision'.[145]

Further reading

J Bowers and E Moran, 'Justification in direct sex discrimination law: breaking the taboo' (2002) 31(4) *ILJ* 307.

S Garben, 'Case Comment on *Bressol*' (2010) 47(5) *CMLR* 1493.

M Connolly, *The English Judiciary, Discrimination Law and Statutory Interpretation* (2018, Routledge) pp. 91–101. www.taylorfrancis.com/books/9780429450808

145 C-73/08 *Bressol v Gouvernement De La Communauté Française* [2010] 3 CMLR 20, para AG46.

3 Discrimination and pregnancy

Introduction

Pregnancy discrimination is something very obviously a target of a sex discrimination law, but not neatly accommodated by the direct/indirect dichotomy, a limitation unforeseen by the drafters. Caselaw struggled with the result, either by accommodating pregnancy into the sex discrimination model with a technically unsatisfactory method, or excluding this obvious policy imperative for want of a technically correct solution. Eventually, courts and/or legislators created models that do not comply with the direct/indirect discrimination model. Parliament's response was a model no longer requiring *less* favourable treatment, something at odds with conventional notions of comparative treatment as discrimination. Meanwhile the European Court of Justice (ECJ) held that pregnancy discrimination is direct sex discrimination because only women can become pregnant and/or there is an indissociable physical nexus between pregnancy and being female. It further holds that discrimination because of a pregnancy-related illness is direct sex discrimination *unless* the discrimination falls outside of a legally imposed maternity period, in which case it is analysed as *indirect* discrimination, despite that only women can suffer pregnancy-related illness and the continuing physical nexus. This all suggests that the direct/indirect model of discrimination is incapable of addressing all the policy goals of discrimination law.

This chapter explores the many attempts to explain the legal response to pregnancy discrimination. It suggests that none can do so in terms of conventional discrimination law. This is because, it is ventured, the underlying policy goals are in fact economic (such as population replacement and the pensions crisis) rather than ones of gender inequality. As such, equality law is not entirely in harmony with its policy goals.

Pregnancy discrimination and the direct/indirect dichotomy

An early conundrum for the courts was how to analyse pregnancy discrimination within the framework of sex discrimination law. In this instance, the matter brought the direct/indirect model to breaking point.

DOI: 10.4324/9781003187547-3

The equal treatment model, being symmetrical, demands (or at least suggests) a comparison between the treatment given to the woman, and that which would have been given to a man in the same circumstances. Of course, as men do not get pregnant, this comparison is not obvious for pregnancy cases. Back in 1980, the EAT in *Turley v Alders Department Stores*[1] held that a claim of sex discrimination on the ground of pregnancy must inevitably fail, for want of a comparator. A similarly doctrinal approach was adopted by a majority of the United States Supreme Court; in *General Electric v Gilbert,* it held that a distinction 'between pregnant and nonpregnant persons' was not one based on sex, as there were 'nonpregnant' women.[2] Unlike the apparently indifferent UK Parliament, Congress promptly remedied the position with the Pregnancy Discrimination Act 1978, which provided that the statutory term 'because of sex' includes 'because of ... pregnancy, childbirth, or related medical conditions'.[3]

A subsequent British attempt at a purposive interpretation merely highlighted the limitation, rather than provided a solution. In 1985, the EAT in *Hayes v Malleable Working Men's Club and Institute*[4] used a 'sick man' as a comparator. Apart from the offence caused by comparing a celebrated event with a negative one, it carried a counter-productive characteristic of incentivising deteriorating work practices for all.[5] Employers could escape liability by showing that they treated their sick male workers equally *badly,* for instance, with a policy of dismissing any worker after four weeks' absence. This defence becomes truly poisonous to the rights of the women the law is supposing to protect, if used by the archetypal sweatshop employer with an all-female workforce. These workers cannot bring a real comparator into court, only a hypothetical one. A tribunal would have the somewhat dubious task of deciding how a sweatshop employer might treat male workers – the evidence being how badly it treats its female workers.

This state of affairs was salvaged by the Court of Justice, when in *Dekker*, it held that as only women become pregnant, discrimination on the ground of pregnancy is direct sex discrimination.[6] As with the US legislation, this rather

1 [1980] ICR 6 (EAT). At the time, the Employment Protect Act 1975, s 34, provided that dismissal for pregnancy constituted an (unlawful) Unfair Dismissal, but the claimant had not acquired the necessary 26 weeks of continuous service for unfair dismissal rights. (See now ERA 1996, s 99 (and s 47C for detriments).) A lay member dissented, applying the 'sick man' approach (see below).

2 429 US 125 (1976), 134–135, citing *Geduldig v Aiello* 417 US 484, 503, n 20 (J Brenhan). The case was not cited in *Turley v Alders.*

3 Amending Civil Rights Act 1964, Title VII, s.701, with a new sub-section (k), USC § 2000e(k).

4 [1985] ICR 703 (EAT).

5 See the infamous *Palmer v Thompson* 403 US 217 (1971); after a court ordered Mississippi City to abandon its racial segregation policy for its swimming pools (four white-only, one black-only), the city administration responded by closing down all its pools instead, a response not offending the US constitutional right to equality

6 Case C-177/88 *Dekker v Stichting Vormingscentrum voor Jonge Volwassen (VJV-Centrum) Plus* [1990] ECR I-3941, para 12. See also *Brooks v Canada Safeway* [1989] 1

crude formula ignored the niceties of symmetry, but, of course, fulfilled the purpose of the legislation, an approach typical of the Court of Justice's jurisprudence. As a consequence, UK legislation was modified with a new formula. It classified 'pregnancy and maternity' as additional protected characteristics, alongside race, sex, disability, etc.[7] But more was needed to prevent further arguments over the impossibility of a comparator. So, pregnancy and maternity discrimination required 'unfavourable' rather than 'less favourable' treatment,[8] thus discarding any comparative element and, with it, notions of less favourable treatment and symmetry. In legislative language at least, the only way to protect women from pregnancy discrimination was with a formula excluding an apparently central tenet of discrimination law.

In the meantime, the Court of Justice continued its *Dekker* logic when it came to a pregnancy-related illness, but only where it fell inside the standard maternity period.[9] From here on, any principles from *Dekker* ceased to bite. With less favourable treatment because of a pregnancy-related illness falling outside of the maternity period, the 'sick man' comparison *should* be made: 'the sole question is whether a female worker's absences, following maternity leave, caused by her incapacity for work brought on by such disorders, are treated in the same way as a male worker's absences'.[10] And on the matter of maternity *pay*, lower-than-normal pay was not discriminatory because *no* comparison was possible: women on maternity leave were 'in a special position which requires them to be afforded special protection, but which is not comparable either with that of a man or with that of a woman actually at work'.[11] This in turn was sidestepped where maternity pay is *related* to the worker's salary.[12] Thus, maternity pay failing to reflect a general pay rise during the maternity period can amount to sex discrimination under the equal pay provisions even though there is no comparator.[13]

SCR 1219, where the Canadian Supreme Court, not constricted by a detailed statutory formula, ruled that under the Canadian Charter of Rights, 'The capacity for pregnancy is an immutable characteristic, or incident of gender and a central distinguishing feature between men and women. A distinction based on pregnancy is not merely a distinction between those who are and are not pregnant, but also between the gender that has the capacity for pregnancy and the gender which does not' (Part VIII). The short Report provides no page or para numbers.

7 See now, Equality Act 2010, s 4.

8 Ibid., ss 17 (non-work) and 18 (work).

9 Case C-399/96 *Brown v Rentokil* [1998] ICR 790. See, M Wynn, 'Pregnancy Discrimination: Equality, Protection or Reconciliation?' (1999) 62 *MLR* 435.

10 Ibid., [26].

11 Case C-342/93 *Gillespie v Northern Health and Social Services Board* [1996] ICR 498, [17].

12 Case C-147/02 *Alabaster v Woolwich plc* [2004] ECR I-3103, paras 47–50. Upon its return, the Court of Appeal implemented this ruling through the Equal Pay Act 1970, by disapplying the Act's requirement for a comparator: *Alabaster v Barclays Bank (No 2)* [2005] EWCA 508. See now Equality Act 2010, ss 73–74.

13 Upon its return, the Court of Appeal in *Alabaster*, ibid., implemented this ruling through the Equal Pay Act 1970, by disapplying the Act's requirement for a

Following *Dekker* and its progeny, numerous thoughtful commentaries tried to reconcile these decisions (and pregnancy discrimination more generally) with the direct/indirect dichotomy. Perhaps the best known was Advocate General Sharpston's 'exact coincidence' explanation, where the advantaged and disadvantaged groups coincided exactly with men and women respectively. The difficulty with this is that not all women are or become pregnant.[14]

Elsewhere, a fifth common view of *Dekker* was that the Court (implicitly) applied the *but for* test popularised by the House of Lords at the time,[15] a test apparently needing no comparator.[16] But many commentators objected to this. The first basis was that the *but for* test is unsuitable for pregnancy discrimination. This is because on one view, its 'ability to connect consequences, however remote, with an original causative characteristic may have to be limited in certain situations', such as the 'choice' of pregnancy.[17] Alternatively, it was because, in pregnancy discrimination scenarios, the *but for* test cannot distinguish between direct and indirect discrimination. This latter observation carries the common practice of expressing the test improperly, or 'passively'. If one asks whether the claimant would have *received* the treatment but for a protected characteristic, the answer can be yes for both direct and indirect discrimination. One should ask, would the defendant *have treated* the claimant so, but for a protected characteristic? This shifts the focus from the *effect* of the treatment to the cause, and without much ado, resolves this difficulty. Thus, the difficulty was not with the test *per se*, but with the imprecision with which it was expressed: the first question cannot distinguish between direct and indirect discrimination. The second question can.[18]

comparator: *Alabaster v Barclays Bank (No 2)* [2005] EWCA 508. See now, Equality Act 2010, ss 73–74.

14 Case C-73/08 *Bressol v Gouvernement de la Communauté Française* [2010] 3 CMLR 559, Opinion of AG Sharpston AG47-AG56. This theory is discussed in Chapter 2, 'The "indissociable" and "exact coincidence" rubrics', p. 19.

15 See *James v Eastleigh BC* [1990] 2 AC 751. The test has since been eclipsed by the 'reason why' approach. See e.g. *Nagarajan v LRT* [2000] 1 AC 501 (HL) 511 (Lord Nicholls); neatly distilled by B Watt, 'Goodbye "but-for", hello "but-why?"?' (1998) 27 ILJ 121.

16 See R Wintemute, 'When is Pregnancy Discrimination Indirect Discrimination?' (1998) 27 *ILJ* 23, 24–25, n 4 and references within; S Honeyball, 'Pregnancy and Sex Discrimination' (2000) 29 *ILJ* 43, 48; E Ellis, 'The definition of discrimination in European Community sex equality law' (1994) 19(6) *EL Rev* 563, 567.

17 Wintemute, ibid., 34. The notion of 'choice' to delineate direct and indirect discrimination was discussed in the recent CJ AG Opinions on the wearing of religious symbols: Case C-157/15 *Achbita v G4S Secure Solutions NV* [2017] IRLR 466; Case C-188/15 *Bougnaoui v Micropole SA* [2017] IRLR 447. See comment, S Fraser Butlin, 'The CJEU confused over religion' (2017) 76(2) *CLJ* 246.

18 Unfortunately, the test's judicial author, Lord Goff, improperly expressed it thus, a feature not noticed by the dissents. See *James v Eastleigh BC* [1990] 2 AC 751, 765 (Lord Goff), 774 (Lord Lowry, dissenting). See further, Chapter 2, p. 34, and M Connolly, *The English Judiciary, Discrimination Law and Statutory Interpretation: Easy Cases Making Bad Law* (Routledge, 2018), Chapter 5, pp. 91–101.

But the more substantial objections centre on the need for a comparison, being 'essential' to the concept of discrimination, something envisaging *different* treatment.[19] This also carries policy-flavoured concerns. Without a comparison, the law is left to identifying 'nasty treatment', an approach leaving too much discretion in the hands of the 'overwhelmingly male' judiciary.[20] To mitigate such a discretion, a comparative element gave the law a necessary measure of objectivity.[21] Thus, commentators attempted to reconcile pregnancy discrimination with the traditional direct/indirect model by preserving a comparative element.

To maintain a comparative element, pregnancy discrimination could work with a new form of 'self comparison', where the comparator is 'pared down' to a (hypothetical) person without the reason (pregnancy) for the treatment.[22] The obvious conclusion here is that such a test searches for *pregnancy* discrimination, rather than *sex* discrimination, thus exposing *Dekker* as better analysed as *indirect* discrimination.[23] A parallel train of thought is that treating a person differently because they have a uterus, or a penis, is a matter of direct discrimination, because of a 'necessary connection' between the treatment and the victim's sex.[24] But pregnancy itself, being a 'choice' is one step removed and so 'problematic' to analyse as direct sex discrimination.[25]

Others identified various scenarios, and allocated them to either their direct or indirect buckets. Refusing to hire, or dismissing, a woman because of pregnancy 'clearly' would be direct. This is because the relevant circumstances are the same as that of the non-pregnant male comparator.[26] But this fails to account for the fact that there are non-pregnant women, including women who will never become pregnant.[27]

A more common scenario, dubbed 'needs based pregnancy discrimination', occurs where, say, an employer treats all workers unfavourably for absenteeism. Here, the 'sick man' comparator is resurrected as a credible one:[28] after all, the

19 R Wintemute, 'When is Pregnancy Discrimination Indirect Discrimination?' (1998) 27 *ILJ* 23, 25; S Honeyball, 'Pregnancy and Sex Discrimination' (2000) 29 *ILJ* 43, 47.

20 E Ellis, 'The definition of discrimination in European Community sex equality law' (1994) 19(6) *EL Rev* 563, 571.

21 Ibid.

22 S Honeyball, 'Pregnancy and Sex Discrimination' (2000) 29 *ILJ* 43, 43 and 49–50.

23 Ibid., 50–52.

24 R Wintemute, 'When is Pregnancy Discrimination Indirect Discrimination?' (1998) 27 *ILJ* 23, 27; B Watt, 'Goodbye "but-for", hello "but-why?"?' (1998) 27 *ILJ* 121, 132. See also, L Flynn, 'Gender Blindness in the Face of Real Sex Differences' (1993) 15 *Dublin U LJ* 1.

25 R Wintemute, 'When is Pregnancy Discrimination Indirect Discrimination?' (1998) 27 *ILJ* 23, 27.

26 Ibid., 30.

27 Ibid., 27.

28 P Davies, *The European Court of Justice, National Courts, and Member States* in Paul Davies, Antoine Lyon-Caen, Silvana Sciarra, and Spiros Simitis (eds) European *Community Labour Law, Principles and Perspectives* (Clarendon Press, 1996), p. 127; R

treatment was because of absenteeism, not pregnancy. In these cases, if direct discrimination were not made out (because men and women were treated equally for absences), then this 'facially neutral' treatment (more likely) leads to a conclusion of indirect discrimination, as any facially neutral absentee policy is likely to adversely affect women. The treatment thus becomes potentially justifiable. As such, *Dekker* and its progeny 'make more sense'[29] if analysed as *indirect* discrimination. (This rather fluid transition between direct and indirect discrimination risks violating Baroness Hale's 'mutually exclusive' canon.[30]) Alternatively, the case law subsequent to *Dekker* shows that the Court had moved to a 'reason why' test, which might have produced a different result in *Dekker* itself.[31]

The fuzzy borders

The first feature to note about this mix of views is that they are laced with two foundational errors. First, most assimilated *Dekker* with the *but for* test, when no such test was expressed by the Court. Its central ruling was this, '[I]t should be observed that only women can be refused employment on the ground of pregnancy and such a refusal therefore constitutes direct discrimination on the ground of sex'.[32] The *but for* test asks whether the employer would have employed her but for her being female. The answer is 'no', as it would have employed a non-pregnant woman (as well as any man).[33] Indeed, in *Dekker*, a woman *was* appointed. The only *but for* question to produce an affirmative answer in this case is this: would the applicant have been employed but for being pregnant? In the context of *sex* discrimination, that is a useless test.

The second error was that the various views assumed that *Dekker* abandoned the comparative element of discrimination. These commentaries spent much time trying to retrieve a comparison in order to reconcile pregnancy discrimination with the direct/indirect dichotomy. This was odd, because the Court in *Dekker* made no such indication, as the central ruling cited above shows. Those subscribing to this apparent heresy rely on a later part of the judgment:

> It should be stressed that the reply to the question whether the refusal to employ a woman constitutes direct or indirect discrimination depends on the reason for that refusal. If that reason is to be found in the fact that the

Wintemute, 'When is Pregnancy Discrimination Indirect Discrimination?' (1998) 27 *ILJ* 23, 34–35.

29 R Wintemute, ibid.

30 *R (E) v Governing Body of JFS* [2010] 2 AC 728 (SC). [57] (Baroness Hale). See further, Chapter 2, 'Introduction'.

31 B Watt, 'Goodbye "but-for", hello "but-why?"?' (1998) 27 *ILJ* 121, 127–128

32 Case C-177/88 *Dekker v Stichting Vormingscentrum voor Jonge Volwassen (VJV-Centrum) Plus* [1990] ECR I-3941, para 12.

33 Assuming both the woman and the man were otherwise qualified for the job.

> person concerned is pregnant, then the decision is directly linked to the sex of the candidate. In those circumstances the absence of male candidates cannot affect the answer to the first question.[34]

This final sentence only dispenses with the need for a real comparator, as one was not available in that case (a non-pregnant woman was hired instead of the claimant). It did not dispense with a hypothetical one: would the employer have refused a man the employment? That, of course, is an incomplete question as it excludes non-pregnant women. The Court's solution to this, it seemed, was to consider pregnancy a characteristic indissociable from sex, a device dispensing with the need to ask how non-pregnant women would have been treated,[35] thus isolating the comparator to only males. Indeed, the subsequent (presumably) codifying Recast Directive expresses sex discrimination as *less* favourable treatment related to pregnancy.[36] All this suggests that *Dekker,* and EU pregnancy discrimination law, remains attached to a comparative element.

In any case, is discrimination law without a comparison such a heresy? Subsequent dicta have suggested that it is not always essential in direct discrimination *generally* (i.e. beyond pregnancy cases). Thus, where an employer dismisses someone stating, 'You're a typical lazy African', or 'You're a typical unreliable woman', a tribunal can dispense with 'arid and confusing disputes about the identification of the appropriate comparator'.[37] This approach is gaining traction. More recently, in the Court of Appeal, where Underhill LJ reasoned,

> [I]t is now very well established that the comparison exercise under section 13(1) (the so-called 'less favourable treatment' question) does essentially the same job as asking whether the treatment complained of was 'because of' the protected characteristic (the so-called 'reason why' question), and that if the latter question is answered the answer to the former will normally follow.[38]

34 Case C-177/88 *Dekker v Stichting Vormingscentrum voor Jonge Volwassen (VJV-Centrum) Plus* [1990] ECR I-3941, para 17.

35 This was the explanation of Advocate General Jacobs in C-79/99 *Schnorbus v Land Hessen* [2000] ECR I-10997, AG33.

36 Directive 2006/54/EC, arts 2(2) and 2(2)(c).

37 *Shamoon v Chief Constable of the RUC* [2003] ICR 337 (HL) [11] (Lord Nicholls); see also [125] (Lord Rodger agreeing on this point). In the context of ECHR, Art 14, *R (Carson) v Secretary of State for Work and Pensions* [2006] 1 AC 173 (SC) [63]–[68] (Lord Walker). See also *Madarassy v Nomura* [2007] ICR 867 (CA) [80]–[84], where Mummery LJ stated [81], 'While it would often be desirable for a tribunal to go through the two stages [the comparison and the "reason why"] … it would not necessarily be an error of law to fail to do so acting on the assumption that the burden may have shifted to the respondent'.

38 *Coffey v Chief Constable of Norfolk Constabulary* [2019] UKCA 1061 [76].

This might provide a practical solution where other black or female staff are not treated so by the same employer. And as noted above, for pregnancy and maternity specifically, the Equality Act 2010 no longer requires a comparison to establish discrimination.[39] There are also powerful conceptual objections to a comparator-driven model of discrimination law, which, in this context, tend to value matters by the 'norm' of the male comparator.[40]

The judgment and reasoning of *Dekker* may not be a technical masterpiece, but it adheres neither to the *but for* test, nor to comparison-free discrimination law. It simply associates pregnancy with (female) sex and compares how a man would have been treated. The technical shortcomings of this formula were exposed when the Court of Justice, post-*Dekker*, had to rule on a variety of pregnancy-related cases. The Court failed to adhere to its logic in cases of pregnancy-related absence, illness, or pay. This exposes the logic of the Court in all the pregnancy cases, which is more policy-based than doctrinal. The various attempts to interpret *Dekker* and its progeny misunderstand civil law practice especially that of the Court of Justice, which is less interested in technical niceties than achieving a legislative purpose, which in turn should advance the goals of the EU Treaties.[41] The only sense that can be made of this case law is that the Court was shaping the yet-to-be-developed pregnancy discrimination law. It did so in a way that English lawyers would consider judicial legislating.[42] Hence, it was rather superficial to attempt explanations of the Court's jurisprudence by reference to values it was not using, explicitly or implicitly.

If one bears in mind that the Court had to reconcile any pregnancy discrimination law with other pregnancy-related rights, its decisions make more sense. Hence, discrimination law in relation to maternity leave was shaped around the minimum standards provided by the Pregnancy Workers Directive.[43] A similar approach is detectable regarding maternity rights.[44] As

39 See text to n 7.

40 See, e.g., S Fredman, *Discrimination Law* (2nd edn, OUP 2011) 11; T Ward, 'Beyond sex equality: the limits of sex equality in the new Europe', in T Hervey and D O'Keeffe (eds), *Sex Equality Law in the European Union* (Wiley 1996) p. 370; R Townshend-Smith, *Sex Discrimination in Employment: Law, Practice and Policy* (Sweet & Maxwell 1989) pp. 25–26; C Cockburn, *In The Way of Women: Men's Resistance to Sex Equality in Organisations* (Macmillan, 1991) 38; N Lacey, 'Legislation against sex discrimination: questions from a feminist perspective' (1986) 14 *JLS* 411, 413–417. For a summary of these views, see M Connolly, *The English Judiciary, Discrimination Law and Statutory Interpretation: Easy Cases Making Bad Law* (Routledge, 2018) Chapter 3, pp. 61–62.

41 See e.g., the comments of Lord Diplock, in *R v Henn and Derby* [1981] 1 AC 850, 905.

42 Thus offending the constitutional doctrine of Separation of Powers: See *Duport Steels v Sirs* [1980] 1 WLR 142 (HL) 157 (Lord Diplock), 169 (Lord Scarman).

43 Directive 92/85/EEC, art 8. See Case C-399/96 *Brown v Rentokil* [1998] ICR 790. For comment, see, M Wynn, 'Pregnancy Discrimination: Equality, Protection or Reconciliation?' (1999) 62 *MLR* 435.

44 Ibid., art 11. Case C-342/93 *Gillespie v Northern Health and Social Services Board* [1996] ICR 498.

Advocate General Léger noted, to give full protection to pregnant women on maternity leave 'would threaten to upset the balance of the entire social welfare system'.[45] In other words, existing pregnancy-related rights mandated a large degree of *different* (rather than *equal*) treatment. Some of this may be negative, say, by barring a pregnant woman from certain tasks for health and safety reasons.[46] Other rights could be labelled as 'positive', in relation to say, maternity leave or maternity pay. Such 'absolute' rights disturb the discrimination model. So much so, that men are barred from utilising its symmetrical nature to claim equivalent rights.[47] Even the role of *pregnancy* discrimination law is relegated to a 'safety net', filling the gaps in the absolute rights, rather than infiltrating them with a prescription of equality principles. And any remaining lacunas could be covered by *sex* discrimination or (gender) equal pay law.[48]

So, while seasoned expert commentators struggled to allocate pregnancy rights and discrimination into their direct/indirect dichotomy, the law moved on, leaving the various theories rather marginalised. None of these commentators are likely seriously to challenge these developments (in fact one, specifically advocated them[49]), as the consequent clarity is likely to satisfy most in terms of policy, if not doctrinal principle.

Of course, the practical significance of this somewhat untidy mix of views flows from the defences available: virtually none for direct, and a rather open-ended one for indirect. Supporters of *Dekker* point to this and a fear that the English judiciary would be far too generous to employer's 'practical' or 'needs based' reasons for treating pregnancy and maternity leave as costly and inconvenient business-related problems,[50] even if this does not square with social

45 Ibid., [48] (AG Opinion).

46 Pregnant Workers Directive 92/85/EEC, arts 3–7.

47 Recast Directive 206/54/EC, art 28; Equality Act 2010, ss 17(6) and 18(7) (ousting s 13 (direct discrimination) in pregnancy cases). See, the US, *Newport News Shipbuilding & Dry Dock Co v EEOC* 462 US 669 (Sup Ct, 1983), less valuable pregnancy benefits for spouses of male employees compared to female employees; held to be sex (pregnancy) discrimination for treating male employees less favourably.

48 And note here that in Case C-147/02 *Alabaster v Woolwich plc* [2004] ECR I-3103, paras 47–50, a failure to link maternity pay to a general pay rise was held, without reference to *Dekker* or its logic, to be direct *sex* discrimination under equal pay legislation (TEC, Article 119, now TFEU, Article 157).

49 S Honeyball, 'Pregnancy and Sex Discrimination' (2000) 29 (1) *ILJ* 43, 52.

50 Noted by R Wintemute, 'When is Pregnancy Discrimination Indirect Discrimination?' (1998) 27 *ILJ* 23, 60 citing, *Webb v EMO Air Cargo (UK) Ltd* [1992] 4 All ER 929, 935–936 (HL); T Gill, K Monaghan, 'Justification in direct sex discrimination law: taboo upheld' (2003) 32(2) *ILJ* 115, 120, noting that attendance 'is a fundamental requirement of the employment contract'. On the other hand, those advocating the 'indirect' model consider that with suitable drafting and guidance, 'tribunals would be naturally cautious of any justification defence and would be wholly alive to pandering to "stereotyping and societal expectations"': J Bowers, E Moran, S Honeyball, 'Justification in direct sex discrimination: a reply' (2003) 32 *ILJ* 185, 187, citing Gill and Monaghan, ibid., 116.

policy. But putting this fear to one side, when faced with a bald test of objective justification, even the wisest judge must accede to an employer's genuine business needs, proportionately implemented.

For the purpose of defining discrimination law, the significance is obvious. The orthodox direct/indirect model has a residual role at best in the areas of pregnancy and maternity policy and consequent rights. Any principled 'equality' doctrine to unite these rights would have to come from elsewhere. At the least, it is fair to conclude that Lady Hale's 'mutually exclusive' canon has no application to pregnancy discrimination. At the highest, the developing law of pregnancy discrimination demonstrates that the canon itself is of little utility.

Conclusion

The major omission from the scholarship and case law is that pregnancy discrimination law is a policy choice. As the discussion above demonstrates, in terms of doctrine, most claims should fail as (direct) sex discrimination, and any conventional model of *pregnancy* discrimination should fail for want of a comparator. Hence, pregnancy 'discrimination' law is not discrimination at all, in the sense of less favourable treatment. The reasons for the adverse treatment generally are either pregnancy per se, or (more commonly) the consequences of pregnancy (or an expectation of those consequences), typically, absence from work. Such cases are logically analysed as indirect (sex or pregnancy) discrimination. When characterised as such, defendants enjoy an objective justification defence. Employers in particular, would readily provide objective business reasons for treating pregnancy and maternity unfavourably. Large employers could deploy sophisticated statistics to demonstrate quite precisely when business requires adverse treatment of pregnant workers, thus fulfilling the legal requirement of proportionally. This approach accords with a basic premise of discrimination law (aside from its more moralistic bases): subjective decision-making can be inefficient, while objective decision-making is more efficient. Here, treating unfavourably pregnancy and maternity *can* be efficient in business terms.[51]

This incongruity with discrimination law is more understandable upon a consideration of its policy drivers. In the latter 20th century, policy has moved to the position where achieving substantive equality for women requires pregnancy and maternity rights. Of course, various theories can be assigned to this, such as population replacement to maintain the economy, especially with an aging population and growing pension crisis.[52] The logic here is that society needs women to form part of the workforce without the accompanying

51 For an extensive study of business efficiency and Title VII (employment) of the US Civil Rights Act 1964, see S Greenberger, 'A Productivity approach to Disparate Impact and the Civil Rights Act of 1991' (1993) 72 *Oregon Law Rev* 253. Cf R Epstein, *Forbidden Grounds: The Case Against Employment Discrimination Laws* (Cambridge: Harvard University Press 1992), esp. pp. 226–229.

52 See e.g. D Coleman, 'Who's Afraid of Low Support Ratios? A UK Response to the UN Population Division Report on Replacement Migration' (2000) Shorter

disincentive to bear and raise children. Thus, pregnancy and maternity rights could be attributed to an economic policy choice, rather one of some moral principle rooted in say, feminism or human rights.[53] This helps explain why pregnancy and maternity rights have the appearance of a coincidental link with equality and discrimination, and the consequent struggle to couch them in terms of discrimination. Policy makers have observed that gender equality produces higher fertility rates and so recommend the proliferation and improvement of those rights.[54]

If the goal is to produce a coherent and accessible definition of discrimination, the analysis above presents a choice. The first is to assert the technical logic, but legislate only for specific defences (if any) for sex discrimination where a factor is pregnancy or maternity. This addresses the concerns that the judiciary (or merely the objective justification defence itself), would be too generous to employers. The alternative is to detach pregnancy and maternity rights from the equality legal spectrum altogether, which actually represents the current position, as pregnancy discrimination law is not in fact discrimination law. This would not detract from any notion of indirect sex discrimination where a factor is pregnancy or maternity, and operating with the standard objective justification defence without any special or dedicated qualification.

Further reading

J Bowers, E Moran and S Honeyball, 'Justification in direct sex discrimination: A reply' (2003) 32*ILJ* 185.

T Gill and K Monaghan, 'Justification in direct sex discrimination law: Taboo upheld' (2003) 32(2) *ILJ* 115.

S Honeyball, 'Pregnancy and sex discrimination' (2000) 29(1) *ILJ* 43.

T Ward, 'Beyond sex equality: the limits of sex equality in the new Europe', in T Hervey and D O'Keeffe (eds), *Sex Equality Law in the European Union* (Wiley1996) 370.

R Wintemute, 'When is pregnancy discrimination indirect discrimination?' (1998) 27*ILJ* 23.

M Wynn, 'Pregnancy discrimination: Equality, protection or reconciliation?' (1999) 62*MLR* 435.

Revised Draft, p. 3; or www.un.org/en/development/desa/population/events/pdf/expert/2/coleman.pdf accessed 16 December 2020.

53 For policy documents assuming population decline is an economic 'problem', and gender equality as a 'solution', especially to 'fertility rates', see e.g. 'The demographic future of Europe – from challenge to opportunity', COM (2006) 571, esp. para 3.1 https://eur-lex.europa.eu/legal-content/EN/ALL/?uri=CELEX:52006DC0571; 'Promoting Solidarity Between the Generations', COM (2007) 244, para 2.2 https://eur-lex.europa.eu/legal-content/EN/TXT/?qid=1553105670267&uri=CELEX:52007DC0244; Green Paper 'Confronting demographic change: A new solidarity between the generations', COM (2005) 94 final, Annex 1 https://eur-lex.europa.eu/legal-content/EN/TXT/?uri=celex:52005DC0094 all accessed 16 December 2020.

54 Ibid.

4 The outer margins of indirect discrimination

Introduction

The seminal case for today's indirect discrimination law, *Griggs v Duke Power*, announced that discrimination law was to address the 'built in headwinds' against minorities and women in employment.[1] In this context, the headwinds can only be identified by their effect, something which is often difficult to capture. Indeed, when the legislation introducing this for the first time was presented to Parliament, the opposition spokesman stated,

> we do not know what it means. Secondly we do not think the Government knows what it means; and, thirdly, if we did know what it meant, we do not think that we would like it, but we cannot be sure.[2]

Nonetheless, by the time the concept reached the United Kingdom, a detailed statutory formula was drafted rendering the concept much more tangible. Despite this, the courts have still struggled with various aspects of the concept. One particular problem is on the outer margins. Unlike the problems highlighted in the previous three chapters concerning the border between direct and indirect discrimination, this problem examines the fuzzy border where indirect discrimination ceases to be discrimination at all. There are three themes here. First, the all-too-common situation where a sole migrant worker is mistreated because of his or her vulnerability as a migrant, usually with some unlawful status. Second, there is the appointment from a circle of family, friends, or personal acquaintances. These situations range from the romantic family business to the most egregious nepotism, presenting the challenge to policy considerations. Third, there is the anomalous situation of the law recognising one-off religions and manifestations for legal protection, but not recognising them for indirect discrimination *because* they are one-offs. Each is taken in turn, after an introduction to the legislation.

1 401 US 424 (S Ct 1971) at 432.
2 SC Deb (B) 22 April 1975, col 36 (Ian Gilmour).

DOI: 10.4324/9781003187547-4

The legislation

Indirect Discrimination is defined in the Equality Act 2010 as follows:

> 19 Indirect discrimination
>
> 1 A person (A) discriminates against another (B) if A applies to B a provision, criterion or practice which is discriminatory in relation to a relevant protected characteristic of B's.
> 2 For the purposes of subsection (1), a provision, criterion or practice is discriminatory in relation to a relevant protected characteristic of B's if—
>
> a A applies, or would apply, it to persons with whom B does not share the characteristic,
> b it puts, or would put, persons with whom B shares the characteristic at a particular disadvantage when compared with persons with whom B does not share it,
> c it puts, or would put, B at that disadvantage, and
> d A cannot show it to be a proportionate means of achieving a legitimate aim.

The formula consists of the following elements: (1) an apparently neutral[3] provision, criterion or practice (PCP), (2) which puts, or would put, (3) the claimant and the claimant's group at a 'particular disadvantage', and (4) cannot be justified (para (d)). The first three complete the claimant's prima facie case, after which the burden shifts to the defendant to justify the challenged practice. Note that disadvantage to the *claimant* (para (c)) should be the same disadvantage suffered by the claimant's group.[4] Otherwise, it requires no further discussion, because it is merely to ensure a claimant has *locus standi* (a right to sue),[5] although note the claimant share the same disadvantage as the group.

On the matter of making a comparison for the purpose of establishing the 'particular disadvantage', guidance is provided by section 23(1):

> On a comparison of cases for the purposes of [indirect discrimination] there must be no material difference between the circumstances relating to each case.

3 Paragraphs (a) and (b) combine to require that the provision, criterion or practice (PCP) applies to persons irrespective of whether they share the claimant's protected characteristic.

4 See case comment, Tarunabh Khaitan, 'Indirect discrimination law: causation, explanation and coat-tailers' (2016) 132 *LQR* 35, 37.

5 The original version of sub-paragraph (2)(c) appearing the SDA 1975 (as s 1(1)(b)(iii)) was said by Government to be for the purpose of providing an individual remedy: see Under-Secretary of State for Employment (John Fraser), HC Deb 18 June 1975, Vol 893, cols 1491–1492 and 1494 https://api.parliament.uk/historic-hansard/commons/1975/jun/18/sex-discrimination-against-women accessed 30 December 2020.

The original UK legislation required that,

> the proportion of persons of the same racial group as [the claimant] … who can comply with [the requirement or condition] … is considerably smaller than the proportion of persons not of that racial group who can comply with it.[6]

The need for a 'considerably smaller' proportion of the claimant's group to be adversely affected had driven the courts to a statistically-minded approach. The 'particular disadvantage' rubric in section 19 liberates this. That said, where the challenged practice is not 'intrinsically liable' to adversely affect the group, English courts default to some form of numerical or statistical analysis. This requires identifying a 'pool' (for the purpose of section 23), comprising the claimant's group and the comparator group. Apart from excluding material differences, the courts have been troubled on how to select the pool, as observed by Sedley LJ:

> [O]ne of the striking things about both the race and sex discrimination legislation is that, contrary to early expectations, three decades of litigation have failed to produce any universal formula for locating the correct pool, driving tribunals and courts alike to the conclusion that there is none.[7]

Thus, for Sedley LJ, there is no single principle. It is a question of fact in each case.[8] That may be largely true, but one technical rule, beyond the material differences rubric, is that the challenged factor(s) should not be used in defining the pool, as this would frustrate the purpose of assessing its impact.[9]

Mistreatment of a sole vulnerable migrant worker

The cases of Onu V Akwiwu and Taiwo V Olaigbe[10]

These joint appeals concerned a particular class of migrant worker, who enter the country under a 'domestic workers visa' (DWV), granted to workers who had already been working abroad for the employer, or the employer's family,

6 RRA 1976, s 1(1)(b)(i). See the substantially same formula for sex, SDA 1975, s 1 (1)(b)(i).
7 *Grundy v British Airways* [2008] IRLR 74 (CA)*Grundy v British Airways* [27].
8 Ibid., [31].
9 'There is no formula for identifying indirect discrimination pools, but there are some guiding principles. Amongst these is the principle that the pool should not be so drawn as to incorporate the disputed condition'. *Allonby v Accrington & Rossendale College* [2001] ICR 1189; *Allonby v Accrington & Rossendale College*, [18] (Sedley LJ).
10 [2016] UKSC 31; [2014] EWCA Civ 279; *Taiwo* [2013] ICR 770 (EAT); *Onu* [2013] ICR 1039 (EAT).

for at least a year. Any vulnerability of this status was aggravated formally by a condition that they could not change their employer without permission from the immigration authorities. This left them particularly dependant on their employers. In both cases the employer had manufactured the claimant's employment history, and so each was working in the UK illegally, adding to their already vulnerable status.

Ms Onu had responsibility for the Akwiwus' daughters, and was required to cook, clean, launder and iron. She had substantial responsibility for the home. She worked an average 84-hour week, and was paid (well) below the national minimum wage. Generally, she was subject to threats and abuse from the Akwiwus. Onu signed a 'contract', stating (a) that if she 'absconded' within a year of starting work Mr and Mrs Akwiwu would report her to the police and the immigration authorities (and told that this meant she would be imprisoned); and (b) that they would retain her passport until the termination of her employment, as they in fact did.[11]

Taiwo's case was very similar, save that she was subjected to verbal *and* physical abuse,[12] had very limited English (another vulnerability exploited by her employer),[13] and was afforded limited access to food, causing her to suffer a 'dramatic loss of weight'.[14]

Eventually, the claimants escaped, found refuge, and brought these cases of discrimination. The claim of direct racial discrimination was rejected at all levels. The claim of indirect discrimination was also unanimously rejected, although with a lot less discussion. Before discussing the problems of indirect discrimination in this case, the consideration of the reasoning behind the direct discrimination decisions needs to be appreciated as the logic of both is interconnected (albeit inadvertently).

Direct discrimination

The claimants presented two arguments. First, that immigration status and nationality were indissociable. Second, immigration status is recognised under Article 14 of the European Convention on Human Rights.[15] This second argument was dismissed, essentially on the basis that, unlike the Convention, the Equality Act 2010 covers only a finite number of protected characteristics which do not include immigration status.[16]

The indissociable argument alludes to established jurisprudence that where an apparently neutral term is indissociable from a protected characteristic the term will be treated as directly discriminatory. Thus, pregnancy discrimination

11 [2014] EWCA Civ 279 [14]; [2016] UKSC 31[8].
12 [2013] ICR 770 (EAT) [6]; [2014] EWCA Civ 279 [15]; [2016] UKSC 31 [4].
13 [2013] ICR 770 (EAT) [13] and [46].
14 [2016] UKSC 31 [4].
15 Ibid., respectively [15]; [16] (*R (Morris) v Westminster CC* [2004] EWHC 2191 (Admin)).
16 Ibid., [19].

amounts to direct sex discrimination.[17] While the Court agreed that immigration was a 'function of nationality', it did not consider the two to be indissociable. In the only speech handed down, Lady Hale underpinned this with two principal and one 'reserve' lines of reasoning. First, just as British nationals would not have been so badly treated, neither would non-British nationals who were lawfully working.[18] This led to the second line: 'The reason why these employees were treated so badly was their particular vulnerability arising, at least in part, from their particular immigration status'.[19]

The 'reason why' (vulnerability) conclusion may be correct in itself. But it would have been better to compare the treatment with that which would have been handed out to somebody in the same circumstances as the claimants, save for their race, in this case non-British. It is quite likely that the defendants would have treated a British person working unlawfully with a similar vulnerability in the same way. This could be, for example, a runaway underage teenager, an escaped prisoner, or somebody working in breach of health and safety rules. Of course, this is speculative, but it would be more speculative to suppose that the defendants would only mistreat non-British vulnerable people. Moreover, this 'reason why' logic sidesteps the 'indissociable' argument. This was addressed with Lady Hale's third 'reserve' line of reasoning.

This line of reasoning was that the decision was consistent with a body of case law. She cited four authorities to address more directly the claimants' 'indissociable' argument. These were *Patmalniece, Schnorbus, Bressol,* and *Preddy v Bull,*[20] with quotations from two.

In *Schnorbus*, Advocate General Jacobs had said there could be direct discrimination where a criterion, not explicitly that of sex, was 'necessarily linked to a characteristic indissociable from sex'.[21] The formula was developed in *Bressol* by Advocate General Sharpston:

> I take there to be direct discrimination when the category of those receiving a certain advantage and the category of those suffering a correlative disadvantage coincide exactly with the respective categories of persons distinguished only by applying a prohibited classification.[22]

17 See e.g. Case C-79/99 *Schnorbus v Land Hessen* [2000] ECR I-10997, Opinion of Advocate General Jacobs, at para 33; *Lee v Ashers* [2018] UKSC 49 [25] (Lady Hale). The 'indissociable' rubric is discussed in Chapter 2, p. 19. Nowadays Pregnancy and Maternity are protected characteristics under the Equality Act 2010 (s 4).

18 [2016] UKSC 31 [26].

19 Ibid., Langstaff J used the same reasoning in the EAT: *Taiwo* [2013] ICR 770 (EAT) [34] and [48]; *Onu* [2013] ICR 1039 (EAT) [50].

20 [2016] UKSC 31 [27]–[30]. Cases cited, respectively, *Patmalniece v Secretary of State for Work and Pensions* [2011] UKSC 11; Case C-79/99 *Schnorbus v Land Hessen* [2000] ECR I-10997; Case C-73/08 *Bressol v Gouvernement De La Communauté Française* [2010] 3 CMLR 20; *Bull v Hall and Preddy* [2013] UKSC 73.

21 Case C-73/08, para 33.

22 Case C-79/99, para 56.

Problems and inconsistencies with these two Opinions of been discussed elsewhere in this book.[23] For the present purpose, Lady Hale's focus is on the symmetry apparently required by AG Sharpston's Opinion. In these cases of alleged nationality discrimination, Lady Hale concluded,

> There was not an exact correspondence between the advantaged and disadvantaged groups and the protected characteristic, as some of those distinguished by their nationality were not disadvantaged, although others were.[24]

Lady Hale did not expressly relate this to the facts (or, as students are taught, 'apply the law'), but the implication is clear. In the *Onu/Taiwo* cases, there was no such symmetry between British and non-British and hence the 'vulnerable migrant worker' status was not indissociable from nationality or race.

The difficulty with this lies in AG Sharpston's Opinion (which was not taken up by the ECJ). Not all women are pregnant, or are pregnant all of the time. Thus, when pregnancy cases are brought as sex discrimination it cannot be said there is an exact correspondence between the advantaged (men) and disadvantaged (women). Some, women will remain unaffected by pregnancy discrimination. Thus, a more accurate definition comes from AG Jacobs, that pregnancy discrimination is 'necessarily linked to a characteristic indissociable from sex'. On this logic, it is plausible to argue that 'DWV discrimination' is necessarily linked to a characteristic indissociable from nationality (non-British). Just as men do not become pregnant, British workers cannot come under DWV status. And just as only some women are pregnant, only non-British workers become DWV. It might be that this point was missed because of the talk of the claimants being mistreated because of their vulnerability. Lady Hale said herself that the reason for the treatment was 'their particular immigration status',[25] which was of course their DWV status. If the reason for the treatment were reworded as DWV status, AG Jacobs' definition would appear to encompass this scenario, although there are distinctions to be considered. First, the proportion of those with DWV status within the protected group (e.g. non-British) is likely to be much smaller than pregnancy/maternity status is among women. Second, the 'necessary link' between pregnancy and sex is an inevitability of nature, rather than a choice of (immigration) law. This second distinction may dissolve in light of *James v Eastleigh BC*, where the House of Lords held that state pension age (law) was 'convenient shorthand' for sex discrimination, a decision Lady Hale acknowledged as falling within AG Jacobs' *and* AG Sharpston's tests.

In sum, for Lady Hale, the reason for the treatment was not indissociable from any protected characteristic of the claimants because first, any comparison

23 See Chapter 2, 'Incorporated and cumulative cases: Direct or indirect?', p. 7.
24 [2016] UKSC 31 [28]
25 Ibid., [26].

showed that the actual reason for the treatment was vulnerability, rather than immigration status. This may have been so, but it sidestepped the claimant's argument. When facing the argument, the ('Sharpston') formula cited by Lady Hale cannot be reconciled with the situation (pregnancy discrimination), it was trying to explain.

As a result of the rejection of the direct discrimination claim, arguments defaulted to indirect discrimination. These proved to be quite elusive and slippery.

Indirect discrimination

Counsel strained to characterise the 'provision, criterion, or practice' (PCP), at first as the 'practice of employing someone who was "on a migrant domestic worker visa"',[26] or (advanced on appeal) 'the mistreatment of migrant workers'.[27] The protected characteristic varied somewhat but settled around nationality or national origin ('non-British'), sub-categories of 'race'.[28]

Langstaff J in EAT dismissed the first PCP as having 'no basis' to establish indirect discrimination, 'for the need for the claimant to have a DWV was not linked causatively to any mistreatment of her'.[29] In other words, the requirement for the DWV (imposed by law, rather than by the employers), did not 'put' the claimants at a particular disadvantage. Their suffering was caused by other matters, essentially the mistreatment.

This reasoning may have informed the advancement of the second PCP. Langstaff J gave two reasons for holding that this was not a PCP at all. First, 'the definition of this PCP inevitably answers the question to be posed: it is entirely circular'. Second, 'the PCP will only apply to those who are migrant workers: it is not on the face of it a neutral criterion which disadvantages some of those to whom it applies disproportionately when compared to others to whom it applies'. As such, 'This cannot be a proper PCP in the circumstances'.[30]

The Court of Appeal, now dealing only with the second PCP, gave equally brief, but rather vague, reasoning. As a matter of policy, 'The factual situation in this case has nothing to do with the kind of mischief which the concept of indirect discrimination is intended to address'.[31] On a more technical note, the Court reasoned that, 'If those acts [of mistreatment] do not constitute direct discrimination because the relevant ground was absent, they cannot be

26 [2013] ICR 770 (EAT) [51]; [2014] EWCA Civ 279 [32].
27 [2013] ICR 770 (EAT) [52]; [2014] EWCA Civ 279 [58].
28 EA 2010, s 9. The claimant's arguments varied somewhat. See [2013] ICR 770 (EAT) [1]; [2014] EWCA Civ 279 [24]: in Onu's case, 'race, ethnic or national origin', but *not*, nationality; in Taiwo's case, nationality ('Nigerians'); and later for both, 'non-British' nationality ([47]). See also UKSC 31 [23], [26]: 'non-British'.
29 [2013] ICR 770 (EAT) [51].
30 Ibid., [53].
31 [2014] EWCA Civ 279 [58] (Underhill LJ).

converted by some process of abstraction into the application of a discriminatory PCP'.[32] This is rather Delphic, and required some expansion of what is meant by 'abstraction'. After all, it is not unusual for a claim of direct discrimination to fail, but then be analysed for indirect discrimination.[33]

By the time the case came to the Supreme Court, the issue was virtually dead, with the claimants' counsel even conceding that 'It is direct discrimination or nothing'.[34] For the record, Lady Hale broadly agreed with the EAT and added, rather dismally, that 'the problem' was that 'no-one can think of' a PCP that these employers would have applied to their employees.[35]

There are a number of aspects to discuss here. The Court of Appeal's dependence on the undefined 'mischief' was a concern. This is considered further below. On either side of that reasoning the EAT and Supreme Court deployed a mechanical approach while wrestling with seemingly elusive and uncooperative facts.

THE PCP: NEUTRALITY AND APPLYING TO ALL

In a nutshell, Langstaff's J logic was that the PCP could not be a neutral, while Lady Hale's was that the PCP did not apply to all. These opinions depend on the primary question of the protected characteristic being supposed. The Equality Act 2010 includes under 'race', colour, nationality, ethnic or national origins.[36] The discussions at all levels meandered around several precise protected characteristics, but settled in the main on 'non-British'.[37]

Langstaff's J logic was that a practice applying only to migrant workers is not a neutral one, assuming that migrant workers can be classed as a protected characteristic: non-British. The judge is on thin ice here, having previously rejected the claim of direct discrimination because the treatment was *not* because of migrant status, but because of vulnerability,[38] a finding endorsed by the Court of Appeal and the Supreme Court.[39] Thus, Langstaff's J logic here appears neat and tidy but a little too clever. The fault lies in the depiction of the PCP. It would be more accurate to depict the defendants' practice as the mistreatment of *vulnerable* or DWV workers; the issue then becomes whether this would put non-British (or migrant) workers at a particular disadvantage. This approach is more readily reconcilable with Langstaff's J approach to the direct discrimination claim.

32 Ibid.
33 See e.g. *R (A) v Governing Body of JFS* [2009] UKSC 15; *Ladele v Islington LBC* [2009] EWCA Civ 1357; C-83/14 *CHEZ Razpredelenie Bulgaria AD v Komisia za zashtita ot diskriminatsia* [2016] CMLR 14.
34 [2016] UKSC 31 [31]. The counsel was Robin Allen QC, who made the same point in the similar case of *Mruke v Khan* [2018] EWCA 280 [11].
35 Ibid., [32].
36 EA 2010, s 9(1).
37 See [2013] ICR 770 (EAT) [1]; [2014] EWCA Civ 279 [24]; [2016] UKSC 31 [23], [26].
38 *Taiwo v Olaigbe* [2013] ICR 770 (EAT) [45]–[48]. See above, p. 52.
39 See also [2014] EWCA Civ 279 [50] and [75]; [2016] UKSC 31 [30].

Lady Hale's focus was on an apparent need that a PCP must apply to all. This is endorsing Langstaff's J logic, but from a different perspective. Whereas Langstaff's J reasoning was based on the notion that the PCP applied too narrowly, Lady Hale based her reasoning on the notion that the PCP was not applied widely enough. She deployed a rather bizarre analogy: 'Requiring all employees to sport a moustache is obviously indirectly discriminatory against women'.[40] The analogy is also wanting for relevance. For a start, such a requirement appears to be a thinly disguised pretext for *direct* sex discrimination. Moreover, the language is looser than necessary to align with Langstaff's J reasoning. Lady Hale probably intended to reject the PCP because it applied exclusively to a group defined by protected characteristic (migrant, or non-British, workers) and not to a wider class of employees. But it appears as if she is saying the PCP must apply to *all* employees of a certain business, and there is a danger this could be mistaken such. This is clearly wrong. Not all apparently neutral requirements apply to all employees. The legislation requires that the PCP applies 'to persons with whom B does not share the characteristic',[41] not that it applies to *all* persons, or *all* employees. More appropriate examples would be strict dress codes applying only to those with public-facing roles. These could encompass bans on non-company and/or religious paraphernalia, such as a headscarf,[42] veil,[43] or turban. Elsewhere, rules against the wearing of turbans[44] or karas[45] might apply for purported health and safety reasons to only those working in certain parts of a factory. Likewise, an employer paying part-time workers disproportionately less than full-time workers applies it to all employees only in the sense that it would apply to a full-time worker should he or she switch to part-time work. Nonetheless it would be treated as indirect sex discrimination under the equal pay regime.

Both Lady Hale's and Langstaff's J reasoning was unconvincing and somewhat convoluted because it was based on a rather unrealistic PCP. As noted above, the choice of 'the mistreatment of migrant workers' as the PCP, with respect, was inaccurate. Assuming that migrant workers could be classed as non-British (a protected characteristic under nationality),[46] mistreatment of

40 [2016] UKSC 31 [32].

41 EA 2019, s 19(2)(a). See also, Race Directive 2000/43/EC, art 2(2)(b) simply requires the challenged practice to be 'apparently neutral' putting people of racial or ethnic origin at a particular disadvantage when 'compared with other persons'.

42 C-157/15 *Achbita v G4S Secure Solutions* NV [2017] 3 CMLR 21.

43 *Azmi v Kirklees MDC* [2007] ICR 1154 (EAT) (only to those employed in teaching).

44 e.g. *Singh v British Rail Engineering Ltd* [1986] ICR 22 (EAT) (only those working under trains required to wear 'bump hat').

45 *Kaur v Brookes* (unreported, 1998), only those in the food processing part of the factory required to remove Kara (bangle). *Leicester Mercury*, 5 and 8 August 1998; *Daily Mail*, 8 August 1998; *BBC News*, 7 August 1998 http://news.bbc.co.uk/1/hi/uk/147040.stm accessed 30 December 2020.

46 See *Orphanos v QMU* [1985] AC 761 (HL) where an EEC residence requirement indirectly discriminated against non-EEC or non-British students.

them is more likely to amount to direct discrimination. Of course, such a PCP omits the essential ingredient of being a *particularly vulnerable* migrant worker.[47] This becomes relevant to the next discussion, regarding the choice and interaction of the PCP, protected characteristic, and particular disadvantage.

CHOOSING THE APPROPRIATE PCP, PROTECTED CHARACTERISTIC, AND DISADVANTAGE

The case was argued (loosely) around the following three elements: 1) The protected characteristic was 'non-British';[48] 2) the PCP was 'mistreatment of migrant workers';[49] and 3) the particular disadvantage was the mistreatment.[50] What the judgments at all levels of appeal lacked was an exploration of the interaction between all three elements, and subsequently, how different permutations might improve the claim. The House of Lords once discussed how the choice of protected characteristic can be critical to the particular disadvantage.[51] Such an analysis applies to the identification of all three elements and how they interact.

A feature of the cases that might have caused this was that the claimants might well have been the sole employees of the respective families. This may have led the Court of Appeal to hold that the mistreatment of migrant domestic workers is neither a provision, requirement, nor a practice. It was merely 'a number of particular acts of mistreatment'.[52]

The 'sole employee' feature may have driven also the limited analysis of any interaction of the elements. As such, one has to hypothesize over whether these employers would apply their PCPs to any 'others' at all. At all three appeal levels, the objection to the 'mistreatment' PCP focussed on mistreating only vulnerable migrants.[53] This assumes that the employers here would not mistreat others in the same way. The Court of Appeal came close to addressing this aspect when dismissing counsel's submission that instead of a single broad PCP of 'mistreating migrant workers', there were a series of particular practices, such as 'a requirement to work an average of 83 hours per week' or 'a policy of retaining an employee's passport'.[54] These were dismissed as reproducing 'the

47 It seems that something like this was suggested, but not taken up. See *Taiwo v Olaigbe* [2013] ICR 770 (EAT), n 5 'in his closing written submissions to the tribunal Mr Milsom argued for a PCP of "mistreating workers requiring a domestic worker visa". This formulation was not however identifiable in the reasoning of the tribunal'.

48 See [2013] ICR 770 (EAT) [1]; [2014] EWCA Civ 279 [24]; [2016] UKSC 31 [23], [26].

49 [2013] ICR 770 (EAT) [52]; [2014] EWCA Civ 279 [58].

50 [2013] ICR 770 (EAT) [52]–[53]. In fact, the EAT was the only appeal court to attempt to specify the disadvantage.

51 For the significance of making the choice see *Orphanos v QMC* [1985] AC 761 (HL) 771, noted, I Leigh, 'Of racial groups and non-groups' (1986) 49 *MLR* 235.

52 [2014] EWCA Civ 279 [58].

53 [2013] ICR 770 (EAT) [52]; [2014] EWCA Civ 279 [58]; [2016] UKSC 31 [32].

54 [2014] EWCA Civ 279 [58].

same error in little … an artificial attempt to generate a PCP out of a series of specific acts against a particular employee'.[55] Subsequently, Lady Hale reasoned, 'By definition, this would not be applied to workers who are not so vulnerable'.[56]

This reasoning is compressed because of the choice of the protected characteristic and PCP. As noted above, the choice of PCP – 'mistreatment of migrant workers' – was flawed because of the chosen protected characteristic, 'Non-British'; it would not apply to the chosen comparative group of 'British'.

The difficulty in these cases is that the facts do not align with the judges' rather mechanical approach. In cases where the claimant is the sole employee, tribunals are obliged to speculate as to how the employers would have treated another, or how any given PCP would have impacted on the claimant's group. There was also a litany of practices and disadvantages, which the lawyers try to wrap up into single bundles, notably here labelled 'mistreatment'.

It appears that everybody lost sight of the itemised forms of mistreatment, or in the case of the Court of Appeal, lost sight of their relevance. It might be that, under the influence of *Bressol* and *Schnorbus*, it was assumed by all that a litany of practices containing directly discriminatory elements should be taken as a single bundle. These have been dubbed 'cumulative' cases.[57] But cases such as Onu's and Taiwo's are different, notably because the 'bundle' chosen did not so readily default to indirect discrimination, as the above rehearsal of the judicial reasoning reveals. So, there is no imperative to gather the individual acts of mistreatment into one bundle.

It was thus permissible to consider the employers' individual acts of mistreatment. One rather obvious practice here, common to cases like these, was the confiscation of vulnerable worker's passport. Assuming that the claimants' protected characteristic is non-British, as a matter of direct discrimination, one would speculate whether the employer would do this to a British vulnerable worker. If the answer were no, then non-British vulnerable workers were being treated less favourably than British ones. If the answer were yes, the question defaults to one of indirect discrimination. If it is thus presumed that the employer would confiscate the passports of both British and non-British vulnerable workers, the next issue is the particular disadvantage caused. Quite clearly, the particular disadvantage for non-British workers will be more severe than for British workers, who are much less likely, for example, to be deterred from escaping without a passport. A similar argument may be made out with the practice of threats of imprisonment, or involvement of the police and immigration authorities.

55 Ibid.
56 [2016] UKSC 31 [32].
57 See e.g. *Patmalniece v Secretary of State for Work and Pensions* [2011] UKSC 11 [31]–[35] (Lord Hope).

INDIRECT DISCRIMINATION AND THE MISCHIEF

It has been argued above, but given the right choice of protected characteristic, treatment/PCP, and disadvantage, the case could have been argued successfully as direct or indirect discrimination. This requires no straining of the facts nor the statutory wording.

However, in addition to its rather fragile doctrinally reasoning, Court of Appeal indicated that in any case, the claims should fail as indirect discrimination because they were not within its 'mischief'. This is of some concern, especially if otherwise sound cases can be rejected for falling outside of some unspecified 'mischief', a rather dated rule of statutory interpretation, largely superseded by the purposive rule. It went without any explanation as to what was considered to be the mischief of the indirect discrimination provisions. The only suggestion came with a hint of what it was not: it had nothing to do with this 'the factual situation', leaving the reader of an appeal judgment only to speculate. The starting point in identifying a 'mischief' is the state of affairs intended to be remedied.[58] There is little in the legislative history, but four points can be inferred from the drafting.

First, the concept of indirect discrimination was first introduced into British legislation with a late amendment to the Sex Discrimination Bill 1975. Only the White Paper to the subsequent Race Relations Bill gave some indication of a policy goal and/or mischief to be remedied. In reference to the 1968 Race Relations Act, the White Paper made it clear that direct discrimination alone was 'insufficient' to address the 'practices and procedures which have a discriminatory effect'.[59] This language was itself lifted from the seminal US case of *Griggs v Duke Power*.[60] Further evidence of the mischief is circumstantial.

On the history of the PCP, the Court of Appeal had given its predecessor (expressed as a 'requirement of condition'[61]) a particularly narrow interpretation, confining it to job requirements that were an 'absolute bar' to a job, thus excluding less formalised practices, such as 'mere preferences'.[62] This was remedied piecemeal as each new piece of EU legislation provided a broader definition, the now-familiar 'provision, criterion, or practice' or PCP. The logical inference here is that the new definition was intended broaden the meaning of the limited scope afforded by the Court of Appeal. Indeed, the statutory phrase employed by the US Civil Rights Act 1964 (upon which *Griggs* was based) was held to cover 'subjective employment practices', which

58 *Jones v Wrotham Park Settled Estates* [1980] AC 74 (HL) 105.
59 Home Office, *Racial Discrimination* (Cmnd 6234, 1975) para 35. The 1968 Act proscribed only direct definition.
60 *Griggs v Duke Power* 401 US 424 (1971) 431.
61 RRA 1976, s 1(1)(b).
62 *Perera v Civil Service Commission (No 2)* [1983] ICR 428 (CA), followed by *Meer v London Borough of Tower Hamlets* [1988] IRLR 399 (CA). For a discussion of the issue, see, M Connolly, *The English Judiciary, Discrimination Law and Statutory Interpretation: Easy Cases Making Bad Law* (2018, Routledge) pp. 154–171; (1998) 27 *ILJ* 133, 'Discrimination law: Requirements and preferences'.

included informal interviews, word of mouth hiring, and even the absence of any safeguards against discrimination.[63]

In the early days of the UK legislation the EAT drew on the American progenitor to identify the purpose or mischief and suggest a liberal interpretation. In *Clarke v Eley (IMI) Kynoch*,[64] Browne-Wilkinson J stated *obiter*:

> The purpose of the legislature in introducing the concept of indirect discrimination into the 1975 Act and the RRA 1976 was to seek to eliminate those practices which had a disproportionate impact on women and ethnic minorities and were not justifiable for other reasons. The concept was derived from that developed in the law of the United States … see *Griggs v Duke Power*. If the elimination of such practices is the policy lying behind the Act, although such policy cannot be used to give the words any wider meaning than they naturally bear it is in our view a powerful argument against giving the words a narrower meaning thereby excluding cases which fall within the mischief which the Act was meant to deal with.[65]

Shortly afterwards, Waterhouse J cited this passage in *Watches of Switzerland v Savell*,[66] where the EAT recognised the employer's practice as a 'vague, subjective, unadvertised promotion procedure which does not provide … any adequate mechanisms to prevent subconscious bias unrelated to the merits of the candidates … for the post'.[67] Sometime later, the Court of Appeal suggested that word of mouth hiring (or 'help a friend') fell within the bounds of the legislation.[68] In the meantime, the Equality Act 2010 was passed with the Long Title including the purpose, 'to increase equality of opportunity'. This suggests that older particular narrow definitions were broadened to this end.

Second, a further liberalising reform was made to the definition of indirect discrimination by the Equality Act 2010. The original definition required that,

63 See e.g. *Watson v Fort Worth Bank* 487 US 977 (US Sup Ct, 1988); *Rowe v General Motors* 457 F 2d 348, at 358–359 (5th Cir 1972); *Montana Rail Link v Byard* 260 Mont 331, at 352 (Sup Ct of Montana 1993), decided under the Montana Human Rights Act.

64 [1983] ICR 165 (EAT).

65 Ibid., 170–171, rejecting an argument that 'Condition' included qualifications for the job and not disqualifications to continue holding the job, where only part-timers (all female) were made redundant. See also: *Steel v Union of Post Office Workers* [1978] 1 WLR 64 (EAT) *Steel v Union of Post Office Workers*, 70–71, where Phillips J cited *Griggs* for 'assistance' in defining the 'heavy onus' of justification, where the preferable rounds were allocated according to length of 'permanent' service, not available to women until 1975; *Snoxell v Vauxhall Motors* [1978] QB 11 (EAT) *Snoxell v Vauxhall Motors*, 29, citing *Griggs*, and another US case which was relevant to the facts ('red circling' defence to equal pay claims): *Corning Glass Works v Brennan* 417 US 188 (Sup Ct, 1974) *Corning Glass Works v Brennan*.

66 [1983] IRLR 141 *Watches*. The claim failed because that procedure did not adversely affect women.

67 Ibid., [17] and [23].

68 *Coker v Lord Chancellor* [2002] ICR 321 (CA) [57]. See further below, pp. 67.

> the proportion of persons of the same racial group as [the claimant] … who can comply with [the requirement or condition] … is considerably smaller than the proportion of persons not of that racial group who can comply with it.[69]

The reformed definition requires that the PCP 'puts, or would put', the claimant and her group, at a 'particular disadvantage'.[70] As Lady Hale once pointed out, this new definition was intended to make it easier to establish indirect discrimination. In particular,

> [i]t was intended to do away with the need for statistical comparisons where no statistics might exist. It was intended to do away with the complexities involved in identifying those who could comply and those who could not and how great the disparity had to be. Now all that is needed is a particular disadvantage when compared with other people who do not share the characteristic in question. It was not intended to lead us to ignore the fact that certain protected characteristics are more likely to be associated with particular disadvantages.[71]

This means that when deciding if there has been the requisite disadvantage, tribunals need not become mired in attempts to identify statistically significant pools for comparison, say between the proportion of Nigerians and non-Nigerians adversely affected by the PCP. Tribunals have some leeway, including whether being, say, Nigerian (or an ethnic sub-group), is 'more likely to be associated with' the particular disadvantages, or that a PCP is 'intrinsically liable' to cause the particular disadvantage to the claimant's group.[72]

Third, the concept of indirect discrimination, as expressed by say, EA 2010, section 19, requires that the defendant 'applies, *or would* apply' the PCP, and (nowadays) that it 'puts, *or would put*' the claimant's group at a particular disadvantage.[73] And so, where in fact the PCP has yet to be applied to anyone bar the sole employee,[74] this permits some speculation as to whom the PCP would be applied and as to whom it would it put at a particular disadvantage.

69 RRA 1976, s 1(1)(b)(i). See the substantially same formula for sex, SDA 1975, s 1 (1)(b)(i).

70 EA 2010, s 19(2)(b). Section 19 is set out in full, above, p. 51. See also Race Directive 2000/43/EC, art 2(2)(b); Recast Directive 2006/54/EC, art 2(2)(b); Framework Directive 2000/78/EC, art 2(2)(b).

71 *Chief Constable of West Yorkshire Police v Homer* [2012] UKSC 15 [14] (Lady Hale), referring to Sir Bob Hepple, *Equality: The New Legal Framework* (Hart, 2011), pp. 64–68.

72 Case C237/94 *O'Flynn v Chief Adjudication Officer* [1996] ECR I-2617, at para 20.

73 EA 2010, s 19(2)(a) and (b) respectively. 'Applies, or would apply' was in the original versions. Section 19 is set out in full, above, p. 51. See also Race Directive 2000/43/EC, art 2(2)(b); Recast Directive 2006/54/EC, art 2(2)(b); Framework Directive 2000/78/EC, art 2(2)(b). Emphasis supplied.

74 This is not a case where the protected characteristic comprises just the claimant, which is not actionable as indirect discrimination: *Eweida v BA* [2010] ICR 890

Fourth, nothing in the current drafting undermines the approach in *Seymour-Smith*,[75] where the House of Lords, following ECJ advice, recognised that a 'small but persistent' disparity could amount to the 'considerable difference' required at the time. It showed that it was legitimate to assess the impact of a practice over a number of years. This is so even where the actual favoured and disfavoured persons in the pool change, because of, say, retirement, death, and recruitment.[76] *Seymour-Smith* was decided upon actual statistics. But nothing in the case said the same approach should not be apposite where the facts are speculative, as the statutory phrase 'or would apply' permits. Thus, an assessment of the impact in *Onu* or *Taiwo* need not be stuck at the one point in time when the claimant was the sole employee.

These developments could not be said to address explicitly cases such as *Onu* and *Taiwo*, but they make clear that the anti-discrimination rubric does not have any 'no-go areas' in terms of policy or mischief. These boundaries are expressed in the legislation.[77]

This returns the matter to the only hint given for Court of Appeal's reasoning: that the Act's mischief has nothing to do with 'the factual situation in this case'.[78] One can only speculate as to what this meant, as this 'factual situation' was not defined nor distinguished from others. The stand-out facts in these cases include many itemised acts of mistreatment applied to a sole and highly vulnerable employee. Given the leaning towards a purposive approach for equality law, it is surprising to see such a factual situation so readily dismissed as having potential for an indirect discrimination claim. On the 'mischief' question specifically, one must ask, what would be the mischief if the 'factual situation' was simply enlarged, to say, the mistreatment of 50 vulnerable migrant workers amongst a large workforce of 1,000 including some 200 non-vulnerable migrant workers? One might readily conclude that such a scenario falls within the mischief of equality law. On this basis, the Court of Appeal

(CA) (religious obligation to display crucifix was a protected characteristic unique to claimant); reversed on other grounds, *Eweida v UK* (2013) 57 *EHRR* 8 *Eweida v UK* (ban on display of crucifix violated Art 9). See further below, p. 73 ('Single person impact and the "*Williamson* anomaly"').

75 Case C-167/97 *R v Secretary of State for Employment, ex parte Seymour-Smith* [1999] ECR I-623; [2000] 1 WLR 235 (HL).

76 In *Seymour-Smith*, ibid., an analysis was made of the impact of the challenged measure upon UK's whole working population over a seven-year period. It showed (approximately) that each year, for every 10 men, 9 women qualified for unfair dismissal rights, thus establishing the prima facie case. M Connolly [2000] 05/2 Jo Civ Lib 212, 217–219; DW Vick, 'Disparate effects and objective justifications in sex discrimination law' (2001) 5(1) *IJDL* 3, 12–14.

77 E.g. EA 2010, s 19 applies to *group* disadvantage: see *Eweida v BA* [2010] ICR 890 (CA), discussed below, p. 73 ('Single person impact and the "*Williamson* anomaly"'). The Act specifies civil activities for inclusion, such as, the Provision of Services and Public Functions (Part 3), Premises EA 2010 (Part 4), Work (Part 5), Education (Part 6), Associations (Part 7).

78 [2014] EWCA Civ 279 [58].

ought to have explained why reducing the scenario to just one worker takes it outside of the mischief of the legislation.

In the context of these claims, this suggests that the 'factual situation' of confinement, dependency, passport confiscation, threats of imprisonment, and abuse - all obvious restrictions to equality of opportunity in employment, are very much within the mischief of the Act, as would be the mistreatment of a subclass of migrant workers. Thus, if the challenged practice(s) met the legal definition, it is no argument that it falls outside of the 'mischief', and even if it did, this would be something more appropriate for the justification defence, where policy can be more readily accessed.

This argument is all the stronger when one considers that it is common practice of the courts to take a purposive approach,[79] something more appropriate than the mischief rule by legislation designed to advance matters rather than merely solve a particular problem. Equality legislation assumes the status quo is intolerable, but sees its goal, which could be loosely put as equality of opportunity,[80] as something aspirational, rather than achievable overnight.[81] Given that both *Taiwo* and *Onu* fell within the EU Race Directive,[82] a purposive approach was compulsory, and the courts should have considered whether the mistreatment of vulnerable migrant workers fell also within the 'spirit' of anti-discrimination law.

There was also a failure to adopt a purposive approach in more general terms. The judgments seemed reluctant to treat the PCP as something rather more fluid than the norm. The English judiciary especially, is used to dealing with more tangible, or fixed, PCPs, such as a job specification, entrance exam, redundancy selection criterion, pay, dress code, and so on. Characterising 'mistreatment' as something applying to all, but adversely impacting on only one group is a slippery business. Nonetheless, equality law should not be restricted because of such difficulties. Otherwise, it creates an incentive for employers (and others bound by equality law) to relegate tangible malpractices to less tangible ones. A restrictive approach here reverts to the *Perera* era, where the English judiciary confined indirect discrimination analysis to only 'absolute bars' to an advantage,[83] thus permitting discriminatory practices to be relegated to 'mere preferences' and escaping liability. The legislation has since admonished this thinking, with the introduction of the more accommodating phrase,

79 For the common law approach nowadays see *R (Quintavalle) v Secretary of State for Health* [2003] 2 AC 687 (HL) [21] (Lord Steyn), citing *Cabell v Markham* 148 F 2d 737 (2nd Cir 1945) *Cabell v Markham*, 739 (Learned Hand J).

80 A common theme for decades. See e.g. *Griggs v Duke Power* (US Sup Ct, 1971) 401 US 424, 431, and nowadays the Long Title to EA 2010.

81 '[I]n modern times many statutes are intended to do much more than merely correct defects in the common law as in Coke's day. Parliament now legislates for us from the cradle to the grave'. Lord Renton, 'The interpretation of statutes' (1982) 9 *J Legis* 252, 258.

82 The Race Directive 2000/43/EC does not apply to 'nationality' (art 3(2)) which is preserved for EU nationals only, TFEU, Art. 45 (ex 39 TEC).

83 See n 62 and accompanying text.

provision, criterion or practice. While 'provision' or 'criterion' could be said to restrict challenges to tangible or fixed barriers, the inclusion of word 'practice' is open to all manner of vague and subjective conduct. If hiring by informal chats, or word-of-mouth recruitment, or the mere absence of an equality policy, can amount to 'practices',[84] then so too should forms of mistreatment, such as threats of imprisonment, confiscation of passports, deprivation of food, and so on.

Conclusion

These cases are characterised by being the sole and particularly vulnerable migrant employee who is subjected to 'mistreatment'. This, and the generalised choice of PCP, combined to deny claims of both direct and indirect discrimination. For direct discrimination, both the EAT and Supreme Court sidestepped the argument that DWV status was indissociable from being a migrant worker. They did this by applying strictly the statutory formula. When actually facing the issue, the Supreme Court alone deployed the unsupported 'Sharpston' test demanding exact symmetry between those affected and the protected characteristic in question. This was to the exclusion of the broader ECJ jurisprudence on pregnancy and sex discrimination, which does not require such symmetry. There also appeared to be an adherence to the ECJ 'cumulative' case law (e.g. *Bressol, Schnorbus*), cases that were clearly distinguishable as they readily defaulted to an indirect discrimination analysis. This was just about the only impediment to itemising the instances of mistreatment, which would have enabled them to speculate as to how the employers would have treated British workers, either for direct or indirect discrimination. Meanwhile, the Court of Appeal's rejection based on the mischief rule was unexplained and has no basis. In fact, one would want to hear compelling reasons why such cases do not fall within the mischief of equality law.

Appointing from a circle of family, friends and personal acquaintances

A significant feature of *Onu* and *Taiwo* was that the employer was only likely to mistreat one employee, or, at most, one at time in succession. For establishing indirect discrimination, a good deal of speculation is required to suppose how the employer 'would apply' any facially neutral practice to others, as required by legislative formula. A similar issue arises with the *appointment* of a worker from within a circle of family, friends and personal acquaintances. Although in

84 See *obiter Coker v Lord Chancellor* [2002] ICR 321 (CA) [57]. For overseas examples, see, *Watson v Fort Worth Bank* 487 US 977 (US Sup Ct, 1988); *Rowe v General Motors* 457 F 2d 348, at 358–359 (5th Cir 1972); *Action Travail des Femmes v Canadian National Railway* [1987] 1 SCR 1114; *Montana Rail Link v Byard* (1993) 260 Mont 331 (Supreme Court of Montana), *Action Travail des Femmes v Canadian National Railway* decided under the Montana Human Rights Act.

these cases the appointment can be something desirable, such an appointment, or mistreatment, both represent a minute proportion of those who otherwise would be qualified to fill the post. In a mirror image of the mistreatment, the advantaged 'group' is likely to comprise just one person, rendering comparisons statistically insignificant and seemingly undermining any claim of indirect discrimination. The fuzzy border here are centres on the law's understanding of 'significant'. Much the same can be said where nowadays tribunals may consider if the practice was 'intrinsically liable' to adversely affect the claimant's group, when, of course, it will affect every otherwise qualified person except for the appointee. This may push tribunals back to a statistical analysis just in order to provide a tangible reason to reject a claim.

However, beyond the legal technicalities, a comparison is less symmetrical with the factual realities. This arises when the appointment is in the more romanticised setting of a family member being brought into the family firm. Indeed, a family business will often advertise itself as such, as this is generally seen in a positive light. This involves, for example, a small business owner appointing his son to learn the ropes with a view to him taking over the business. Discrimination law generally applies to the giving of jobs, but not the handing over of a business. On the other hand, when scaled up society can see such appointments as nepotistic, 'old school tie', or 'jobs for the boys'. Both scenarios may have been on the mind of the Court of Appeal when entertaining an allegedly nepotistic appointment.

In *Coker v Lord Chancellor*,[85] a 'desirable' appointment was made. The Lord Chancellor recruited someone known to him, Garry Hart, as his political advisor. There was no formal recruitment process (arguably no process at all), other than it was essential to appoint a long-standing acquaintance in whom Lord Chancellor had trust and confidence. Such appointments were exempt from the normal recruitment requirements of merit on the basis of fair and open competition, set out in the Civil Service Order in Council.[86] With dreary predictability, the white male Lord Chancellor appointed another white male. The appointment was challenged as indirectly discriminating on grounds of sex and race. Unlike *Onu* and *Taiwo*, the case predated the legislative reforms, and the claim had to satisfy the rather constrained definition. For example, the Sex Discrimination Act 1975 provided:

> A person discriminates against a woman in any circumstances relevant for the purposes of any provision of this Act if …
>
> (b) he applies to her a requirement or condition which he applies or would apply equally to a man but:

85 [2002] ICR 321 (CA) (Lord Phillips MR, giving the Court's judgment). The House of Lords refused leave to appeal, ibid., [58].

86 Ibid., [14]–[15].

i which is such that the proportion of women who can comply with it is considerably smaller than the proportion of men who can comply with it, and
ii which he cannot show to be justifiable irrespective of the sex of the person to whom it is applied, and
iii which is to her detriment because she cannot comply with it.[87]

The Race Relations Act 1976 provided the same formula, suitably adapted.[88] In short, any 'requirement or condition' was one which a 'considerably smaller' proportion of the claimant's group could comply. This of course suggests a statistical approach was the only one, which was apparent in the Court of Appeal's rejection:

> The test of indirect discrimination focuses on the effect that the requirement objected to has on the pool of potential candidates. It can only have a discriminatory effect … if a significant proportion of the pool are able to satisfy the requirement. Only in that situation will it be possible for the requirement to have a disproportionate effect on the men and the women, or the racial groups, which form the pool. Where the requirement excludes almost the entirety of the pool it cannot constitute indirect discrimination within the statutes.[89]

There are two matters to note in this paragraph. First, it does not indicate whether the '*significant* proportion' is meant in the sense used by statisticians, the law, or the layperson.[90] It was probably meant in the legal sense, given the legislative formula in play and no express reference to *statistical* significance. And, elsewhere, when referring to the legislation, the judgment observed that a challenged practice should 'have the specified disproportionately adverse impact'.[91] This tallies with the final sentence of the reasoning, which appears to be saying in a roundabout way that because only a minute proportion were favoured by the requirement (to be otherwise qualified and 'personally known the Lord Chancellor',[92]) it could not amount to a considerable difference (the legislative benchmark).

87 SDA 1975, s 1(1)(b).
88 RRA 1976, s 1(1)(b).
89 [2002] ICR 321 (CA) [38] (Lord Phillips MR, giving the Court's judgment). The House of Lords refused leave to appeal, ibid., [58].
90 For an appraisal of the consistency with which the courts approach (discrimination) statistics, see K O'Donovan and E Szyszczak, *Equality and Sex Discrimination Law* (Oxford: Blackwell, 1988) p. 104; M Connolly, *The English Judiciary, Discrimination Law and Statutory Interpretation: Easy Cases Making Bad Law* (2018, Routledge) pp. 174–182.
91 [2002] ICR 321 (CA) [57].
92 The rather artificially and inflated pool was used in the case, although with 'reservations': [2002] ICR 321 (CA) [35].

This leads to the second matter. The final sentence could be taken to mean that as a matter of principle, a challenged practice excluding 'almost the entirety of the pool' could never be challenged. This principle would apply with all the more force where the success rate of the favoured group is 100 per cent.[93] *As a principle*, this cannot hold, especially with a pool of large numbers. Or, put another way, where the numbers are *statistically* significant. This can be illustrated with *McCausland v Dungannon DC*.[94] The claim was that a job requirement for a chief works manager to be an existing worker in local government indirectly discriminated against Catholics. The other (unchallenged) requirement was a 'standard occupational classification' (SOC) of 1, 2 or 3. The pool chosen was the whole Northern Ireland workforce with the SOC 1, 2 or 3. The number of SOC 1, 2 or 3 workers in Northern Ireland comprised 28,159 Catholics and 50,170 Protestants. The number of SOC 1, 2 or 3 workers in local government comprised 423 Catholics and 1,039 Protestants. The comparison was between the proportion of Catholics, and the proportion of Protestants, who could comply with the requirement to be in local government. The proportions were 1.5 per cent and 2.1 per cent respectively. The ratio reveals a considerable difference. The Catholic percentage (1.5) is just 71 per cent of the Protestant percentage (2.1). Hence (roughly) for every ten Protestants who qualified, there were seven Catholics (a ratio of 10:7). This reasoning would apply where the numbers of the advantaged group were reduced to a smaller proportion of the pool and would only cease at the point where they became statistically insignificant. *McCausland* illustrates that where the advantaged group forms a minute proportion of any pool,[95] a principle ruling out 'minute proportions' cannot prevent the establishment of a prima facie case. Cases will turn on the particular facts.

Nevertheless, the Lord Chancellor's one-off appointment was not statistically significant, and on that basis, there is no prima facie case based on statistics. But that should not be the end of the enquiry. The Court overlooked another method of analysis at hand. It was noted above that *Seymour-Smith* could help broaden the analysis for establishing the particular disadvantage for the mistreatment of a sole employee. It could be just as useful here. The House of Lords, following the ECJ, recognised that a 'small but persistent' disparity could amount to the requisite considerable difference.[96] Consequently, it was legitimate to assess the impact of a practice over a number of years. This is so even where the actual favoured and disfavoured persons in the pool change, because

93 See *Greencroft Social Club v Mullen* [1985] ICR 796 (EAT), below n 100.

94 [1993] IRLR583 (NICA). Heard under the Fair Employment (Northern Ireland) Act 1989, outlawing discrimination on grounds of religious belief or political opinion.

95 It was 3.6 per cent. In numbers the advantaged group was 1462 out of the pool of 78,329.

96 Case C-167/97 *R v Secretary of State for Employment, ex parte Seymour-Smith* [1999] ECR I-623; [2000] 1 WLR 235 (HL).

of, say, retirement, or death.[97] Thus if, over the years, successive Lord Chancellors had appointed special advisors in this way, or indeed *all* government ministers had done so, a longer view was in order, rather than a snapshot of a single appointment of one person. Some evidence of this was before the Court, who were made aware that the practice had been in place for decades.[98] Thus, a more sophisticated challenge to the widespread government practice of appointing from those 'personally known' to the relevant minister might reveal a small but persistent difference, sufficient to raise a prima facie case. No such argument was deployed, nor considered, in *Coker.*

The discussion so far has centred on Lord Phillips' analysis of the *appointment.* It has been argued that the analysis was misplaced. In his commentary to the case, Michael Rubenstein wrote,

> [T]he Court of Appeal seems to be answering the wrong question.... The applicants were not challenging the appointment of Mr Hart as such – the reduction of the 'elite pool ... to a single man'. They were challenging the selection arrangements whereby the potential candidates were confined to an 'elite pool'. The statutes rightly treats these as separate and distinct causes of action.[99]

On this basis, the advantaged group would comprise the 'elite pool', rather than the sole appointee. This might disturb Lord Phillips' analysis, but not enough to undermine it. After all, the advantaged group, now numbering, say, 10 or 20 persons, remains a tiny proportion of Lord Phillips' enormous disadvantaged group. It could be argued instead that the *disadvantaged* group should be reduced, comprising only those otherwise qualified for the job (i.e. all the attributes required save for being personally known to the Lord Chancellor). We could speculate that this pool might contain, say, 50 persons, half of whom were women. The proportion of male qualifiers (comprising the single

97 In *Seymour-Smith* (n 96) an analysis was made of the impact of the challenged measure upon UK's whole working population over a seven-year period. It showed (approximately) that each year, for every 10 men, 9 women qualified for unfair dismissal rights, thus establishing the prima facie case. M Connolly [2000] 05/2 Jo Civ Lib 212, 217–219; DW Vick, 'Disparate effects and objective justifications in sex discrimination law' (2001) 5(1) *IJDL* 3, 12–14.

98 This method of appointment of special advisors was practiced since the 1960s and formalised in 1978; there 30 recorded in 1974: [2002] ICR 321 [14]. Post-*Coker* figures show an increase to 69 in 2010, and 108 in 2019: respectively https://assets.publishing.service.gov.uk/government/uploads/system/uploads/attachment_data/file/62379/special-advisers-in-post-28-october.pdf; https://assets.publishing.service.gov.uk/government/uploads/system/uploads/attachment_-data/file/854554/Annual_Report_on_Special_Advisers.pdf > both accessed 30 December 2020. None of this shows the number of *appointments*, of course, but is an indicator; moreover, the number of appointments should have been obtainable.

99 [2002] IRLR (Highlights: January) 3.

successful candidate, Mr Hart) would have been one in 25 (4 per cent), whilst the proportion of female qualifiers would have been zero.[100] This is a significantly greater disparity than that in *McCausland*. If the *advantaged* pool were expanded to comprise the 'elite pool', the disparity would be reduced. This of course would depend on the numbers involved, and indeed the proportion of women and ethnic minorities in the advantaged pool.

Nevertheless, Lord Phillips' analysis was convenient, as it facilitated the distinction between one-off family appointments and broader nepotistic practices used by larger employers. The Court was aware that judgment for the claimant would have 'wide-ranging' implications for family appointments.[101] It made clear that its statistical analysis would also protect such appointments.[102] In a postscript, Lord Phillips MR (speaking for the Court) drew the dividing line:

> It is possible that a recruitment exercise conducted by word of mouth, by personal recommendation or by other informal recruitment method will constitute indirect discrimination.... If the arrangements made for the purpose of determining who should be offered employment or promotion involve the application of a requirement or condition to an applicant that he or she should be personally recommended by a member of the existing workforce that may, depending of course on all the facts, have the specified disproportionately adverse impact.[103]

The suspicion must be that the decision was driven, at least in part, by a policy to insulate from discrimination law the recruitment of friends and family, even as one-off appointments, or in very small numbers.

100 Even under the old definition, a claim can succeed if the proportion of the claimant's group who can comply is zero. In *Greencroft Social Club v Mullen* [1985] ICR 796, only members were entitled to a disciplinary hearing. Women were not admitted as members, so the proportion of women who were entitled to the disciplinary hearing was zero. The EAT found that the disciplinary hearing rule adversely affected women. In his commentaries to *Coker* in the IRLR, Michael Rubenstein noted, 'The prohibition of discrimination in selection arrangements – a concept which lies at the heart of discrimination law – can be circumvented by the simple expedient of not having any selection arrangements' ([2001] IRLR 116, at 115) and '[T]he Court of Appeal seems to be answering the wrong question of whether it was indirectly discriminatory to appoint Mr Hart rather than whether the tribunal was right to find the arrangements for selection were indirectly discriminatory. The applicants were not challenging the appointment of Mr Hart as such – the reduction of the "elite pool ... to a single man". They were challenging the selection arrangements whereby the potential candidates were confined to an "elite pool". The statutes rightly treat these as separate and distinct causes of action' ([2002] IRLR, at 3).

101 [2002] ICR 321 (CA) [8].

102 Ibid., [39].

103 Ibid., [57].

Legislative reforms

Since *Coker* was decided, both the EU the UK's statutory formulas for indirect discrimination have been somewhat loosened. The facially neutral conduct, rigidly characterised in the UK legislation as a 'requirement or condition',[104] has been replaced by the more open 'provision, criterion or practice' (PCP), while the statistically-minded 'considerably smaller'[105] rule has given way to a 'particular disadvantage'.

The introduction of the PCP, notably the 'practice', frees the courts from having couch any challenged practice as a 'requirement', such as 'being personally known to the Lord Chancellor'. It became easier instead to characterise the practice as, for example, a subjective, unadvertised or vague promotion procedure without mechanisms to ensure appointment on merit and without discrimination.[106] Notable here is the possibility of challenging an *omission*, such as the absence of an equality policy. For a case like *Coker*, the 'practice' could be identified simply as the exemption from the Civil Service Order in Council.[107]

Allied to this, the 'particular disadvantage' rule dispenses with any notion that a case must be brought on statistics, no matter how artificial that exercise may become. Indeed, *Coker* was based on guesswork as to the pool of otherwise qualified candidates,[108] while it was not clear if the advantaged 'group' was a number of persons qualified for the post *and* known to the Lord Chancellor, or just Garry Hart. In any case, the new formula legitimises such guesswork, and even frees the courts from having to mimic statistical reasoning. Such guesswork would not be necessary should the tribunal instead take the 'intrinsically liable' path. As Lady Hale once observed, the new formula was 'not intended to lead us to ignore the fact that certain protected characteristics are more likely to be associated with particular disadvantages'.[109] But this can still lead to much the same problem as the supposition becomes that the practice is intrinsically

104 SDA 1975, s 1(1)(b); RRA 1976, s 1(1)(b).

105 SDA 1975, s 1(1)(b)(i); RRA 1976, s 1(1)(b)(i). For a while, EU legislation required a 'substantially higher proportion': Burden of Proof Directive 97/80/EC, art 2(2).

106 See *Watches of Switzerland v Savell* [1983] IRLR 141 [17] and [23]. For examples from the US, see *Watson v Fort Worth Bank* 487 US 977 (US Sup Ct, 1988); *Rowe v General Motors* 457 F 2d 348, at 358–359 (5th Cir 1972); *Action Travail des Femmes v Canadian National Railway* [1987] 1 SCR 1114; *Montana Rail Link v Byard* (1993) 260 Mont 331 (Supreme Court of Montana).

107 See *Coker* [2002] ICR 321 (CA) [14]–[15].

108 Set by the IT as: first-class common sense, judgment and ability to assess situations; a profound knowledge of how a broad area of government works in practice; a commitment to New Labour; a comprehensive knowledge of the whole politics of the law; all the qualities and experience of the law necessary to offer sound political advice across the whole range of the work of the Lord Chancellor's Department. Notably, no numbers were estimated, nor an attempt to analyse this group's composition by sex or race. Cited and accepted ibid., [33].

109 *Chief Constable of West Yorkshire Police v Homer* [2012] UKSC 15 [14].

liable to disadvantage everybody otherwise qualified, rather than any particular protected group.

The difficulty of identifying a PCP

Another consequence of the employment or recruitment of just one person is that it is difficult to articulate a (facially neutral) practice that applies, or would apply, to all. In the Court of Appeal in *Coker* found 'great difficulty' in understanding how the tribunal below found one, 'The reality is that he has applied no requirements or conditions to anyone. [The Lord Chancellor] has simply offered someone known to him a job'.[110] Again, Michael Rubenstein observed sharply,

> The prohibition of discrimination in selection arrangements – a concept which lies at the heart of discrimination law – can be circumvented by the simple expedient of not having any selection arrangements.[111]

In *Onu and Taiwo*, it may be recalled, the Supreme Court was resigned to the admission that nobody could think of a practice that applied 'to all'.[112]

This reveals another fuzzy border. As the nature of the practice reduces its target, eventually to just one person, the ability to classify it as a practice peters out. But case law has failed to provide any threshold here, either in terms of statistical or legal significance of the numbers.

Single person impact and the '*Williamson* anomaly'

A flipside of *Coker,* if you like, is where a facially neutral practice *disfavours* just one person. In *Eweida v British Airways,*[113] a ban on visible jewellery for uniformed customer-facing staff adversely affected a Christian who insisted on displaying a small cross. Although she could not show this was a requirement of her Christianity, the Court of Appeal accepted this as a legitimate manifestation of her religion.[114] However, it went on to hold that the ban did not raise a prima facie case of indirect discrimination because it affected only the claimant. There was no evidence that anyone else among 30,000 workforce ever made

110 Ibid., [23]. As the ET's finding was not perverse, the Court proceeded on this basis that the requirement was that 'only those personally known to the Lord Chancellor will be considered' (ibid., [24]).
111 [2001] IRLR (Highlights: March) 115.
112 [2016] UKSC 31 [32]. See above, p. 57.
113 [2010] ICR. 890 [12]–[17] (CA).
114 Cf the US case, *Wilson v United States West Communications* 58 F 3d 1337, a Roman Catholic worker made a religious vow to wear an anti-abortion button displaying a colour photograph of a foetus and two anti-abortion slogans. Although the evidence showed that the wearing of the badge was within the vow, the *displaying* of it was not, and so outside of the meaning of 'religion'.

such a request to display a small cross. This follows the wording of the Equality Act 2010, and the parent Directive, which both demand *group* disadvantage indicated with the plural *persons*, rather than 'person'. For example, section 19 of the Equality Act 2010 requires, that the provision, criterion or practice is applied to 'persons with whom [the claimant] does not share the characteristic', and that it 'puts, or would put, persons with whom [the claimant] shares the characteristic at a particular disadvantage'.[115] Likewise, the Parent Framework Directive requires, 'an apparently neutral provision, criterion or practice [that] would put persons having a particular religion or belief … at a particular disadvantage'.[116]

The Strasbourg Court[117] found that the UK legal system had not done enough to protect Eweida's Article 9 (freedom of religion) rights, and found no need to explore the discrimination claim. This has left courts and legislators in a difficult position, as the domestic and EU legislation has no equivalent of Article 9. Further, other, protected characteristics in the conventional discrimination frameworks (e.g. sex, race, disability, sexual orientation, age) are not represented by an equivalent to Article 9 at the human rights level. In other words, 'religion' stands alone with the status of a human right *and* a protected characteristic.

Three issues flow from this situation. The first is the control that Article 9 has over the definition of religion or belief as a protected characteristic. The second is whether the Strasbourg decision should be implemented by re-drafting the legislation. The third is how courts and tribunals should respond.

On the first issue, the House of Lords has held under Article 9, a religion, or its manifestation, can be a one-off, something not shared by anyone else. In *R (Williamson) v Secretary of State for Employment*,[118] Lord Nicholls advised,

> [R]eligious belief is intensely personal and can easily vary from one individual to another. Each individual is at liberty to hold his own religious beliefs, however irrational or inconsistent they may seem to some, however surprising.

This means that 'emphatically, it is not for the court … to judge its "validity" by some objective standard'. A court should scrutinise a person's claimed religious belief only to ensure good faith and that it is 'neither fictitious, nor capricious, and that it is not an artifice'.[119] By section 3 of the Human Rights

115 Eweida's claim was brought under its structurally similar predecessor, Employment Equality (Religion or Belief) Regulations 2003, SI 2003/1660, reg 3.
116 Framework Directive 2000/78/EC, Article 2(2)(b).
117 [2013] IRLR 231.
118 [2006] 2 AC 246 [22] (HL).
119 Ibid., [22], citing *Syndicat Northcrest v Amselem* (2004) 241 DLR (4th) 1 (Sup Ct of Canada), [52]–[54] (Iacobucci, J.). See e.g. *X v UK* (App No 7291/75) (1977) 11 DR 55, where the (European Human Rights) Commission found no evidence of the existence of the claimed 'Wicca' religion.

Act 1998: 'So far as it is possible to do so, primary legislation and subordinate legislation must be read and given effect in a way which is compatible with the Convention rights'. Failing this, by section 4, a court must issue a declaration of incompatibility. Domestic courts are obliged by the Act (s 2) to take into account the case law of the European Court on Human Rights, which treats the Convention as a 'living instrument' and rarely constrains itself to a literal approach. Thus, domestic courts ought to adopt this expansive approach when interpreting the Equality Act 2010.

As such, even if they were minded to do so, courts could not demand that recognition of a religion or belief depends on group membership. And so, the Equality Act 2010 carries the strange '*Williamson* anomaly' of recognising a one-off religion or one-off manifestation as a protected characteristic, but denying it the protection of indirect discrimination. Moreover, this means that UK legislation is not fully compliant with Article 9 of the Convention of Human Rights. This in turn points to the second issue of the possible options for the statutory drafters.

The options would seem to be:

1 Redraft/redefine indirect discrimination for religion only.
2 Redraft/redefine indirect discrimination for religion and belief only.
3 Redraft/redefine indirect discrimination for all protected characteristics.
4 Redraft religious discrimination law to include the US style 'reasonable accommodation' doctrine.
5 Add protection to the employment regime, extending the protection to dismissal and detriments. This would be similar to the reaction to the decision in *Redfearn v UK*,[120] where discrimination law could not help the worker dismissed his membership of a racist political party, but the Strasbourg Court found for him under Article 11 (Freedom of Association). But this would not address issues arising beyond employment.

All bar option 3 are confined to just one protected characteristic. Option 4 is realistic, it being the usual practice in the United States.[121] It is roughly parallel to section 15 of the Equality Act 2020, 'Discrimination Arising from the Disability'. This this draws on a feature of indirect discrimination, in that the conduct is aimed at a manifestation of the protected characteristic. But it also draws on direct discrimination, as it is not group based; individuals need only prove harm to themselves. The advantage of this option is that it is already established would readily provide a solution for cases such as *Eweida*.

120 [2013] IRLR 51. See also *HM Prison Service v Potter* [2006] UKEAT/0457/06/DM. Employment Rights Act 1996, s.108(4) (dismissal 'related to' political opinion is automatic unfair dismissal).

121 Civil Rights Act 1964 Title VII s 701(j) 42 USC s 2000e(j). See further, Chapter 6 'Problems with perceived discrimination', n 3.

In the absence of statutory reform, the third issue is to look to the courts. Could a court allow a claim when the adverse impact is just upon one person? This was argued in *Eweida* and the Court of Appeal dispensed with it abruptly, holding that it would render a significant part of the legislative formula otiose. Sedley LJ reasoned that the result would be that no claimant would ever have to show group disadvantage.[122] But this is not the case. All the formulas dating over the years required that the challenged practice puts or *would put* persons who share the claimant's protected characteristic at a disadvantage. This allows a tribunal to envisage the impact *as if* the persons were in the purview of the defendant, for example, Christians wanting to display crucifixes within the workforce at British Airways. The Court of Appeal found that this 'loads far too much on the word "would"'.[123] But this is to unload the word to the point where it instead becomes meaningless, or otiose, a 'cardinal sin' of statutory interpretation.[124] Sedley LJ was concerned about the evidential implications, supposing anyone in the world shared Miss Eweida's religious practice, and placing 'an impossible burden on employers to anticipate and provide for what may be parochial or even factitious beliefs in society at large'.[125] The phrase 'or would put' should be confined to those real people to whom the challenged practice potentially applies.[126] Again, this merely sends the problem to the other extreme. Demanding more than one real potential victim places an impossible burden on the claimant, who generally would have fewer resources than the defendant. In this case it would mean the claimant contacting every one of the 30,000 employees and asking if they shared her commitment to display a small cross because of their Christianity. Although it might not be a requirement of the religion, nor practised by all members, it is not unusual for Christians to display a small cross. Certainly, it is not such a rare and unusual phenomenon to demand proof that others share the manifestation. It is much the same for other religious manifestations, such as turbans or karas for Sikhs, various coverings and clothing for Muslim women.[127] In such cases, the courts have not searched the whole of the workforce or school cohort for others sharing the same manifestation. The only difference between these instances and Eweida's case is that the adherents consider that they feel are *required* by their respective religions to adopt the manifestation. Nonetheless, not all Sikhs or Muslims observe these practices, just as not all Christians display a crucifix,

122 *Eweida v British Airways* [2010] ICR. 890 [12].
123 Ibid., [17] (Sedley LJ)
124 *Re Florence Land Co* (1878) 10 Ch D 530 (CA), 544 (James LJ). See also *Hill v William Hill (Park Lane) Ltd* [1949] AC 530 (HL) 546–547 (Viscount Simon).
125 Ibid., [18].
126 Ibid., [17].
127 See, respectively, *Singh v British Rail Engineering* [1986] ICR 22 (EAT), *Mandla v Dowell Lee* [1983] AC 548 (HL) (turbans); *R (Watkins-Singh) v The Governing Body of Aberdare Girls' High School* [2008] EWHC 1865 (Admin) (Kara); *R. (Begum) v Denbigh High School Governors* [2007] 1 AC 100 (HL) (jilbab: a long coat-like garment, worn by some Muslims, which effectively concealed the shape of the female body).

or worship on Sundays. English courts have recognised other manifestations of Christianity while adhering to the requirement of group disadvantage. It was not required, for example that the sanctity of marriage or not working on Sundays were manifestation shared by other members of the workforce.[128] Moreover, the law does not require that manifestations of religion are obligatory. Indeed, neither the Court of Appeal nor the Strasbourg court doubted that Eweida's desire to display her crucifix was a manifestation.

Beyond the protected characteristic of religion, the anomaly of the Court of Appeal's decision here is even starker. Suppose a work practice would put mothers of young children at a disadvantage. It would make no difference to the prima facie case of indirect discrimination if only one woman within the workforce had young children. In *Edwards v London Underground (No 2)*,[129] the claimant had previously organised her shift pattern to accommodate her child care needs but, unlike the other 20 female train operators and all of the 2,023 male train operators, she was unable to comply with new rostering arrangements. Despite being the only person put at a disadvantage by the new rostering arrangements, 'The high preponderance of single mothers having care of a child is a matter of common knowledge'.[130]

Sedley's LJ evidential concerns were presented as a matter of substantive law. But in *Eweida* it was no such thing. Uniquely it seems, Eweida had to prove that others it within her workforce shared the same manifestation, when in all other cases no such demand has been made where the manifestation is 'common knowledge'. All that was required here is a reading of the statutory word 'persons' to include hypothetical members of the workforce and/or persons more generally.

Nonetheless, Sedley LJ was quite correct to point out as a matter of substantive law indirect discrimination requires group disadvantage. And so with an actual 'one-off' religion, belief, or manifestation, indirect discrimination provides no remedy if the scenario falls beyond the outer margin of the statutory definition of indirect discrimination. The option here for the courts is to read down the statutory definition to comply with Article 9, using the interpretive commandment from the Human Rights Act 1998, section 3.

On this, in *Godin-Mendoza v Ghaidan*,[131] Lord Nicholls said 'The precise form of words read in for this purpose is of no significance. It is their substantive effect which matters'.[132] This tells us that courts should not be fettered by an impossibility of a grammatical solution and that section 3 goes further merely than resolving ambiguities in legislation. However, the interpretation

128 See respectively, *Pendleton v Derbyshire County Council, The Governing Body of Glebe Junior School* (EAT, 29 March 2016) Appeal No. UKEAT/0238/15/LA; *Mba v Merton LBC* [2013] EWCA Civ 1562 [35] (Elias LJ).

129 [1999] ICR 494 (CA).

130 Ibid., [24] (Potter LJ).

131 [2004] 2 AC 557. See also *Vodafone 2 v Revenue and Customs Commissioners* [2010] Ch 77 (CA) [38].

132 Ibid., [35].

should 'go with the grain of the legislation'[133] and not be against a fundamental feature of it or amount to a decision better suited for Parliament. This would effectively mean opening up a group-based provision to include individual cases, something that would resemble the 'reasonable accommodation' doctrine suggested above is a statutory amendment. This would be quite a dramatic step, especially given this is not an obvious drafting error,[134] but rather an absence of foresight. Redrafting s.19 to include individual disadvantage goes against the established formulas of indirect discrimination at both domestic and EU levels. But it would not 'go against the grain' of the statute as a whole, given (i) its overall scheme to promote equality and outlaw discrimination, (ii) that it includes (the roughly parallel) 'discrimination arising from disability', (iii) remove the anomaly that one-off religions, beliefs, and manifestations are recognised but not subject to indirect discrimination law, and (iv) its ancestor in the US, the Civil Rights Act 1964, was held to cover 'one-off' practices,[135] whilst the (US) EEOC Code provides:

> The fact that no religious group espouses such beliefs or the fact that the religious group to which the individual professes to belong may not accept such belief will not determine whether the belief is a religious belief of the employee or prospective employee.[136]

This brings the matter back to the '*Williamson* anomaly'. These are credible policy and technical drivers to invoke section 3 and recognise one-off religions, beliefs, and manifestations for indirect discrimination analysis. Until such a time as the introduction by Parliament of a 'reasonable accommodation' provision, or the invoking of the Human Rights Act 1998, the anomaly will exist. In the meantime, the Court of Appeal's decision in *Eweida* should be marginalised as one turning on an interpretation of the evidence, or simply overruled for being out of line with parallel cases on other protected characteristics.

Conclusion

It is clear that the law has struggled to cope confidently with the three scenarios. The main theme has been aligning the statutory formula with policy. This was typified at one point, when the Court of Appeal in *Onu* and *Taiwo* alluded to, but failed to define, the 'mischief'. One would suppose the policy very

133 Ibid., [121] (Lord Roger).
134 See e.g. *Rowstock v Jessemey* [2014] 1 WLR 3615 [45(5)].
135 *Frazee v Illinois Department of Employment Security* 489 US 829 (Sup Ct, 1989) 'Sunday working'; *Wilson v United States West Communications* 58 F 3d 1337 (8th Cir, 1994) 'Anti-abortion badge'; *American Postal Workers Union v Postmaster General* 781 F 2d 772 (9th Cir 1986) (handling draft papers).
136 EEOC Code of Practice, Title 29 Labor, § 1605.1. See www.gpo.gov/fdsys/pkg/CFR-2011-title29-vol4/xml/CFR-2011-title29-vol4-part1605.xml and generally EEOC.Gov accessed 30 December 2020.

much supports the vulnerable migrant workers, yet even their counsel and a seemingly sympathetic Supreme Court could not master the technicalities of the formula to find a remedy. The 'family and friends' appointment scenarios produced a policy-heavy judgment from the Court of Appeal in its attempts to leave undisturbed the romantic family business practices while addressing 'built in headwinds' of egregious nepotism. Some would argue the Court got the balance wrong in its decision, and it certainly struggled to square its policy utterances with the technicalities of the statutory formula, or indeed any broader notion of indirect discrimination. Finally, the normally masterful Sedley LJ, seemingly distracted by the evidential aspects of proving one-off religious discrimination, failed to align the law with policy, despite there being a relatively simple answer in the statutory formula.

The cases show that the law is yet to command a firm dividing line between what it considers to be actionable discrimination, and non-this country conduct.

Further reading

M Connolly, 'Commentary, R v Secretary of State for Employment, ex parte Seymour-Smith' [2000] 05/2 Jo Civ Lib 212 217–219.

DW Vick, 'Disparate effects and objective justifications in sex discrimination law' (2001) 5(1) *IJDL* 3.

For an appraisal of the consistency with which the courts approach (discrimination) statistics:

K O'Donovan and E Szyszczak, *Equality and Sex Discrimination Law* (Oxford: Blackwell, 1988) 104.

On the 'particular disadvantage' for indirect discrimination:

T Khaitan, 'Indirect discrimination law: Causation, explanation and coat-tailers' (2016) 132*LQR* 35, 37.

5 Objective justification

Introduction

Over the years of Britain's membership of the European Community/Union, there have been many references to the ECJ to clarify the meaning of particular aspects of the discrimination provisions, with the Court generally giving a more liberal interpretation than the domestic courts had suggested would be their preference. One element of the law largely untouched by this process is the objective justification defence to claims of indirect discrimination. This is because the domestic courts have maintained a fiction that their interpretation is consistent with the EU formula. For no apparent reason, the domestic courts have reworded the EU formula whilst labelling it as being no different. This presents yet another fuzzy border, this time regarding the significant shades of difference between the EU and UK notions of the objective justification defence. An additional dimension to this issue is that, given the judiciary's assertion that all is harmonious, it is all too easy for Parliament to assume all is well and that there is no need to intervene.

EU lawyers in general, and discrimination lawyers in particular, will be familiar with the '*Bilka* test' of objective justification,[1] which is the expression of the Court of Justice's general principle of proportionality[2] in the context of (employment) discrimination law. Many will know also that this represents the 'business necessity defense' devised by the United States' Supreme Court, which developed the notion of indirect discrimination ('disparate impact'), beginning with *Griggs v Duke Power*.[3] It is unfortunate (for many) that for decades British courts have been proffering a diluted version of the defence while asserting this is consistent with *Bilka* and its progenies. This chapter explores these cases, their decisions, reasoning, and language, to expose these shortcomings as inconstant with EU law, as well as principle and policy. It concludes that the only realistic solution is a forthright legislative restatement of the test, with the introduction of a statutory rule of interpretation mandating a

1 Case 170/84 *Bilka-Kaufhaus v Weber von Hartz* [1984] ECR 1607, para 36.
2 See the *Cassis de Dijon* case, C-120/78 (*Rewe-Zentral AG v Bundesmonopolverwaltung für Branntwein*) [1979] ECR 649.
3 401 US 424 (1971).

DOI: 10.4324/9781003187547-5

liberal and purposive interpretation of all equality law, which will align more closely British and EU interpretations and applications of this law, even while remaining beyond the jurisdiction of the Court of Justice.

The concept of indirect discrimination

Statistics reveal a racially unbalanced workforce, or gender pay gap; yet there is no evidence of any facially discriminatory cause. What to do? The concept of indirect discrimination was developed to address such scenarios. If claimants can lay *a* cause at the employer's door, say, word of mouth hiring, an entrance exam favouring whites, or a pay regime favouring predominantly male occupations, then a prima facie case of discrimination can be established. This is so where the employer had no discriminatory intent and there were many causes beyond the employer's control. For instance, an employer may not be responsible for the inferior education of minorities, who are now disfavoured by its (unnecessary) entrance exam,[4] nor for women choosing lower paid (but equally skilled) occupations according to cultural norms.[5] Nonetheless, the law provides the victims with a cause of action against the employer.

But the employer has a defence. If it can show that the cause is an employment practice appropriate and necessary to achieve a legitimate employment goal, then there is no liability. This is key. Without the defence, employers would be obliged to hire by quota, politically and economically unthinkable in any western economy. But the precise application of the defence plays a role in resolving any unnecessary pay gaps and other workplace imbalances. Thus, the focus of this law is on discriminatory *effects* and responsibility, rather than cultural norms and culpability. A consequence of this is that there should be no margins or leeway to the defence. Such margins are margins for the identified discriminatory effects to perpetuate. Not only is this contrary to principle and policy, it is, it has been argued, economically inefficient.[6]

This notion of necessity was inherent in the development of the law of indirect discrimination, which began in the United States Supreme Court. In *Griggs v Duke Power*, after identifying practices that are 'fair in form but discriminatory in operation', the Court turned to the defence, announcing, 'The touchstone is business necessity'.[7] In other words, once the claimant has made out a prima facie case (that the employer's practice adversely affects a protected group) the burden shifts to the employer to show that 'the challenged practice

4 See e.g. *Griggs v Duke Power* 401 US 424 (US Sup Ct, 1971).
5 See e.g. *Enderby v Frenchay HA* Case C-127/92, [1994] ICR 112.
6 See e.g. P Caldwell, 'Reaffirming the disproportionate effects standard liability in Title VII Litigation' (1985) 46 *U Pitt L Rev* 555; S Greenberger, 'A Productivity approach to Disparate Impact and the Civil Rights Act of 1991' 72 *Oregon Law Rev* 253 (1993). Cf R. Epstein, *Forbidden Grounds: The Case Against Employment Discrimination Laws* (Cambridge: Harvard University Press 1992), esp pp. 226–229.
7 401 US 424 (1971) 431.

is job related for the position in question and consistent with business necessity'.[8]

One consequence of this 'necessity' aspect is that a claimant may prevail if there exists a less discriminatory alternative means to achieve the same legitimate goal. Even small adjustments to the means can make a significant difference. One such practice is 'banding'. This can be useful for entrance and promotion exams, and is used in the United States (an example is provided below). Here, strict ranking scores can be placed into bands, and selection then made from these bands, where that would reduce the discriminatory impact. At first sight, this might seem to offend the symmetrical principle of direct discrimination law, by deliberately *disfavouring* the advantaged-but-protected group, say men, or whites. As such, this would not be a less discriminatory alternative.[9] Indeed, it would appear to introduce another fuzzy border. But this need not be so, as explained in the American case law:

> Banding is premised on the belief that minor differences in test scores do not reliably predict differences in job performance. It also recognizes that an individual is unlikely to achieve an identical score on consecutive administrations of the same examination. Because some measurement error is inevitable, strict rank order promotions will not necessarily reflect the correct comparative abilities of the candidates. The smaller the difference between observed scores, the more likely it is a result of measurement error, and not a variance in job-related skills and abilities.[10]

Similarly, the judge and jurist, Posner J, rejected an argument that banding amounted to unlawful discrimination with the assertion that, 'In fact it's a universal and normally an unquestioned method of simplifying scoring by eliminating meaningless gradations'.[11] Banding has become well enough known in the US jurisprudence, that a defendant refusing to adopt it where appropriate would be liable.

More generally though, how would a court, or claimants, evaluate the employer's testimony that it had considered (and evaluated) all alternatives, when the requisite knowledge, expertise, and resources, are likely to be in the hands of the employer? An employer could omit a less discriminatory, but 'inconvenient', alternative without the claimant or the court becoming any wiser. Some class actions, and/or union-funded actions may well have the resources to evaluate the employer's assertions and practices. But that is an element of fortune, not law. The US Supreme Court has offered a partial

8 See now, Civil Rights Act 1991, s 703(K)(1)(A); 42 USC 2000e-2.

9 See the controversial five–four holding by the US Supreme Court in *Ricci v DeStefano* 557 US 557 (2009), where test results were abandoned because of their discriminatory impact on minorities; this was direct discrimination against the now-disfavoured whites.

10 *Officers for Justice v San Francisco* 979 F 2d 721 (9th Cir, 1992) 723–724.

11 *Chicago Firefighters Local 2 v City of Chicago* 249 F 3d 649 (7th Cir, 2001) 656.

solution, which again finds a place on the procedural landscape of shifting burdens. The requirement for business necessity is augmented with the Alternative Practice doctrine. Here, should a prima facie case be met with an apparently good business necessity defence, the plaintiff may still prevail by proposing an alternative business practice with a less discriminatory effect.[12] The rubric generally used was set in *Albermarle Paper Co v Moody*[13] where the Court stated that the alternative should 'also serve the employer's legitimate interest in 'efficient and trustworthy workmanship'.[14] Again, without the expertise or funding, a claimant may find this too difficult a burden to discharge,[15] but it increases the chances of an employer having to adopt a less discriminatory alternative, and once some alternatives (such as banding) are discussed in litigation, they will become common knowledge, enabling better-informed courts to evaluate the employer's defence.

An example of a successful demonstration of an alternative practice (of banding) arose in *Bridgeport Guardians v City of Bridgeport*[16] where tests used in the promotion of police officers to the rank of sergeant were challenged. One hundred and seventy persons applied for 19 posts and the results showed that the tests had a disparate impact on blacks and Hispanics, with only 30 per cent and 46 per cent respectively passing in comparison with 68 per cent of whites. But the real impact was worse than that because the nineteen best performers were selected, leaving *no* minorities with promotion. The employer successfully justified the tests as a reliable and accurate predictor of job performance. However, what these figures did not reveal was that, of all those passing, the marks were extremely close. The plaintiffs put forward evidence that the difference between a few marks was insignificant. Accordingly, the plaintiffs suggested that the marks should be banded: that is, marks within, say, eight per cent of each other, placed in a single band. Then the successful candidates could be selected from those bands, using other (non-discriminatory) factors for selection. In this way the best performers were selected without a disparate impact. The Court found that the use of banding would alleviate the disparate racial effect of the examination without imposing any significant burden on the defendants whilst serving their legitimate interests.[17]

This Alternative Practice doctrine has not been adopted by the EU or British schemes, although a strictly applied 'necessity' limb of *Bilka*[18] ought to achieve the same result. This places an even stronger emphasis on a strict scrutiny of the employer's defence. Thus, if the anti-discrimination legislation is to address properly the gender pay gap and other discriminatory patterns, the judiciary must demand the least discriminatory alternative.

12 Since recognised in the Civil Rights Act 1991, s 105; codified as 42 USC s 2000e-2(k)(1)(ii).
13 422 US 405 (1975).
14 Ibid., 425 citing *McDonnell Douglas Corp v Green* 411 US 792, 802 (Sup Ct, 1973).
15 See e.g. *Allen v City of Chicago* 351 F 3d 306 (7th Cir, 2003).
16 933 F 2d 1140 (2nd Cir 1991).
17 Ibid., 1145 and 1148.
18 Case 170/84 *Bilka-Kaufhaus v Weber von Hartz* [1984] ECR 1607.

The legislation

The discrimination Directives nowadays state that a defendant may 'objectively justify' a challenged practice by showing a *legitimate aim*, and that *the means of achieving that aim are appropriate and necessary.*[19] This formula codifies Court of Justice case law, originally formulated in *Bilka-Kaufhaus v Weber von Hartz*, which held that a challenged practice is justified if,

> the means chosen … correspond to a genuine need on the part of the undertaking, are appropriate with a view to achieving the objectives pursued and are necessary to that end.[20]

It would seem that for an aim to be legitimate, it must 'correspond to a genuine [or "real"[21]] need of the undertaking'. The test was been transposed into the British legislation, nowadays the Equality Act 2010, as 'a proportionate means of achieving a legitimate aim'.[22] Although the expression 'proportionate' compresses the *Bilka* elements of 'appropriate' and 'necessary', the formula was intended to implement the EU formula.[23] Of course, this compression of language presents an opportunity to dilute its meaning, although cases doing so have not alluded to the different wording.

The British *judicial* dilution of this defence has stemmed from two of its features. First, and almost universally, the domestic courts perpetuated a notion that 'necessary', means '*reasonably* necessary', which provides some leeway to discriminate. Second, on occasions, there has been some confusion between aims and means, which again, has provided some leeway. Allied to both of these issues is a balancing test, which has the potential to provide even more leeway.

Necessary and reasonably necessary

At first sight, the addition of 'reasonable' might be just a way of denoting the test as an objective one.[24] But that has not how the phrase has been used.

19 See e.g. Council Directive 2000/43/EC, art 2(2)(b).
20 Case 170/84, [1984] ECR 1607 para 36. See also [1986] CMLR 701; [1987] ICR 110.
21 Some reports translate this passage as 'the measures chosen … correspond to a real need'. Presumably, 'genuine' and 'real', and 'measures' and 'means, are interchangeable terms in this context. See [1986] IRLR 317 or the official transcript http://curia.europa.eu/juris/liste.jsf?oqp=&for=&mat=or&lgrec=en&jge=&td=%3BALL&jur=C%2CT%2CF&num=170%252F84&page=1&dates=&pcs=Oor&lg=&pro=&nat=or&cit=none%252CC%252CCJ%252CR%252C2008E%252C%252C%252C%252C%252C%252C%252C%252C%252C%252Ctrue%252Cfalse%252Cfalse&language=en&avg=&cid=19359423 accessed 23 December 2020.
22 EA 2010, s 19(2)(d).
23 *Explanatory Notes* to EA 2010, para 81.
24 In a case predating *Bilka*, Browne-Wilkinson J reasoned that EU law outlawed only *intentional* indirect discrimination (*Jenkins v Kingsgate* [1981] ICR 715 (EAT) 725–727), thus suggesting that the test was subjective. It has since been held to be

Instead, it has been used to qualify 'necessary' with a notion of reasonableness, and in doing so provided employers with some leeway, which is leeway for unnecessary discrimination.

A short history is required to understand how this has come about. The original British discrimination legislation used the rather open-ended phrase, 'justifiable irrespective of sex [or race]'.[25] In the early years, tribunals (influenced by *Griggs*), equated this with 'necessity'; in other words, the challenged practice had to be no more than necessary to achieve the aim. For example, in *Steel v Union of Post Office Workers*[26] the President of the EAT, Phillips J, citing *Griggs*,[27] wrote of the defendant's 'heavy' onus of justification, which included showing that the challenged practice was 'genuine' and 'necessary'. Among other things, the tribunal should weigh the need for the practice against the discriminatory effect, and 'distinguish between a [practice] which is necessary and one which is merely convenient, and for this purpose it is relevant to consider whether the employer can find some other and non-discriminatory method of achieving his object'.[28]

In 1982, however, the Court of Appeal in *Ojutiku v Manpower Services Commission*[29] *contrasted* 'necessity' with the statutory word *justifiable*. Kerr LJ stated that 'justifiable … clearly applies a lower standard than … necessary'.[30] Eveleigh LJ considered it to mean 'something … acceptable to right-thinking people as sound and tolerable'.[31] Following this, Balcombe LJ, in *Hampson v Department of Education*,[32] conflated the justification process to a single 'balancing' test, which weighs the discriminatory effect of the challenged practice against the *reasonable* needs of the *employer*.[33]

In the meantime, the Court of Justice was developing a differently formulated justification test, expressed in *Bilka*, which gradually found its way into the domestic legislation. As the influence of EU law grew, domestic courts were forced to reconcile the *Hampson* test with this formula. If there were a

objective, allowing 'after-the-event' justifications: Joined Cases C-4/02 and C-5/02 *Schönheit v Stadt Frankfurt am Main* [2006] CMLR 51, paras 86–87. But see the caution in *Ministry of Defence v O'Brien* [2013] UKSC 6, [48] (Lord Hope and Baroness Hale): 'in this as in any other human rights context, this court is likely to treat with greater respect a justification for a policy which was carefully thought through by reference to the relevant principles at the time when it was adopted…'

25 SDA 1975, s 1(1)(b); RRA 1976, s1(1)(b).

26 [1978] ICR 181 (EAT).

27 401 US 424 (1971). See above, text to n 7.

28 [1978] ICR 181 (EAT) 187–188.

29 [1982] ICR 661 (CA). In Parliament, the Government resisted amendments to the Sex Discrimination Bill that would have replaced 'justifiable' with 'necessary'. Lord Harris stated that where a body offered reduced fares for pensioners, the policy might be justifiable, but not necessary (362 HL Deb 14 July 1975 cols 10116–10117).

30 Ibid., 670.

31 Ibid., 668.

32 [1989] ICR 179 (CA).

33 *Hampson v Department of Education* [1989] ICR 179 (CA) 196.

pivotal point in this process, leading to today's position, it came in the Court of Appeal's (re)formulation in *Barry v Midland Bank*.[34] After citing the *Bilka* and *Hampson* tests, Peter Gibson LJ, speaking for the Court, said,

> In our judgment it would be wrong to extrapolate from those words written in that context that an employer can never justify indirect discrimination in a redundancy payment scheme unless the form of the scheme is shown to be necessary as the only possible scheme.

Thus, he surmised, the 'true position' was that the objective must be legitimate and 'the means used are appropriate to achieve that objective and are *reasonably* necessary for that end'.[35] Peter Gibson LJ cited in support the House of Lords authority, *Rainey v Greater Glasgow Health Board*.[36] In *Rainey*, Lord Keith in fact had to decide whether the defence was subjective or objective (or both).[37] Citing the recently decided *Bilka*, he concluded it must be objective, and in this context, labelled *Bilka's* requirement accordingly as 'reasonably necessary'.[38] Thus, Peter Gibson's LJ reformulation, giving employers some leeway, had no basis in precedent. There is nothing in the Court of Justice language or jurisprudence to support such an approach.[39] In fact, his judgment reconciled *Hampson* and a test of *reasonable* necessity with *Bilka* for no other reason than he said it was so. The rubric has gained traction through nothing more than repetition, with even the Supreme Court culpable. In *Ministry of Justice v O'Brien*[40] for instance, the Supreme Court quoted the familiar EU justification '*Bilka*' test provided by the Court of Justice for the case in hand,[41] and in the next summarising paragraph added the qualifier 'reasonably' for no given reason.[42]

34 [1999] ICR 319 (CA), affirmed on different grounds [1999] ICR 859 (HL).
35 Ibid., 336. Emphasis supplied. The House of Lords dismissed an appeal on the basis (four–one) that the scheme did not discriminate and so did not consider justification, or (Lord Nicholls) was justified under the principle that 'The more serious the disparate impact … the more cogent must be the objective justification': [1999] ICR 859 (HL) 870–871. The principle 'reasonably necessary' was not discussed.
36 [1987] AC 224 (HL).
37 As had been queried by Browne-Wilkinson in *Jenkins v Kingsgate* (EAT) [1981] ICR 715 (EAT) 725–727. See n 24 above.
38 [1987] AC 224, 235–239.
39 A search of EU case law (30 December 2020), using the terms 'reasonably necessary' and 'discrimination' produced four cases, none of which concerned employment or the discrimination directives. The cases were, C-61/77; C-218/11; C-86/82(Opinion); C-524/04 (Opinion).
40 [2013] UKSC 6. See also *Homer v Chief Constable of West Yorkshire* [2012] UKSC 15 [23] (Baroness Hale).
41 Case C-393/10, [2012] ICR 955 [64].
42 [2013] UKSC 6 [45] (Lord Hope and Baroness Hale, writing the Court's judgment).

It is no surprise then, that the fiction of conformity continued in the Court of Appeal, with an unabashed Maurice Kay LJ asserting that this leeway can only be afforded with the qualified formula: 'The test does not require the employer to establish that the measure complained of was "necessary" in the sense of being the only course open to him'.[43] More recently, Slade J in the EAT asserted, 'neither domestic nor European jurisprudence regard the existence of a possible alternative non-discriminatory means of achieving the aim of a measure or policy to be determinative against justifying a discriminatory PCP'.[44]

This is a looser test than one requiring that the means used discriminates no more than necessary, and provides a similar leeway to the *Hampson* test. There are boundaries of course, albeit somewhat more generous to the employer: '*Reasonably* necessary' did not mean that a defendant could justify a measure simply by showing it was one of a band of reasonable responses which a reasonable defendant (e.g. an employer) would adopt, as in unfair dismissal;[45] in one rare instance Sedley LJ suggested that tribunals should consider 'fairly obvious alternatives'.[46] But the leeway remained. In contrast to a strict necessity test, defendants were not bound to show that the practice was the only possible one available.[47] As Maurice Kay LJ reminded tribunals in *Cadman v Health and Safety Executive,* 'The difference between "necessary" and "reasonably necessary" is a significant one'.[48]

Indeed, a few examples will illustrate the significance of the distinction between the original and modified tests. First, two cases pre-dating the *Ojutiku* pronouncements. In *Steel v Union of Post Office Workers,*[49] preferable postal rounds were awarded according to length of service as a 'permanent status' employee. As women historically had been prevented from acquiring permanent status, they were disadvantaged. Phillips J held that the justification would include a consideration of whether it was necessary to allot postal walks by seniority and, if so, whether the seniority rule could be revised so that women would be given credit for their temporary service. In other words, if there existed a less discriminatory alternative, it should be adopted.

In *Bohon-Mitchell v Common Professional Examination Board,*[50] the Board maintained that persons with a degree in a non-law subject should to take a

43 *Cadman v Health and Safety Executive* [2004] EWCA 1317 (CA) (Maurice Kay LJ) [30]–[31]. See also, *Hardys v Lax* [2005] ICR 1565 (CA) (Pill LJ) [32]; *Ladele v Islington LB* [2010] IRLR 211 (CA) [47]–[48] (Lord Neuberger MR). For a view that it is 'impossible' to gauge the seriousness of the discriminatory effect under the *Hampson* test, see *British Airways v Grundy (No 2)* [2008] IRLR 815 (CA), [4] (Sedley LJ).

44 *Kapenova v Department of Health* [2014] ICR 884 (EAT) [83].

45 *Hardys v Lax* [2005] ICR 1565 (CA) (Pill LJ) [31]–[32].

46 *Allonby v Accrington and Rossendale College* [2001] ICR 1189 (CA), [28].

47 *Hardys v Lax* [2005] ICR 1565 (CA) [32].

48 [2004] EWCA 1317 (CA) [31].

49 [1978] ICR 181 (EAT).

50 [1978] IRLR 525 (IT).

12-month course in academic law before being able to sit the Bar Finals. But those with a non-British or non-Irish degree were required to complete a 21-month course. Save for one year, Ms Bohon-Mitchell had been living in England since 1972 and was married to an Englishman. In 1978 she applied to take her Bar Finals and as an American graduate, she was required to sit the 21-month course. Upon her complaint for indirect discrimination on grounds of nationality or national origin, the Board tried to justify that requirement on the ground that barristers needed a wide knowledge of the English way of life (the aim), and the simplest way of identifying those without such experience was by their degrees (the means). Applying the standards set by *Steel*, an industrial tribunal held that the requirement to sit a 21-month course was not justified because it was not *necessary* to achieve the aim. Instead, each candidate's familiarity with the English way of life could be assessed on a case-by-case basis.[51] If the tribunal had applied the *Hampson* test, or asked if the means were *reasonably* necessary, it may well have concluded that the requirement was justified. The evidence was that just eight out of 191 applicants with a non-law degree had overseas degrees. Probably fewer than that eight had been resident in Britain and were therefore 'familiar with the English way of life'. In any case, in terms of numbers, the discriminatory effect was relatively minor. If this discriminatory effect were weighed against the inconvenience of changing the system, a court may well find that defendant's administrative needs justified the practice, or was a reasonable way to achieve the aim. In other words, discrimination would persist because that would be more convenient for the Board.

Finally, a more recent Court of Justice decision nicely exposes the difference In *Enderby v Frenchay Health Authority*,[52] the defendant Health Authority was trying to justify a 40 per cent difference in pay between speech therapists (98 per cent female) and pharmacists (63 per cent female). As women were over-represented in the lower paid group, the Health Authority was obliged to justify the difference. It argued that market forces caused the difference. But the evidence was that only an extra ten per cent pay was needed to recruit a sufficient number of pharmacists. Thus, there existed a less discriminatory alternative of paying the pharmacists a ten per cent premium. In the UK, the EAT[53] applied the *Hampson* test and weighed the 40 per cent difference in pay against the need for sufficient pharmacists. Given that stark choice, the EAT held that the difference in pay was justified. In other words, the leeway provided by the less strict *Hampson* approach meant that employers were not bound to use the least discriminatory practice available. The ECJ held that the pay difference could only be justified to the proportion that market forces required (ten per cent). The existence of the less discriminatory alternative

51 Ibid., [29].
52 Case C-127/92, [1994] ICR 112.
53 [1991] ICR 382.

meant that the practice (a 40 per cent pay difference) could not be justified. For the ECJ, proportionality meant *no more than* necessary:

> If, as the question referred seems to suggest, the national court has been able to determine precisely what proportion of the increase in pay is attributable to market forces, it must necessarily accept that the pay differential is objectively justified to the extent of that proportion. When national authorities have to apply Community law, they must apply the principle of proportionality.[54]

The cases demonstrate that the application of a strict test enables courts to demand equally effective (if inconvenient) alternatives and dictate that there is no more discrimination than necessary. As well as having a fragile, if not non-existent, legal basis, the deviant notions of 'reasonableness' and 'balance' create yet more fuzzy borders.

Confusing aims and means

The *Bilka* test distinguishes between aims and means. It seems that once an aim is considered 'legitimate' it is untouchable (save for the balancing test, explained above). This permits employers a certain amount of latitude and discretion on how to run their affairs, although of course, there are limits. As seen above, the aim should correspond to a genuine need.[55] Once this legitimacy is established, the analysis turns to the *means* of achieving the aim, and this is where most cases on justification are decided. As *Enderby* in particular demonstrated, the means must be suitable and the least discriminatory method of achieving the aim. Here, employers have a lot less latitude, and arguably, none at all. Thus, it is vital to distinguish the aim(s) and means in any one case.

The latitude afforded with the aim has enabled appeal courts to reject claims on the basis that a tribunal cannot substitute its own (less discriminatory) aim for that of the employer. This is apparent from three important cases on this matter. First, in *Barry v Midland Bank,*[56] a severance payment based on two criteria – the salary at the time of termination *and* length of service – was challenged for adversely affecting women, who were more likely to have moved to part-time status and whose salary-related payment was therefore lower, despite having worked full-time for a period in the past. Ms Barry herself had worked full-time for 11 years, moving to part-time for a further two years following the birth of her child. Her (equal pay) claim of indirect sex discrimination failed at every stage of the appeal process. The House of Lords dismissed her appeal on the basis (four–one) that the scheme did not discriminate and so did not warrant justification. Only Lord Nicholls decided that

54 Case C-127/92, [1994] ICR 112, para 27.
55 [1984] ECR 1607, para 36. See also [1986] CMLR 701; [1987] ICR 110.
56 [1997] ICR 192 (EAT); [1999] ICR 319 (CA); [1999] ICR 859 (HL).

the practice required justification. The aims of the scheme were to compensate for the loss of job and recognise loyalty, which tallied respectively with the two criteria (the means). The claimant's suggestion that the bank could have calculated the payment according to hours worked was rejected. Lord Nicholls reasoned,

> To decide otherwise would be to compel the bank to abandon its scheme and substitute a scheme where severance pay is treated and calculated, not as compensation for loss of a job, but as additional pay for past work. That could not be right.[57]

This dictum has been taken as a principle to reverse some first instance decisions for substituting the employer's aim for another of the tribunal's choosing. In *Land Registry v Benson*,[58] the employer, a self-financing government body, decided to merge two offices and reduce staff following a considerable operational loss (nearly £80m). It devised a scheme offering voluntary early retirement to employees aged over 50, and (less generous) redundancy to those under 50. It allocated a £12m budget for the scheme. More volunteered than the budget could afford, and so the employer selected only from those under 50 for redundancy, as that was cheaper. Those aged over 50 claimed for indirect age discrimination, in that they were denied the opportunity to benefit from the scheme, in comparison to the younger workers (the claimants were later dubbed the 'unfairly non-dismissed'[59]). The employment tribunal found that reducing staff costs was a legitimate aim, but that the employer not shown that it was necessary to limit its spending on the scheme to £12m: it had the resources to accept all the applications. The EAT (Underhill J) reversed, holding that fixing the budget to £12m was a legitimate aim: 'Like any business, it was entitled to make decisions about the allocation of its resources'.[60] In effect, the tribunal had substituted the employer's scheme for one of its own.[61]

The most recent instance, *Harrod v Chief Constable of West Midlands Police*,[62] reached the Court of Appeal (Elias, Underhill, and Bean LJJ). Following the 2010 general election, police forces were required to make budget cuts of 20 per cent over four years. Five police forces opted to retire all officers eligible for compulsory retirement under regulation A19 of the Police Pensions Regulations 1987.[63] This provided that a police force may, 'in the general interests of efficiency', require the compulsory retirement of an officer who would be

57 Ibid., 872.
58 [2012] ICR 627 (EAT). See also *Chief Constable of West Midlands Police v Blackburn* [2008] ICR 505 (EAT) (Elias J).
59 Cavanagh QC, as counsel in *Harrod v Chief Constable of West Midlands Police* [2017] EWCA 191, cited [25].
60 [2012] ICR 627 [34].
61 Ibid., [39].
62 [2017] EWCA 191.
63 SI 1987/257.

entitled to receive a pension of at least two-thirds of his average pensionable pay. Such a pension entitlement could be acquired only with at least 30 years of service. This meant only those aged 48 or more could be retired. Although a 'substantial majority' of officers retire voluntarily after 30 years,[64] regulation A19 was applied to all eligible officers, forcing some into compulsory retirement. This blanket application of regulation A19 made more savings than was required.

Officers aged 48 and over brought a claim of indirect age discrimination. It was agreed that the dismissals adversely affected those aged 48 and over, and so the case turned on the element of justification. An employment tribunal found the dismissals were not justified, as the forces could have made the required savings by a less discriminatory means, such as identifying those willing to take voluntary retirement, career breaks, part-time working. The EAT reversed, with Langstaff J holding that these 'entirely speculative' alternatives could not provide the required certainty, as officers could change their minds about any of those three options.[65] The Court of Appeal upheld the EAT reversal, holding that it was not for the tribunal to substitute an alternative scheme.

So far, so clear. It seems straightforward: once an aim is identified as 'legitimate' it becomes unassailable. But a common difficulty in coming to these decisions was distinguishing between aims and means. As Underhill J confessed in *Benson*: 'The truth is that the distinction between means and aim is not always easy to draw'.[66] But this did not seem to matter for the judges in these cases. Elias J once noted that the distinction was 'a matter of semantics'.[67] Underhill J has observed more than once that, 'the dichotomy of "aim" and "means" is not always clear cut and the two elements can sometimes reasonably be formulated in more than one way'.[68] Thus, he advised with a flourish, 'Tribunals need not cudgel their brains with metaphysical inquiries about what count as aims and what count as means as long as the underlying balancing exercise is carried out'.[69]

Rather than provide a solution to tribunals (and other interested parties), this presents a problem. If it matters little, or is impossible to classify, which features of a defence are aims and which are means, how is a tribunal supposed analyse them, when according to *Bilka*, the aims must be legitimate but the means proportionate (or appropriate and necessary)? In *Benson* and *Harrod,* all the forums pondered at length over which was which. It is inevitable that this will lead to confusion. In *Harrod,* for instance, Langstaff J, considered the aim to be 'at least that of achieving efficiency'.[70] In the Court of Appeal, Elias LJ

64 Cited [2015] ICR 1311 (EAT) [37].
65 [2015] ICR 1311 [46].
66 [2012] ICR 627 [33].
67 *Loxley v BAE Systems Land Systems (Munitions & Ordnance) Ltd* [2008] ICR 1348 [37].
68 *Land Registry v Benson* [2012] ICR 627 (EAT) [36], citing *Pulham v Barking and Dagenham LBC* [2010] ICR 133 (EAT) [15]. Cited with approval by Bean LJ, *Harrod v Chief Constable of West Midlands Police* [2017] EWCA 191, cited [26].
69 Ibid., *Pulham* [2010] ICR 133 (EAT) [15].

appeared to agree, declaring: 'The dismissals are on grounds of efficiency'.[71] Meanwhile, Underhill LJ stated, 'In my view the right way to characterise the forces' aim is that they wished to achieve the maximum practicable reduction in the numbers of their officers'.[72] Bean LJ was less specific. His leading judgment did not expressly identify an aim. The closest he came was when he said,

> The decision to reduce officer headcount to the fullest extent available was taken in the interests of achieving certainty of costs reduction and it was not for the Tribunal to devise an alternative scheme involving the loss of fewer posts.[73]

Given that it was held a mistake for the tribunal to devise another scheme (as it is not for the tribunal to substitute the defendant's aim for its own), it is implicit here that Bean LJ considered the aims to be the 'fullest' possible reduction in officer headcount in the interests of achieving 'certainty of costs reduction'.

Not only is this speculation producing a variety of views confusing for interested parties, it can incorporate mistakes. For instance, Underhill and Bean LJJ both assumed that it was an aim to achieve to maximum possible reduction of staff. This was not the case. The forces were under instruction to make a 20 per cent saving. There was no edict to achieve this with staff cuts, and certainly not to reduce the staff beyond that necessary to achieve the saving. Quite the opposite, one would imagine. Hence, a reduction of officers was just one of many cutbacks, including spending on buildings, IT equipment and vehicles; this was in addition to the dismissal of some civilian staff. Clearly, the 'aim' was to save money, and arguably to do so with certainty. Yet, the evidence was that more than the necessary numbers of officers were dismissed. By characterising the 'maximum reduction' as an 'aim', Underhill and Bean LJJ detached this action from the required question of proportionality. With some clarity around the means and aims, the Court of Appeal may have realised that it was necessary to select only the number of 'A 19' officers needed to meet the required savings and certainty. The two-thirds pension entitlement laid down in regulation A19 was a threshold, not an absolute rule. Thus, depending on the calculations, the forces could have selected all those with say, at least three-quarters pension entitlement.

Meanwhile, in *Benson*, after considering the features of the need to break even (at least), including the office merger scheme, staffing costs reduction, £12m budget, and method of selection, Underhill J said, 'The uncertainty about how to characterise them ... does not, fortunately, matter since in our view all the various potential elements are plainly legitimate'.[74] The error here,

70 [2015] ICR 1311 [9].
71 [2017] EWCA 191 [44].
72 Ibid., [38].
73 Ibid., [30].
74 [2012] ICR 627 (EAT) [34].

albeit of the same flavour, was slightly different. Instead of wrongly classifying the features of the case, Underhill LJ measured them all by the standard required for aims, again detaching them from the question of proportionality.

The irony here is of course, after criticising the tribunal below for devising an alternative aim, these judges fare only a little better in speculating themselves as what were the aims. Thus, as well as being more diligent in identifying the aims and means, further clarity would be achieved by expecting defendants to identify their own aims. The indeterminable speculation on the defendant's aim (s) has not only led to confusion and errors, it is wrong in principle. The tribunals' task is to scrutinise the defence provided, not to help draft a party's pleadings.

The continued use of the balancing test

Assiduous readers of the law reports (concerning discrimination) would have noticed judges occasionally reverting to the *Hampson* 'balancing' test rather than, or alongside, the 'reasonably necessary' rubric. It seems they consider these expressions to mean one of the same thing.[75] It is arguable, that the *Hampson* formula perhaps betrays another departure from *Bilka,* because it requires only that the employer's needs are 'reasonable', and not 'real' or 'genuine'. This is hard to sustain though, as 'fake', spurious or 'non-real' needs are hardly likely to be accepted as 'reasonable', no matter what the discretion. But the unnecessary exchange of 'real' for 'reasonable' can only add to the confusion by the British judiciary's rewriting of *Bilka.*

In relation to *Bilka's* requirement regarding the means, the language used in either (domestic) test shares the same feature of discretion, or 'leeway'. As such, it should make little difference which test is used, save in one way. The *Hampson* test permits tribunals to vitiate the employer's aim by another route. Where the aim is legitimate, but the only means to achieve the aim 'outweighs' it because of its overwhelming discriminatory effect, then the aim itself is vitiated.

In *Allen v GMB,*[76] when negotiating with their employer, the claimants' trade union prioritised pay protection and future pay for all its members over

75 In *Barry v Midland Bank* [1999] ICR 859 (HL) 870, Lord Nicholls assumed the *Bilka* test to mean, 'The more serious the disparate impact on women … the more cogent must be the objective justification', thus conflating *Bilka* and *Hampson.* When *Barry* was in the Court of Appeal, Gibson LJ assumed that *Hampson* and 'reasonably necessary' both correctly reflected the *Bilka* test: [1999] ICR 319 (CA) [43]. The most direct of these opinions came from Gage LJ in *Hardys v Lax* [2005] ICR 1565 (CA) [59], 'In my view the reasonably necessary test is much the same as a test of proportionality and rather different to a margin of appreciation'. See also *Benson* [2012] ICR 627 (EAT) [37] (Underhill J); *Harrod v Chief Constable of West Midlands Police* [2015] ICR 1311 (EAT) [34] (Langstaff J); *British Airways Plc v Grundy* [2008] EWCA Civ 875 [28] (Sedley LJ); *Allonby v Accrington and Rossendale College* [2001] ICR 1189 (CA), [27]–[28] (Sedley LJ).

76 [2008] EWCA Civ 810.

compensation (back pay) for unequal pay in the past, affecting just the female members, who were the claimants. The reason was that the union did not wish to antagonise the employer in its aim to achieve the best possible deal overall. In pursuit of their goal, the union persuaded the claimants to agree to the negotiated deal. In doing so, the union wrongly told the claimants that no better deal could have been achieved for them by litigation. The claimants sued their union for indirect discrimination.[77] Reversing the employment tribunal's decision for the claimants, the EAT (Elias J) found that although the union's priorities were legitimate aims,[78] the means used, albeit dishonest, were the only way to achieve the goal. Hence, there was no less discriminatory alternative. To hold otherwise would be substituting the union's aims for its own,[79] violating a seemingly cardinal rule.[80] The Court of Appeal restored the tribunal's decision holding that if the means are disproportionate, then they cannot be justified. Maurice Kay LJ said 'although the objective was a legitimate one, it was not the only possible legitimate one. If it were achievable only by disproportionate means, then it would not be susceptible to justification. To conclude otherwise would be to license disproportionality'.[81] The Court of Appeal came to this decision without citing *Hampson* or the balancing test. But in effect, that is what it used. Elias's J decision was perfectly logical on the wording of *Bilka*, but clearly unpalatable for the Court of Appeal. Of course, the decision could readily be explained as one hostile to trade unions, and Elias's J holding may have stuck otherwise. Nonetheless, it does show the utility of a balancing test and distinguishing it from *any* notion of necessity, which is confined to the means.

It is inconceivable that in such a situation, where a relatively modest aim inevitably creates a considerable adverse impact, that the Court of Justice would adhere to the semantics of the *Bilka* test in preference to its more general principle of proportionality. The nearest case to this scenario arose *Rinke*.[82] Here, the requirement for some full-time work by two Council Directives[83]

77 The ET rejected a direct discrimination claim on the basis that the 'reason why' was 'was not the genders of the people in those groups. It was an attempt to keep the peace and to appear to as many people as possible to have done a "good job" as a Union in representing the interests of all members' (para 3.181, cited [2007] IRLR 752 (EAT), [25]). Surely this should have been appealed, as it is no defence to treat a protected group less favourably to placate others: see e.g. *James v Eastleigh BC* [1990] 2 AC 751 (HL); *R v CRE ex parte Westminster City Council* [1985] ICR 827 (CA); and for a virtually identical situation in the context of race, see the US case, *Goodman* v *Lukens Steel* 482 US 656 (Sup Ct, 1987).

78 [2007] IRLR 752 [18]–[19].

79 Ibid., [83].

80 See e.g. *Barry v Midland Bank* [1999] ICR 859 (HL); *Land Registry v Benson* [2012] ICR 627 (EAT); *Chief Constable of West Midlands v Blackburn* [2008] ICR 505 (EAT); *Harrod v Chief Constable of West Midlands Police* [2015] ICR 1311 (EAT), all discussed above, p. 89 et al.

81 [2008] EWCA Civ 810 [33].

82 Case C-25/02 *Rinke v Ärztekammer Hamburg* [2003] ECR I-8349.

83 Council Directives 86/457 and 93/16.

on the training of doctors, was claimed to offend the EU's general principle of (sex) equality. The Court weighed the policy (harmonising training across the EU, thus facilitating free movement of doctors, as well as better preparation to fulfil the particular function) against the discriminatory impact. Although it concluded that the Directives were justified, it showed a willingness of the Court to take this approach.[84]

This shows that the balancing test is distinguishable from the 'reasonably necessary' approach, in that it has some utility in addressing the gender pay gap and other discriminatory patterns. Hence the suggestion made back in 1978 by Phillips J,[85] and more recently by the Supreme Court[86] that the courts should use *both* tests would seem to be the most effective way to satisfy the policy of addressing all discrimination.

Such a dual approach ought to have jarred Lord Nicholls's reasoning in *Barry v Midland Bank*,[87] especially when scrutinising a scheme under a 'fundamental' rule of EU law, such as sex discrimination.[88] When invoking the 'substitution' rule, Lord Nicholls speculated that the claimant's suggested alternative (of severance payments calculated by hours worked) would be more discriminatory, as women were more likely to have worked fewer hours over the same time period.[89] Yet, although Lord Nicholls recited a balancing test, in deference to the substitution rule he failed to apply it. Had he done so, he may have considered that the discriminatory impact of the Bank's scheme outweighed its aims (of compensation for loss of job and rewarding loyalty). As such, he may have asked the (well-resourced multi-national) bank to calculate and compare the adverse impact of alternative aims, such as paring down to original aim to a reward of loyalty calculated on the length of service.

Court of Justice referrals

One might suppose that this state of affairs has persisted for so long because of an absence of a referral to the Court of Justice. The stark signal given in *Enderby* back in 1993 would seem to have bypassed the British judiciary. The only other referral close to the matter, in 1999, illustrates this, with the House of Lords, upon its return, thoroughly misrepresenting the ECJ's ruling. The case was distinguishable as it concerned a social policy justification where the

84 Case C-25/02, paras 37–38. For a detailed argument that the *Hampson* balancing test has potential to be stricter than *Bilka*, see JA Lane, R Ingleby, 'Indirect Discrimination, Justification and Proportionality: Are UK Claimants at a Disadvantage?' (2018) 47 (4) *ILJ* 531.

85 *Steel v Union of Post Office Workers* [1978] ICR 181 (EAT) 187–188.

86 *Homer v Chief Constable of West Yorkshire* [2012] UKSC 15 (Baroness Hale) [19], [24] and the cases cited within.

87 [1999] ICR 859 (HL). See above, text to n 56.

88 See e.g. Joined Cases C-4/02 and C-5/02 *Schönheit v Stadt Frankfurt am Main* [2006] 1 CMLR 51 [85] and the cases cited therein.

89 Ibid., 871. See also [1999] ICR 319 (CA) 329–330 (Peter Gibson LJ).

Court of Justice can provide defendants with some leeway. Nonetheless, it illustrates the UK's looser and somewhat muddled approach to justification.

A social policy justification is used normally by Governments defending a domestic measure against superior EU discrimination law. Where a defence is based on social policy, the *Bilka* test is modified. Defendants must still show that the practice reflects a necessary aim of its social policy and is suitable and necessary for achieving that aim, but at the same time, they are afforded a broad margin of discretion in choosing the appropriate means to achieve that policy. In *R v Secretary of State for Employment, ex parte Seymour-Smith*,[90] the extension of the qualification period for Unfair Dismissal rights from one to two years was challenged as indirectly discriminating against women, who are more transient in the workforce.[91] Upon referral from the House of Lords, the Court of Justice recited the *Bilka* test and the margin of discretion, but added, with an allusion to the defence proffered by the Government, the margin of discretion is not so broad to have the effect of frustrating the implementation of the fundamental principle of equal treatment: 'Mere generalisations … are not enough'.[92]

The Government's argument was that the legislation would encourage recruitment, although it offered no evidence that, after six years, it had made any impact. Upon return, the House of Lords held that the Government had justified the legislation. Lord Nicholls cited the Court of Justice ruling on the margin of discretion, but omitted its reference to *Bilka*, necessity, and the ruling against 'mere generalisations'. This selective interpretation was enough for Lord Nicholls to conclude that the burden on the Government was not 'as heavy as previously thought'.[93] Read as a whole the ECJ's judgment clearly envisaged that the measure must be 'necessary' to achieve an aim.[94] Even on Lord Nicholls's less stringent test, the decision was surprising. After all, the Government offered no evidence to support its assertion of increasing employment. The decision might be explained by the marginal adverse effect of the legislation (about eight per cent less women than men qualified for unfair dismissal rights). But on a national scale, it meant that for no good reason, for some fourteen years, hundreds of thousands of British women worked without the protection of Unfair Dismissal rights. Of course, the ultimate beneficiary in this case was not the defendant (the UK Government), as there was no evidence of improved employment nationally, but Britain's employers, who were given more leeway to dismiss more conveniently and cheaply, a process already proven to adversely affect women.

90 Case C-167/97, [1999] ICR 447.
91 It was reduced to one year in 1999 (SI 1999/1436), and restored to two years in 2015 (SI 2012/989).
92 Case C-167/97, paras 69–77.
93 [2000] ICR 244, 261
94 See e.g. Case C-167/97, [1999] ICR 447, para 65.

Although this was not a singular employment case where an unabated *Bilka* test should apply, the signal sent out by Lord Nicholls's judgment chimed with the diluted approach already growing in the British courts.

Conclusion

As well as preserving the fiction of compliance, this language of compromise puts an unnecessary judicial gloss on the statutory words and Court of Justice jurisprudence. 'Proportionate' and 'necessary' do not mean *nearly* proportionate, or *reasonably* necessary. A strict approach does not mean that businesses would be forced to spend great sums for a marginal reduction in a discriminatory impact: economic reasons are acceptable as a legitimate aim.[95] These cases demonstrate that the British judiciary's interpretation of the notion of objective justification falls short of principle, policy, and the EU jurisprudence. They also show an unexplained makeshift (and not very adept) sleight of language employed to disguise this.

The American 'banding' and Alternative Practice cases, in addition to *Enderby*, demonstrate that even marginal or subtle adjustments can make a significant impact in reducing discrimination, without damaging the employer's business. The British approach at best rules out all bar 'fairly obvious alternatives'.[96] At its worst it happily speculates over the employer's aims to find a justification, and steadfastly refuses to interfere with them should that produce a less discriminatory alternative. The only adventurous decision here was to give the otherwise permissive *Hampson* balancing test its full potential against a trade union,[97] raising suspicions that employer's costs or inconvenience are weighing heavily in the court's thinking, if not its expressions.

Despite dicta to the contrary,[98] it is arguable that cases such as *Benson*, Barry,[99]*Harrod* and *Enderby* (in the EAT), as well as *Seymour-Smith*, were in fact decided on a notion of reasonableness rather than proportionality. If allowed to carry on this way without an alignment with EU law, there is a danger of the courts drifting past the already-loose boundaries expressed and assuming the 'band of reasonable responses' test from unfair dismissal, in line with the common law tradition of *Wednesbury* reasonableness,[100] rather than the civil law concept of proportionality.

95 See e.g. *Bilka* Case 170/84, [1984] ECR 1607, para 36.
96 *Allonby v Accrington and Rossendale College* [2001] ICR 1189 (CA), [28].
97 *Allen v GMB* [2008] EWCA Civ 810.
98 *Hardys v Lax* [2005] ICR 1565 (CA) (Pill LJ) [31]–[32].
99 Assuming a prima facie case were established. The House of Lords (four–one) reversed the Court of Appeal on this point.
100 *Associated Provincial Picture Houses Ltd v Wednesbury Corporation* [1948] 1 KB 223, 230 (CA)*Associated Provincial Picture Houses Ltd v Wednesbury Corporation*, holding that for judicial review the courts would interfere only if a decision were so unreasonable that no reasonable authority could never have come to it.

In the absence of a reference to the Luxembourg Court, which in any case in the past have proved ineffectual, the only solution is statutory reform. For this to occur, Parliament needs to be aware of the problem. For this to even be contemplated, Parliament needs to be aware of the courts' pretence that its approach to justification is in accordance with EU law. This presents another hurdle. Should this be overcome, the existing British legislation, in particular the Equality Act 2010, section 19, requires redrafting, with *both* aspects (*Hampson* and *Bilka*) of the justification defence included as mandatory steps in the process. It is in fact helpful that the existing definition does not align to this. The compressed formula ('proportionate means of achieving a legitimate aim'), means that a redraft, expressing the elements 'appropriate' and 'necessary', will present a clear signal that the courts must change their approach. In addition, the requirement of *strict* necessity should be included, and a procedural requirement that the 'legitimate aims can only be those pleaded. Finally, it would be helpful if the Equality Act 2010 contained an interpretive clause that the Act should be given a purposive interpretation. This should help align the UK justification test with that of the EU, irrespective of any EU, or ECJ, jurisdiction. Without such a reform, the UK courts are likely to continue to drift with their 'reasonably necessary', 'balancing test', and quite possibly a 'band of reasonable responses' mantra. Not only is this present situation unrepresentative the principles of discrimination law, it is also a cloud of uncertainty, or a bundle of fuzzy borders.

Further reading

JA Lane and R Ingleby, 'Indirect discrimination, justification and proportionality: Are UK claimants at a disadvantage?' (2018) 47(4) *ILJ* 531.

6 Problems with perceived discrimination

Introduction

It can happen that a defendant discriminates against a person because he thinks, or perceives, incorrectly, that the person has a protected characteristic. For instance, an employer may reject a job application from a white man, wrongly thinking he is black, because of his African-sounding name.[1] Similarly, a publican may refuse to admit two straight men, wrongly perceiving them to be gay, or (in the wake of the 9/11 attacks), a Sikh man wearing a turban, mistaking him for a Muslim.[2]

The matter involves alternative meanings ascribed to the notion of direct discrimination. On the one hand, the UK and EU versions are form-based, requiring less favourable treatment (which involves a comparison) *because of* a protected characteristic. On the other, the 'because' question is intensified, and the focus remains largely on the defendant's subjective reasons for acting, thus facilitating the notion that there can be liability because of the defendant's reason for acting. This focus of the defendant's motive is favoured by the US Federal courts *but* as the (US) Civil Rights Act 1964 insists that the treatment is because of the *victim's* race, religion, or sex,[3] it is difficult to draw from the Act a general notion of perceived discrimination.

By contrast, the UK and EU form-based definitions present an inverted formula. While the 'because' element does not insist that the victim holds the relevant protected characteristic, the necessary comparison suggests that the victim, or someone else, does so. Of course, with perceived discrimination no one in the scenario holds the relevant protected characteristic. For the UK, this is against a seemingly contradictory backdrop of a statutory purpose expressed

1 Equality Act 2010, Explanatory Note 63.

2 Human Rights Watch, '"We are not the enemy" hate crimes against Arabs, Muslims, and those perceived to be Arabs or Muslims after September 11', Vol 14 no G November 2002, p. 15 www.hrw.org/reports/2002/usahate/ accessed 30 December 2020.

3 e.g. Civil Rights Act 1964, Title VII, s 706 (codified 42 USC s 2000e-2): 'It shall be an unlawful employment practice for an employer … to discriminate against any individual … because of *such individual's* race, color, religion, sex, or national origin'. Emphasis supplied.

DOI: 10.4324/9781003187547-6

in accompanying texts and case law that the legislation is intended to cover perceived discrimination. The matter is further complicated for disability discrimination, where the particularly complex definition of disability renders it near-impossible to hold that a defendant perceived all the elements of this complex definition.

After a brief account of this law's underpinning theories, policy, and origins, this chapter notes the fuzzy borders with perceived discrimination under the US Civil Rights Act. It highlights the shortcomings of the statutory formulas, in relation to the 'closed' and 'open' definitions of direct discrimination, the comparison for less favourable treatment, and perceived disabilities (including disfigurements). It identifies various technical niceties deployed to overcome these shortcomings, and mistakes made in doing so, or indeed in unnecessarily restricting its application, notably for perceived disability discrimination (for which a technically sound method is proposed).

Origins and theories

There is little scholarship offering a theoretical basis for perceived discrimination. The unhelpful drafting of the US Civil Rights Act and absence of expressed Congressional purpose (save for disability[4]), has prompted most scholarship to promote a 'perception theory' with a view to challenging the literal interpretation taken by most courts.[5] One justification is rooted in the post-war theory of race, shifting away from biological or genetic definitions towards a cultural concept, or a social construct. This involves more subjective views of race, which in turn can be linked to one's perception.[6] This 'social construct' theory could apply, to greater or lesser degrees, to other suspect classes, such as sex, gender identity, sexual orientation, age and disability.[7] It can manifest with stereotyping, something closer and more familiar to discrimination law, but in perception cases, the mistake relates to the protected characteristic itself, rather than a manifestation of it. This would be, for example, presuming a Sikh is a Muslim, rather than presuming that an actual Muslim is sympathetic to terrorism. Of course, this stereotype may well follow, but it is based on the victim's perceived religion, rather than his actual one.

4 See below, p. 126.

5 See e.g. DF Flake, 'Religious Discrimination Based On Employer Misperception' (2016) *Wisconsin Law Review* 87; A Onwuachi-Willig, ML Barnes, 'By any other name?: On being "regarded as" black, and why Title VII should apply even if Lakisha and Jamal are white' (2005) *Wisconsin Law Review* 1283; DW Greene, 'Categorically black, white, or wrong: "Misperception discrimination" and the State of Title VII Protection' (2013) 47(1) *University of Michigan Journal of Law Reform* 86, 131; CR Senn, 'Perception over reality: Extending the Ada's concept of "regarded as" protection under federal employment discrimination law' (2009) 36 *Florida State University Law Review* 827.

6 See e.g. DW Greene, ibid., 131.

7 For the 'social model' of disability law, see n 109.

The social construct theory had some traction in the development of perceived discrimination in the UK. The first hint was made in 1983. When distinguishing between scientific and cultural definitions of 'ethnic' in the Race Relations Act 1976, Lord Fraser opined,

> A person may treat another relatively unfavourably 'on racial grounds' because he regards that other as being of a particular race, or belonging to a particular racial group, even if his belief is, from a scientific point of view, completely erroneous.[8]

This observation was cited in 2003 in the Explanatory Notes to British legislation introducing sexual orientation and religion or belief discrimination laws, 'people will be able to bring a claim even if the discrimination was based on (incorrect) assumptions about their sexual orientation/religion or belief'. In addition, individuals would not be required to disclose their sexual orientation, or religion or belief, when making a claim: 'it will be sufficient that they have suffered a disadvantage because of the assumptions made about their sexual orientation/religion or belief'.[9]

This last example reveals another basis of perception theory, a policy particularly relevant to harassment and sexual orientation, highlighted by Sedley LJ in 2008,

> [People] … may desire to keep their orientation to themselves but still be vulnerable to harassment by people who know or sense what their orientation is. It cannot possibly have been the intention, when legislation was introduced to stop sexual harassment in the workplace, that such a claimant must declare his or her true sexual orientation in order to establish that the abuse was 'on grounds of sexual orientation'.… The case would have been exactly the same if [the claimant] … had elected, for whatever reason, to remain silent about his actual sexual orientation.… And the same would be the case if he were actually gay or bisexual but preferred not to disclose it.[10]

Thus, perceived discrimination (and harassment) could be said to be underpinned with a notion of dignity, in this case one of privacy. For the same policy reason, respect for privacy should apply to other protected characteristics. For instance, a worker being abused with mental-health epithets should be able

8 *Mandla v Dowell Lee* [1983] 2 AC 548 (HL) 563.

9 Explanatory Notes to the Employment Equality (Religion or Belief) Regulations 2003, 2003/1660 and Employment Equality (Sexual Orientation) Regulations 2003, 2003/1661, paras 24–25. This Note cited in support Lord Fraser's dictum cited above, from *Mandla v Dowell Lee* [1983] 2 AC 548 https://webarchive.nationalarchives.gov.uk/20050303225921/www2.dti.gov.uk/er/equality/so_rb_longexplan.pdf both accessed 30 December 2020.

10 *English v Sanderson Blinds* [2008] EWCA 1421 [39].

to complain without disclosing any mental health impairments of their own. Others may prefer to keep private matters of religion, race, gender, or age. The principal aim of this policy is to protect those with an actual protected characteristic, but by doing so, it throws a protective blanket over all those on the receiving end of discriminatory treatment, whether or not they possess a relevant protected characteristic. In other words, the privacy policy is *not* a basis of perception theory. Rather, perception theory is a collateral beneficiary of a policy primarily aimed at those with an actual protected characteristic.

That said, a broader notion of dignity could certainly underpin perception theory in other circumstances. These can manifest where the misperception itself violates the victim's dignity. This could be for reasons of the victim's empathy with, or indeed, antipathy towards, the perceived identity. For example, it could be an affront to an Italian worker's Latin identity, to treat her badly on the mistaken basis that she was Spanish.[11] In a predominantly Christian culture, it could be an affront to a Sunni Muslim's Islamic identity to confuse him with a Shia Muslim, or indeed, a Sikh.

Related to these notions of dignity, or perhaps a consequence of them, is a necessary shift of focus away from the actual protected characteristic of the victim towards the motive of the defendant. A hint of this was apparent in the ECJ judgment in *Coleman v Attridge Law*,[12] where the court stated, 'The principle of equal treatment enshrined in the directive in that area applies not to a particular category of person but by reference to the grounds mentioned in Art.1'.[13] This was influential in the UK's extension of perceived discrimination to cover more protected characteristics.[14] It nudges UK and EU law towards the US approach regarding direct discrimination ('disparate treatment') which principally requires for liability a discriminatory motive. Hence, in the US, disparate treatment is commonly labelled 'intentional discrimination'.[15] This approach was neatly captured by a US Federal Court of Appeals, reasoning that the statutory word 'discrimination'

> refers to the practice of making a decision based on a certain criterion, and therefore focuses on the decisionmaker's subjective intent. What follows, the word 'because', specifies the criterion that the employer is prohibited

11 See e.g. *LaRocca v Precision Motorcars* 45 F Supp 2d 762 (D Neb. 1999), discussed below, text to n 34.
12 Case C-303/06, [2008] 3 CMLR 27.
13 Ibid., paras 38 (and 50). The 'grounds' alluded to were sexual orientation, religion or belief, disability, and age ('Framework' Directive 2000/78/EC, art 1). This might explain the retention of the 'closed' definition for Marriage and Civil Partnership (EA 2010, s 13(4)) and Pregnancy or Maternity (ss 17, 18).
14 See Written Statement by Leader of the House of Commons (Harriot Harman), HC Deb 2 Apr 2009, Col 88W https://publications.parliament.uk/pa/cm200809/cmhansrd/cm090402/wmstext/90402m0003.htm accessed 30 December 2020.
15 In contrast to 'nonintentional discrimination' (or 'disparate impact'), the US counterpart to the UK's indirect discrimination.

> from using as a basis for decisionmaking. The laws, therefore, focus on the employer's subjective reasons for taking adverse action against an employee, so it matters not whether the reasons behind the employer's discriminatory animus are actually correct as a factual matter.[16]

These are strong arguments for recognising perceived discrimination, and on occasion, have even nudged some US courts to recognise perceived discrimination, albeit via a circuitous route? But this is not without objections. One line of resistance, noted by DW Greene, is that its recognition will encourage 'individuals with deceitful motives … to disingenuously frame employment discrimination claims as stemming from misperceptions about their respective identities'.[17] Greene cited a US case, *Wood v Freeman Decorating*, an *actual* discrimination claim based on the plaintiff's self-proclaimed Native American identity. The defendant employer countered with evidence that the plaintiff had once self-identified as Hispanic on a military admissions form on which American Indian was a choice. His only proof was his adopted mother's hearsay admissions to him that his natural parents were Native American. In other words, this 'self-classification … was an insincere and self-serving attempt to capitalize on alleged racially offensive conduct toward, and statements about, Native Americans'.[18] This may be so, but if the objection is to recognising perceived discrimination, it misses the point. The incentive to falsify one's suspect class to coincide with the treatment complained of is the *failure* of the law to recognise perceived discrimination. Further, there is no need to falsify one's protected characteristic where the issue is the *defendant's* perception, rather than the victim's actual or invented ethnicity. Accordingly, in *Wood*, the court rejected the defence, holding that the plaintiff's racial identity was irrelevant, '[P]laintiffs who are not members of [a] protected class have standing to challenge racially discriminatory conduct in their own right when they are the direct target of discrimination'.[19] This neatly sidestepped the 'actual' discrimination element of the Civil Rights Act's formula, by focussing on two other aspects: the nature of the conduct and the Act's procedural provision requiring locus standi (or 'standing').[20] As Wood was harmed by the

16 *Fogleman v Mercy Hospital* 283 F.3d 561 (3d Cir 2002) 571 (discussing perceived disability victimisation, rather than discrimination per se). See also Flake (n 5) 128.

17 DW Greene, 'Categorically black, white, or wrong: "Misperception discrimination" and the State of Title VII Protection' (2013) 47(1) *University of Michigan Journal of Law Reform* 86, 136.

18 DW Greene, ibid., 138, citing Defendant's Motion to Dismiss, *Wood v Freeman Decorating* No. 3:08-CV-00375-LRH-RAM, 2009 WL 4836455 (D Nev, July 30, 2009).

19 *Wood v Freeman Decorating* No. 3:08-CV-00375-LRH-RAM, 2010 WL 653764 (D Nev Feb 19, 2010), at pp. 4–5 citing *RK Ventures v City of Seattle* 307 F 3d 1045, 1055 (9th Cir, 2002).

20 See e.g. Civil Rights Act 1964, Title VII (employment), s 706 (codified as 42 USC s 2000e-(5)(f)(1)), Fair Housing Act 1968 (formally Civil Rights Act 1968), s 810 (a) (42 USC s 3610(a)).

discriminatory conduct, he had standing to sue. A less venturesome basis for the decision was that the employer 'associated' Wood with Native Americans, and so the decision could be explained on the widely recognised basis of associative discrimination.[21] The relationship between associated and perceived discrimination is explored below.[22]

Another line of resistance lies in the focus on the defendant's state of mind. Recognising perceived discrimination involves a shift of emphasis from form to motive, or in the (UK) statutory language, from the comparison to the 'because' question. Indeed, it is arguable that it dispenses with a comparison altogether (see below[23]) leaving the defendant's state of mind as the *only* ingredient. Whatever, there is no doubt that liability for *perceived* discrimination depends much more on the defendant's 'guilty' state of mind than ordinarily required for other forms of direct discrimination. This 'guilty mind' notion has been strongly rejected by the UK judiciary in favour of something akin to strict liability. The irony here is that this approach was taken to simplify the law and make it *easier* to claim direct discrimination. Notably, it was intended to thwart 'benign motive' defences. (These can range from employers acceding to customer preferences,[24] to protecting women, or particular nationals, from harassment or even endangerment.[25]) However, these two extremes may not be as polarised as first appears. The UK courts still require evidence of a defendant's 'mental processes' where the discrimination was 'not obvious'.[26] It has even been suggested that in 'obvious' cases tribunals can 'avoid arid and confusing disputes about the identification of the appropriate comparator'.[27] In other words, a comparison is not always necessary. Meanwhile, American jurisprudence, which *requires* a discriminatory motive for direct discrimination, simultaneously recognises, distinguishes, and rejects, attempted benign motive defences.[28] As such, the two approaches are not wholly irreconcilable. Recognition of perceived discrimination may exhibit some disrespect to the UK statutory formula and deviate from its jurisprudence, but it need not carry a risk of importing benign motive defences.

Irrespective of any doubts, Parliament ploughed ahead. In addition to the 2003 Explanatory Note (above), the notion was recognised in the main body of legislation for the first time in the 2006 Equality Act (outlawing religious discrimination in goods, services, and premises); here a rider to the definition of

21 *Wood v Freeman Decorating* (D Nev Feb 19, 2010) (n 19) p. 4.
22 See p. 114, '*Perceived discrimination as associative discrimination*'.
23 Text to n 27.
24 *R v Birmingham City Council, ex parte EOC* [1989] AC 1155 (HL) 1193–1194 (Lord Goff). See *Segor v Goodrich Actuation Systems Ltd* (EAT, 2012) UKEAT/0145/11/DM (US arms contract stipulated 'no French nationals').
25 *Amnesty International v Ahmed* [2009] IRLR 884 (EAT).
26 See e.g. *Nagarajan v LRT* [2000] 1 AC 501, 510–511 (Lord Nicholls).
27 *Shamoon v Chief Constable of the RUC* [2003] ICR 337 (HL) [11] (Lord Nicholls). See further below, p. 115.
28 e.g. *Diaz v Pan Am* 442 F 2d 385 (5th Cir 1971), certiorari denied, 404 US 950 (1971) (preference for female air stewardesses).

direct discrimination provided, 'a reference to a person's religion or belief includes a reference to a religion or belief to which he is thought to belong or subscribe'.[29] Such legislative adoptions of perceived discrimination created an anomaly. For sex, gender reassignment, age, and disability, liability was confined to treatment because of the *victim's* protected characteristic.[30] These anomalies were swept away by the Equality Act 2010, providing a harmonised more 'open' definition of direct discrimination. As noted above, this extension was a response to the ECJ edict that, 'The principle of equal treatment enshrined in the directive in that area applies not to a particular category of person but by reference to the grounds mentioned'.[31] The statement was made when deciding that a worker without a disability suffered discrimination when the treatment was because of her child's disability, so it was not directly on the point of perceived discrimination. Nonetheless, the Explanatory Notes to the Equality Act 2010 made clear that perceived discrimination now applied to all but a select few of the protected characteristics covered by the Act.[32]

The fuzzy borders, uncertainties and shortcomings

The 'closed' definition and manifestations as cues for perceived discrimination

So far, so good, or so it seems. But there are some fuzzy borders in this apparently universal panacea to the issue. First, it is *arguable* that the 'closed' definition (still current in the United States[33]), requiring that the treatment is because of the *victim's* protected characteristic need not frustrate many cases of perception discrimination. The key here is the 'cue' for the mistake. If the cue could be characterised as a suspect ground, and the treatment is because of this cue, then the treatment is because of the victim's *actual* suspect ground. In the examples presented at the start of this chapter, these would be the *actual* African-sounding name, an effeminate demeanour, or the turban. The logic here is that a defendant acting upon these factors is acting upon race, sexual orientation, or religion, as the case may be. This amounts to *actual*, rather than perceived discrimination. This logic was played out in the US Federal District

29 EA 2006, s.45(2), in force 30 April 2007, repealed 30 September 2010 by the EA 2010 (sch 27(1) para 1) which absorbed religious discrimination in goods, services, and premises (s 29).

30 Respectively, SDA 1975, s 1(1)(a), 2A(1)(c); Employment Equality (Age) Regulations 2003, 2006/1031, reg 3; DDA 1995, s 3A(1). Also not covered was sexual orientation discrimination in the goods, services, and premises: The Equality Act (Sexual Orientation) Regulations 2007 SI2007/1263, reg 3(1).

31 Case C-303/06 *Coleman v Attridge Law* [2008] 3 CMLR 27, paras 38 (and 50).

32 Equality Act 2010, Explanatory Note 63. The Act fell short of specifying 'perceived discrimination' in the main text, for fear of inadvertently narrowing the scope of the general edict against direct discrimination: Equality Bill Deb 17 June 2009, cols 253–254 (Solicitor-General). Excluded from this are Marriage and Civil Partnership (s 13(4)) and Pregnancy or Maternity (ss 17, 18).

33 Save for disability. See below, p. 126.

Court in *LaRocca v Precision Motorcars*.[34] Here, a worker of Italian heritage was harassed with derogatory remarks associated with being Mexican, such as 'spic', 'bean dip' and 'wetback'. The cue for the mistake was the worker's 'dark brown skin', which is a matter of race (colour being an express sub category).[35] Thus, there was *actual* discrimination because of the *victim's* race, albeit a different race from that expressed by the conduct complained of.

This logic depends on a particular analysis of the facts. The *treatment* complained of is because of both perceived *and* actual protected characteristics. This analysis divides the nature of the treatment from its trigger, with only the trigger being directly related to the victim's protected characteristic. While it is commonplace for treatment to be for more than one reason, it is well established that there can be liability where just one of those reasons is discriminatory.[36] Policy dictates this, overriding any issues regarding the comparison.[37] This logic extends to 'crossover' cues, where the trigger belongs to one protected characteristic and the treatment to another. Say, a Middle Eastern man (nationality) is mistaken for a Muslim (Religion), or likewise a white British woman is mistaken for a Christian.

However, the matter of remedies could prove less certain. Here, the causative question may more finely evaluated. For mixed-reason cases, where the treatment complained of amounts to a clear-cut single event, such as hiring and firing, it is relatively straightforward to establish rules for compensation. Under UK equality law, for example, compensation may be reduced to reflect the chances of being hired, or retained, if the discriminatory element were absent.[38] In the United States, while likewise there can be liability in mixed-reason cases, there is *no* compensation if the decision would have made without the discriminatory factor.[39] But beyond any question of liability, any analogy with mixed-reason cases more contestable.

34 45 F Supp 2d 762 (D Neb 1999).

35 Civil Rights Act 1964, Title VII, s 706 (codified as 42 USC s 2000e-2): 'It shall be an unlawful employment practice for an employer … to discriminate against any individual … because of such individual's race, color, religion, sex, or national origin'. See also, EA 2010, s 9(1): 'Race includes – (a) colour; (b) nationality; (c) ethnic or national origins'.

36 See *Owen and Briggs v James* [1982] ICR 618 (CA) 621, 'poor employment record, "interview demeanour", and race'.

37 If in *Owen and Briggs*, ibid., a comparator is endowed with the 'relevant circumstances' of say, 'poor interview demeanour' and unemployment record, there would be no finding of less favourable treatment, as this person would have been rejected also. Discussed in Chapter 7, pp. 147.

38 *Chagger v Abbey National* [2010] IRLR 47 (CA) [55]–[60]. Where there was a racial element in the selection for redundancy, the worker's compensation could be reduced to reflect the chances that he would have been retained absent the racial element. Such a reduction in *Owen and Briggs v James* would not be so palatable (her award was not reduced, ibid., 621). For a criticism of the but-for approach in this context, see *Price Waterhouse v Hopkins* 490 US 228 (1989), discussed in Chapter 8 'Age discrimination and retirement', pp. 172.

39 Where the employer makes out an 'affirmative defense', the remedies are restricted to declarations, injunctions and costs: Civil Rights Act 1964, Title VII, s 706 (42 USC s.2000e-5(g)(2)(B)).

The question in these perceived cases with an 'actual trigger', is whether the victim should be compensated for the 'perceived treatment'. In mixed-reason cases, there is no compensation for the lawful reasons. If the analogy is extended to remedies for perceived discrimination, there should be no compensation for the 'perceived treatment', it being lawful in itself (it not being because of the victim's protected characteristic). Given that – in most cases at least – no harm was done by the mistake in itself, why should a person be compensated for treatment on a ground they do not possess, if the face of the clear words of the statute? On the other hand, the 'perceived treatment' would not have occurred 'but for' the actual trigger. Thus, the harm was done as a result of the actual discrimination. Moreover, the causative chain was not merely foreseeable, or flowing directly from the wrong, it was within the control of the defendant. This view relies on a different analysis of the facts. Instead of liking this to mixed-reason cases, it places the different reasons as a causal chain, rather than aligning behind a single event.

Aside from this doubt over remedies, a finding of perceived discrimination on the closed definition has potential for two more fuzzy borders.

First, it would not always be easy to characterise a cue as a suspect ground. Unlike skin colour, many such cues are merely manifestations of the protected characteristic, such as a crucifix, slow-walking, a turban, an accent,[40] a veil,[41] and so on. Ordinarily, treatment because of such characteristics would be addressed as *indirect* discrimination (requiring that the claimant *must* belong to the relevant suspect class). The (US) closed definition of direct discrimination requires treatment because of the victim's suspect status, not a manifestation of it. The manifestation cues the treatment because of a suspect class to which the victim does *not* belong. Drawing a clear line between 'suspect-status cues' and 'manifestation cues' will not always be easy. The misperception itself underpins this. If the cue were so closely associated with the relevant protected characteristic, why did the defendant associate it with another?

The second fuzzy border is that area lying between tangible cues and the situation where the defendant could not express *why* he was mistaken. Somewhere in between, there could be faint, or partial cues, for the treatment, such as a glimpse of crucifix, a hint of a limp, dark skin, or an apparent foreign accent combined with a misleading stereotype seen by the defendant in a recent TV show.

In sum, for the closed definition, where the treatment must be because of the *victim's* protected characteristic, this is a convenient solution and it accords with a notion of dignity. But it comes with fuzzy borders over compensation,

40 For treatment because of the accent itself, see *Sheffield CC v Norouzi* [2011] IRLR 897 (EAT); see also the case of Chetankumar Meshram, rejected from a (Talk Talk) call centre because his accent 'was not English enough'. A Bedford industrial tribunal awarded him £5000 for direct and indirect discrimination. *The Times* 28 November 2007, p. 27.

41 See *Azmi v Kirklees MDC* [2007] ICR 1154 (EAT) for an unsuccessful argument that barring a teacher from wearing a veil was *direct* religious discrimination; instead it was analysed as (justified) indirect discrimination.

whether the cue could be classed as a protected characteristic, and whether it could be sufficiently evidenced as a trigger. Thus, this solution is far from complete or certain.

This solution (with its fuzzy borders) goes only to the 'because' question. It still faces obstacles common to both the closed and open definitions. These concern, first, the comparison, and second, the whole notion of perceived *disability* discrimination.

The comparison

Both the EU and UK legislative formulas for direct discrimination appear to demand that a comparison is made. EU legislation requires a consideration of a how another person would have been treated in a 'comparable situation'. For instance, the Race Directive provides:

> [D]irect discrimination shall be taken to occur where one person is treated less favourably than another is, has been or would be treated in a comparable situation on grounds of racial or ethnic origin.[42]

A slightly more detailed version is provided in the UK. First, section 13 of the Equality Act 2010 defines direct discrimination thus:

> (1) A person (A) discriminates against another (B) if, because of a protected characteristic, A treats B less favourably than A treats or would treat others.

The 'less favourable' element involves a comparison. For this, section 23(1) provides:

> On a comparison of cases for the purposes of section 13 … there must be no material difference between the circumstances relating to each case.

Although this seems to mandate a straightforward symmetrical 'like for like' comparison, section 23 must be read with care. The 'circumstances' in each case cannot be 'materially different', although this cannot include the protected characteristic in question, otherwise the comparison, exactly replicating the claim, would test nothing. Ordinarily, this means that the comparator does not share the same protected characteristic as the claimant.[43] Thus, a rejected black applicant for a job would be compared with the successful white applicant who was equally- or lesser-qualified. The comparison need not be as rigid as this. The UK courts will entertain an imperfect comparator, if that is the best available and is probative.[44]

42 Race Directive 2000/43/EC, art 2(2)(a).
43 Explanatory Notes to the EA 2010, para 91.
44 *Carter v Ahsan* [2008] 1 AC 696 (HL), [36] (Lord Hoffman); *Hewage v Grampian Health Board* [2012] UKSC 37.

Where no actual comparator is available, the phrase from section 13 'or would treat others' allows for the creation of a hypothetical comparator. But the comparison is not limited to identifying an individual (real or hypothetical) without the protected characteristic in question. In *Showboat Entertainment Centre v Owens*,[45] a white manager of an amusement centre was dismissed for refusing to obey an instruction to ban black youths. For Browne-Wilkinson J, 'The only question in each case is whether the unfavourable treatment afforded to the claimant was caused by racial considerations'.[46] On the comparison, he said, 'Only by excluding matters of race can you discover whether the differential treatment was on racial grounds'.[47] This permitted changing not the race of the comparator, but his *attitude* to race, thus envisaging a white manager willing to implement his employer's racist instruction,[48] who of course, would not have been dismissed. A finding of discrimination against the white manager followed.

For perceived discrimination, the comparison is less concrete, if not fictitious. If the claimant has no relevant *actual* protected characteristic, then what of the comparator? The only protected characteristic 'matters' in question belong to the alleged discriminator. It would be necessary to alter some characteristic of the alleged discriminator, an exercise that risks becoming entangled with the conduct to be tested. Direct discrimination requires a comparison of how the defendant treated (or would have treated) *others.*[49] It is not how an alternative defendant would have treated the same person. Thus, in any comparison, the circumstances of A (the defendant) should not be changed. The question should be, *treated less favourably than whom*? Upon this logic, it seems that the legislation does not allow for perceived discrimination. A similar point was raised in *Grieg v Community Industry*,[50] where an employer argued that its refusal to employ a woman on an all-male decorating team should be compared with a refusal to employ a man on an all-female team. The EAT rejected such a comparison because it involved changing the *defendant's* circumstances. The proper comparison should be how the employer would have treated a different applicant, here a man, applying for the *same* job.[51] The same logic would apply to the provision of services or accommodation. The owners of a 'gay bar', for instance, could not escape liability for direct discrimination for excluding heterosexuals by arguing that they would be admitted to its other 'straight' bar.[52]

45 [1984] ICR 65 (EAT).
46 *Showboat Entertainment Centre v Owens* [1984] ICR 65 (EAT), 71.
47 Ibid., 73.
48 Ibid., 73. The unlawful act of 'Instructing to discriminate' is nowadays enforceable by individuals, rather than solely by an enforcement body: EA 2010, s 111.
49 EA 2010, s 13 (see above). EU legislation carries a similar requirement. See e.g., Race Directive 2000/43/EC, art 2(2)(a); Framework Directive 2000/78/EC, art 2 (2)(a), which refer to treatment of 'another'. See also, *Lee v Ashers* [2018] UKSC 49 [44]–[45] (Lady Hale).
50 [1979] ICR 356 (EAT).
51 Ibid., 360–361.
52 For segregated education, see *HM Chief Inspector of Education v Al-Hijrah School* [2017] EWCA Civ 1426 [53].

Beyond a case like *Grieg*, where the tribunal rejected changing the circumstances of the *job*, there is a further danger when changing the circumstances of the *defendant* himself. The danger here is where a person acts on the basis of their own protected characteristic. Say, a person's religious conviction dictates that he cannot employ anyone known to have committed adultery (or some other classification not deemed a protected characteristic).[53] Here, a person qua adulterer could argue he was rejected 'because of' religion. This is based on changing the circumstances of the defendant, to an employer without such a religious conviction, who would not reject our adulterer. On this basis, a person without a protected characteristic, rejected 'because of' his adultery, could claim he was rejected because of 'religion'.[54] Likewise, a customer cannot complain of religious discrimination if a Muslim shopkeeper refuses to sell alcohol out of his religious conviction. As well as contrary to the statutory language, such claims cannot be within its policy objectives.

This was confirmed by the Supreme Court in *Lee v Ashers*, which, it may be recalled, centred on a religious-based refusal to ice a cake with a pro-gay marriage logo. (The refusal was held not to be because of the sexual orientation of the customer or anyone else with whom he was associated.) The Supreme Court held that the refusal could not be categorised as unlawful *religious* discrimination based on the baker's own religious belief.[55]

Nevertheless, given its judicial support and Explanatory Note accompanying the Equality Act 2010,[56] it would take a recalcitrant court to reject a perception claim because a comparison cannot be made. On this basis, tribunals and courts must distinguish on policy grounds between conduct because of the defendant's job description, type of service, or own protected characteristic, and conduct because of one's own misperception. In the first reported UK case on perceived discrimination, *Chief Constable of Norfolk Constabulary v Coffey*, the EAT simply asked, 'How would the defendant have treated a person he did not perceive to have the protected characteristic in question?'[57] That is linguistically neat, notably by removing the protected characteristic 'matters' from the comparable scenario, in line with Browne-Wilkinson's J logic in *Showboat v*

53 Under the Equality Act 2010, s 8, the protected characteristic of 'marriage' only applies to the claimant's marriage, and not that of a third party (nor to those not married). Thus, a single person committing adultery does not fulfil this protected characteristic. In *Gan Menachem Hendon v De Groen* [2019] ICR 1023 the EAT found that a rule requiring *all* staff not to cohabit out of marriage was not discriminatory because, it seems, it was based solely on the employer's religious belief.

54 See *Gan Menachem Hendon v De Groen* [2019] ICR 1023 (EAT), where workers were expected not to cohabit outside of marriage.

55 *Lee v Ashers* [2018] UKSC 49 [44]–[45]. The Supreme Court's reasoning was largely based on the differently-worded Northern Ireland legislation, but the logic was applied to the Equality Act 2010 by the EAT in *Gan Menachem Hendon v De Groen* [2019] ICR 1023. *Lee v Ashers* is discussed in [2021] 72(1) NILQ 29.

56 See above, pp. 99.

57 [2018] ICR 812 (EAT) [62] (Judge Richardson) approved [2019] UKCA 1061 [77].

Owens. It may be enough to fulfil the legislative intent, but it cannot disguise that this comparison involves changing nothing bar the *defendant's* circumstance (her perception); it does not compare how the same defendant would have treated a different person; instead, it compares how a *different* defendant would have treated the *same* person. Alternatives to this *Coffey* comparison are discussed below, after a consideration of the comparison in relation to disability discrimination.

The comparison and disability

Coffey was a disability discrimination case, but the matters raised, and the solutions provided, apply to all protected characteristics. That said, there is an additional fuzzy border for disability cases. Section 23(2)(a) contains a rider specifically for disability discrimination: 'The circumstances relating to a case include a person's abilities'.[58] Bearing in mind that section 23(1) requires that 'there must be no material difference between the circumstances relating to each case', one must ask: What does the rider add? Even without the rider, a comparator's abilities would be deemed to be materially relevant and so should be included.

In *High Quality Lifestyles v Watts*,[59] the claimant worked with persons with learning difficulties. Occasionally he could be bitten or scratched. The claimant was HIV positive, but had not disclosed this to his employer. When his employer discovered his HIV status, it dismissed him. The EAT held that the claimant was dismissed because of the risk of transmission, and not because of his HIV. The (hypothetical) comparator was a person without HIV, but with an equally communicable disease (the 'abilities').[60] Given the edict in section 23(1), it is feasible that even without the rider the comparator in *Watts* would be the same, as a comparator without a communicable disease would be 'materially different'. The best explanation for its inclusion would seem to be 'for the avoidance of doubt' and to emphasise, or make explicit, the distinction between disability and *abilities*.[61]

Alternatives to the **Coffey** *comparator for all protected characteristics*

At the root of these problems, for all protected characteristics (and closed or open definitions), is the impossibility of a conventional comparison because the

58 The counterpart EU Framework Directive 2000/78/EC carries no such rider, although it is implicit in the 'comparable situation' aspect, and could even be accommodated in the Occupational Requirement 'defence' (art 4(1)).

59 [2006] IRLR 850 (EAT).

60 Ibid., [48]. The employer *was* liable for what is now discrimination arising from disability (EA 2010, s 15).

61 Indeed, a previous Code of Practice appeared to take this line, 'It is, however, made explicit in the Act that the comparator must have the same relevant abilities as the disabled person'. *Code of Practice Employment and Occupation* (2004) London: TSO (ISBN 0 11 703419 3) para 4.17. The antecedent DDA 1995, s 3A(5) integrated the rider into its definition of direct disability discrimination.

claimant in perceived cases has no actual protected characteristic, which places the comparator in exactly the same position and so can test nothing. The judicial response, from the EAT in *Coffey*, changes the *defendant's* circumstances, rather than other circumstances more closely associated with the claimant, which would apply to *all* protected characteristics, not just disability.

Three alternatives are considered below.

Manifestations and attributes

Identifying manifestations, attributes, or cues, as the trigger for the mistake was discussed above as a partial solution to the requirement of the closed definition that the victim holds the protected characteristic at which the treatment was directed.[62] Such manifestations could also provide the basis of the comparison.

So, the first alternative could be returning to the *claimant's* comparator's circumstances and changing some related characteristics. As noted above, it will often be the case that the misperception was triggered by an attribute of the claimant, say, a crucifix, a headscarf, a turban, or less tangible features, such as an effeminate mannerism or an African sounding name. Here, the comparison could be with how a person without the relevant attribute would have been treated.

Of course, such a list could tail off into such intangible or unspecifiable matters, that no defendant could express *why* he was mistaken. It might also be that the defendant, for reasons of embarrassment, say, would not admit to what triggered his mistake.

Moreover, the precariousness of such comparisons, using manifestations, is that these are not 'prohibited' factors per se,[63] and so such a test is vulnerable to attack as excluding such factors from the comparison would render it 'materially different' (prohibited by EA 2010, s 23). A few of these comparisons could succeed on the basis that the attribute is 'indissociable' from the protected characteristic, just as pregnancy is a proxy for sex,[64] and, in the past, 'marriage' was for sexual orientation.[65] Take the example of a shopkeeper refusing to serve a Sikh man, because he mistook the man's turban to mean he was a

62 See pp. 105.

63 Less favourable treatment because of a headscarf need not amount to direct discrimination. Assuming a non-Muslim comparator *with* a headscarf would not be 'materially different' (EA 2010, s 23) depending on the allegation and circumstances. See e.g. *Azmi v Kirklees MBC* [2007] IRLR 484 (EAT). Although, as the CJEU advised, singling out an individual Muslim for a headscarf ban (in reaction to a customer's preference) *could* amount to direct discrimination: C-188/15 *Bougnaoui v Micropole SA* [2017] 3 CMLR 22, para 34; see also AG Sharpston's discussion, paras AG 87–88. In such a case, the comparator would *not* have a headscarf.

64 Case C-177/88 *Dekker v Stichting Vormingscentrum voor Jonge Volwassen (VJV-Centrum) Plus* [1990] ECR I-3941, para 12.

65 See e.g. *Bull v Hall* [2013] UKSC 73, predating the introduction of the Marriage (Same Sex Couples) Act 2013. Discussed in Chapter 7.

Muslim. In a claim for direct perceived discrimination 'because of' *religion*, ordinarily, the comparator would be a person *with* a turban, but of a different religion. This would not even reveal if the shopkeeper objected to Islam (as well as turbans), as both would be refused. So, suppose the comparator has no turban (and a different religion). This might reveal that the shopkeeper objected to turbans. Although being turbaned is not a specified protected characteristic, it is arguable that being indissociable from religion, it amounts to one.

Of course, as the list tails off to such attributes as a crucifix or headscarf (which could be purely decorative), or an effeminate mannerism or an African sounding name, the indissociable argument lacks credibility.

Attached to this is a policy issue, albeit based on the assumption that a comparison is mandatory even in the face of patent discrimination. If changing the attribute were the only way a legitimate comparison could be made, defendants would be advised not admit to having been influenced by one. It would be better to say, 'I thought he was a Muslim. I don't know why. I just had a feeling'. Despite this confession to the 'because' (or 'reason why') element, without the cue, there can be no comparison using the attribute and so the claim would necessarily fail. It would take some chutzpah to launch a defence like this, but such technical tactics are not unprecedented.[66]

In sum, the problems with changing the attribute that triggered the treatment is that it distorts the statutory language, is only a partial solution, and a (theoretical) incentive for defendants not to disclose what triggered their perception and consequent treatment. Upon this, it would seem preferable adopt the *Coffey* formula, which although again distorting the statutory language, has a capacity to embrace cases with or without a cue, meaning it does not carry the other two problems. What comes out of this is that section 23 was drafted without perceived discrimination in mind, despite the strong policy commitment expressed elsewhere, notably in successive Explanatory Notes.

Perceived discrimination as associative discrimination

Many instances of perceived discrimination could also be categorised as associative discrimination,[67] save that the association is mistaken. Associative discrimination occurs where the treatment is because of the victim's association

66 The list is long. A few lowlights are included here. *Simon v Brimham Associates* [1987] ICR 596 (CA) ('Are you Jewish' treated all applicants equally); *Stewart v Cleveland Guest (Engineering)* [1996] ICR 535 (EAT) (Pornographic posters treated men and women workers equally); *De Souza v Automobile Association* [1986] ICR 514 (CA) ('Get this typing done by the wog', 'considered' but did not 'treat' the claim less favourably, because she inadvertently overheard it); *Plessy v Ferguson* 163 US 537 (1896) (endorsing 'separate but equal' streetcar racial segregation). See generally, M Connolly, *The English Judiciary, Discrimination Law and Statutory Interpretation: Easy Cases Making Bad Law* (2018, Routledge), especially Chapters 4 and 10.

67 See 'The associative discrimination fiction: Part 1' (2021) 72(1) NILQ 29.

with a person holding the relevant characteristic. Say, a white worker is dismissed because she married a black man.[68] For the comparison here, the race (or other relevant protected characteristic) of the associate is changed. A finding of the 'because' question follows. Transplanted into perception theory, this means that the treatment was because the defendant associated the victim with those of the relevant protected characteristic. It may be recalled that this was an alternative finding by a US court, in *Wood v Freeman Decorating*,[69] where Native-American discrimination against a person whose racial origins were disputed. It was held that regardless of the claimant's actual racial origin, he was associated with Native-Americans. A comparison here would change the race (or other protected characteristic) of the associative group. This prompts the comparative question: would the defendant have treated the claimant so if he were instead associated with white Americans? There are three difficulties here.

First, this would apply only to some perceived cases. For instance, suppose a Catholic graduating from well-known Mormon college was refused a post because the employer wrongly assumed that the applicant was a Mormon, whom he distrusted. It would be straightforward here to change the religion of the college. As such, the applicant would not have been refused on religious grounds. The cue for the treatment was the religion of the college. *This* is not a perception of the defendant, but a fact. It is also a religious fact, in the same way that the black man is a racial fact. This makes it credible to exclude it from the comparison, as the one thing we know that can be changed for the comparison is the relevant protected characteristic. It might be that a turbaned Sikh refused a service because the shopkeeper associated him with Islamic terrorists could succeed under this theory. Here, the cue is this turban, and assuming that turbans were indissociable from religion, the comparative Islamic terrorists would not be known to wear turbans. In which case to shopkeeper would serve the turbaned Sikh. Of course, as noted above, as the attributes that triggered the treatment cease to be indissociable with a protected characteristic (headscarves, crucifixes, African sounding names) this theory is inapplicable.

This is because of the second difficulty, which is more fundamental. In many cases, the comparison is how a different *defendant* would treat the same claimant. Unless cued by some manifestation or attribute, being indissociable from a relevant protected characteristic, any mistaken association is made by the defendant, and so the objection reverts to that mentioned above,[70] that the proper question is how the same defendant would have treated a different person. For example, if a comparison had been made in *Wood*, it would change the race of the third-party Native Americans. This is not asking how the same defendant would have treated the claimant had the Native Americans had been

68 See e.g. Lord Simon, *obiter, Race Relations Board v Applin* [1975] 2 AC 259 (HL) 289–290 (on the premise that foster parents discriminated against a local authority for refusing to foster children of colour).

69 No. 3:08-CV-00375-LRH-RAM, 2010 WL 653764 (D Nev Feb 19, 2010) p. 4. See above, text to n 19.

70 See ' The comparison', p. 109

white Americans, but asking how the defendant would have treated the claimant had the *defendant* associated the claimant with white Americans.

The third difficulty relates to the 'because' question, which although not part of comparative element, is included here for completeness. The UK Supreme Court has required a degree of proximity for associative discrimination. Consequently, a bakery's refusal to ice a cake with a pro-gay marriage logo was not close enough to be associated with sexual orientation.[71] This objection is surmountable though. There is nothing inherent in 'reason why' question that limits proximity, if the protected characteristic was indeed the reason for the treatment.[72]

Bypassing the comparison

The second alternative is more radical, but may relieve us of the linguistic gymnastics required for the above analyses, be it the *Coffey* comparator or the 'cue' alternative. Browne-Wilkinson's J suggestion in *Showboat v Owens* that, 'The only question in each case is whether the unfavourable treatment afforded to the claimant was caused by racial considerations',[73] implied not just an imaginative, or flexible, comparison was permissible, but in some cases, a comparison was unnecessary. In accord with this was Lord Nicholls' *obiter dictum* (noted above[74]), that where a prohibited reason for the treatment is identifiable, a tribunal can 'avoid arid and confusing disputes about the identification of the appropriate comparator'.[75] Indeed, this approach, taken by the ET in *Coffey*, was approved by the Court of Appeal, where Underhill LJ stated,

> [I]t is now very well established that the comparison exercise under section 13(1) (the so-called 'less favourable treatment' question) does essentially the same job as asking whether the treatment complained of was 'because of' the protected characteristic (the so-called 'reason why' question), and that if the latter question is answered the answer to the former will normally follow.[76]

That perhaps overstates the matter in two ways. First, it overstates the status of Lord Nicholls' dictum. Section 13 does not express the two elements as alternatives. Accordingly, there is House of Lords *authority*, from *Glasgow CC v Zafar* (notably given by Lord Browne-Wilkinson), that a comparison must be

71 *Lee v Ashers* [2018] UKSC 49.
72 The 'close enough' rubric from *Lee v Ashers* is discussed in 'The associative discrimination fiction: Part 1' (2021) 72(1) NILQ 29.
73 *Showboat Entertainment Centre v Owens* [1984] ICR 65 (EAT) 71.
74 Text to n 27.
75 *Shamoon v Chief Constable of the RUC* [2003] ICR 337 (HL) [11]. See also *Islington LBC v Ladele* [2009] ICR 387 (EAT) [37]–[39] (Elias J); *JP Morgan Europe Ltd v Chweidan* [2011] EWCA Civ 648 [5] (Elias LJ).
76 [2019] UKCA 1061 [76].

made.[77] In that case (as in many) it was to distinguish less favourable treatment from *unreasonable* treatment,[78] but there will be other reasons why both questions must be addressed. It is true that the authority of *Zafar* has been diminished with the passing of EU-derived rules on evidence, but this relates more to the Lords' judgment on the 'because' question.[79] In any case, the (procedural) rules, now in section 136 of the Equality Act 2010, dictate the shifting burdens on proving discrimination, as defined (substantively) in section 13 and EU law, both of which require the treatment to have been less favourable.[80]

Notwithstanding these caveats, Lord Nicholls' dictum, though probably not intended at the time, could not be more appropriate for perception cases. Where there is sufficient evidence of the reason for the treatment, it may be practical to take the seemingly permissible route of bypassing the comparison and with it the 'arid and confusing disputes about the identification of the appropriate comparator'.

Second, it is an overstatement to suppose that the two elements do 'essentially the same job'. Lord Nicholls' suggestion was simply encouragement for tribunals to otherwise identify the reason for the treatment, with an 'examination of all the facts of the case'.[81] He did not suggest ignoring the comparison in all circumstances, and nor would it be logical to do so, even if it were not a statutory requirement. There will be 'obvious cases', of course. A shopkeeper may state to an overweight Sikh man, 'I'm not serving Muslims'. On the other hand, the shopkeeper may state, 'I'm not serving people like you'.[82] Thus, evidence of the defendant's state of mind, or 'mental processes', is required. This may be acquired from an 'examination of all the facts of the case' without a comparison. The shopkeeper may have a history of Islamophobia, but none of anti-Sikhism, for example. In other cases, there may be evidence of a phobia towards transgender persons (but not homosexuals), or a resistance to the expense of making reasonable adjustments,[83] or that an employer considers that a multi-ethnic workforce 'always brings trouble and discord'.[84] Where there is

77 *Glasgow CC v Zafar* [1998] ICR 120 (HL) 124.
78 Ibid.
79 *Igen v Wong* [2005] ICR 931 (CA), annex to the judgment.
80 In *Efobi v Royal Mail* [2019] ICR 750, the Court of Appeal held a claim of (actual) direct discrimination failed for want of a credible comparison. Permission to appeal to the Supreme Court was granted https://www.supremecourt.uk/docs/permission-to-appeal-2019-1011.pdf *Efobi* (CA) followed *Ayodele v Citylink* [2017] EWCA Civ 1913, where leave to appeal was refused by the Supreme Court. 29 November 2018 https://www.supremecourt.uk/docs/permission-to-appeal-2018-11-2019-01.pdf both accessed 30 December 2020.
81 *Shamoon v Chief Constable of the RUC* [2003] ICR 337 (HL) [11].
82 See *R (E) v Governing Body of JFS* [2010] 2 AC 278 (SC) [21] (Lord Phillips).
83 A conclusion of the ET in *Chief Constable of Norfolk Constabulary v Coffey* cited [2019] UKCA 1061 [78], approved [76].
84 See R Epstein, *Forbidden Grounds: The Case Against Employment Discrimination Laws* (Cambridge: Harvard University Press 1992), especially pp. 496–499 asserting the benefits of exclusion. Cf S Greenberger, 'A productivity approach to disparate impact and the Civil Rights Act of 1991' 72 *Oregon Law Rev* 253 (1993).

a shortfall of other evidence for the 'reason why' question, a comparison may be the only source, or a necessary one for the accumulation of evidence to get 'over the line'.

A particular instance for the need for a comparison was proposed by the EAT in *High Quality Lifestyles v Watts.*[85] This was to resolve any 'causative' disputes over the 'reason why' question:

> For example, a surgeon with hepatitis, and a dentist with tuberculosis, suspended because of the risk of transmission, would be able to show that but for their having the disease, they would not be at risk of transmission, and would not have been suspended.[86]

The suspension was causally connected to the disease, as without the disease, there would be no risk of transmission. Hence, the comparison was necessary to identify the reason for the dismissal, which was the risk of transmission. As such, the comparator would be a surgeon or dentist without the particular disability but with an equally communicable disease; this comparator would have been suspended also. Assume now that the employer was mistaken about the worker's HIV status, and dismissed him because of the risk of communicating the disease. The same 'causative' argument could be deployed here, and so a comparison would be necessary, the most realistic being a *Coffey* comparison. This proposal is not so strong, given that the courts have virtually abandoned the 'but for' test in favour of the 'reason-why' approach,[87] which is more capable of isolating the immediate reason.

Conclusion

In order of preference, bypassing the comparison where there is sufficient evidence of the 'reason why' question would seem to be the most practical approach, albeit by ignoring a statutory element of 'less favourable'. In cases with insufficient 'reason why' evidence, a *Coffey* comparator should be deployed. The 'attributes' approach should be reserved for the rarest of cases, where there is sufficient nexus between the attribute and the protected characteristic.

It can be concluded then, that the policy imperative to recognise perceived discrimination requires that statutory elements should be ignored, or imaginatively manipulated. This shows that a standard statutory formula, with its requirement for less favourable treatment, falls well short of its policy aims. That said, the problems do not end here. More general issues surround the matter of perceived *disability* discrimination.

85 [2006] IRLR 850 (EAT). See above, text to n 59.
86 Ibid., [49].
87 See e.g. *Nagarajan v LRT* [2000] 1 AC 501, 510–511 (Lord Nicholls).

Perceived disability discrimination

As already discussed, the comparison throws up particular issues for disability discrimination because of the need to distinguish between a disability and its effects. However, perceived disability discrimination presents a more general problem. In most cases at least, with the 'functional definition' of disability, it will be impossible the say that a defendant held in his mind the particularly complex statutory definition of disability. A parallel problem exists for the exceptionally drafted edict regarding severe disfigurements, which is discussed after a consideration of the functional requirement.

The functional requirement

Nonetheless, policy dictates that perceived disability discrimination is as important as any other. Issues of dignity and stereotyping have a particular resonance for disability. As the US Supreme Court once stated, 'Congress acknowledged that society's accumulated myths and fears about disability and disease are as handicapping as are the physical limitations that flow from actual impairment'.[88] A more challenging issue than the comparison, it seems, stems from the statutory definition of the protected characteristic itself. As a reminder, for the UK Equality Act 2010, the statutory definition of disability provides, by section 6:

> A person (P) has a disability if –
> a) P has a physical or mental impairment, and
> b) the impairment has a substantial and long-term adverse effect on P's ability to carry out normal day-to-day activities.[89]

Here, 'long-term' means at least twelve months,[90] and 'day-to-day' includes work activities, even if specialised and not undertaken by the general population.[91]

The difficulty here was voiced, *obiter*, by Underhill J in 2010:

> If a manager discriminates against an employee because he believes her to have a broken leg, or because he believes her to be 'depressed', the

88 *School Board of Nassau County v Arline* 480 US 273, 284 (1987), commenting on the Rehabilitation Act 1973 (29 USC s 706), the predecessor to the Americans with Disabilities Act 1990, below, test to n 123.

89 EA 2010, s 6(1).

90 EA 2010, sch.1, para.2(1): an impairment has a long-term effect if: (a) it has lasted at least 12 months; or (b) the period for which it lasts is likely to be at least 12 months; or (c) it is likely to last for the rest of the life of the person affected.

91 Case C-13/05 *Chacon Navas v Eurest Colectividades SA* [2006] 3 CMLR 1123, para 38; Case C-335/11 *HK Danmark v Dansk almennyttigt Boligselskab ('Ring')* [2013] 3 CMLR 21, paras 38–39; *Chief Constable of Norfolk Constabulary v Coffey* [2019] UKCA 1061 [53].

> question whether the effects of the perceived injury, or of the perceived depression, are likely to last more or less than 12 months may never enter his thinking, consciously or unconsciously (nor indeed, in the case of perceived 'depression', may it be clear what he understands by the term).[92]

This could be read to mean that unless a person is well-versed in the complex legal definition(s) of a particular protected characteristic, that person cannot perceive that someone has a disability. Bear in mind that the statutory definition of disability is accompanied by a Schedule, dedicated secondary regulations, *and* guidance.[93] There are also exceptions[94] and a discrepancy between EU law and section 6, whose 'normal day-to-day activities' must be read to include 'the full and effective participation of the person concerned in professional life on an equal basis with other workers'.[95] One must presume this would include specialist and/or infrequent work abilities that are far removed from normal, everyday, activities. This matter is complicated further by uncertainties over post-Brexit interpretations.[96]

All of this indicates that perceiving a disability is a good deal more complex than where a person misperceives that another is, say, Muslim, older, homosexual, or Pakistani. In an apparent, but unacknowledged, revision of his earlier dictum, Underhill LJ more recently approved a statement made in the EAT, that the perception will not depend on the defendant's knowledge of disability law. Instead, it will depend on whether he perceived the victim 'to have an impairment with the features which are set out in the legislation'.[97]

For employers in particular, this apparent transfer of legalese to the background of the threshold requirements should make it harder to deny perception discrimination where the activities in question are those needed for performing the job. Employers ought to have knowledge of their own job descriptions, and if 'day-to-day activities' includes 'professional life', there should be no need for the employer to perceive anything broader than the job description in mind. For permanent, or long-term,

92 *J v DLA Piper* [2010] ICR 1052 (EAT) [62].

93 Respectively, EA 2010, sch 1, Part 1; Equality Act (Disability) Regulations 2010, SI 2010/2128; 'Guidance on matters to be taken into account in determining questions relating to the definition of disability', made under EA 2010, s 6(5). See www.gov.uk/government/publications/equality-act-guidance accessed 30 December 2020.

94 For example, Cancer, HIV infection and multiple sclerosis are deemed to be disabilities without more: EA 2010, sch 1, Part 1, para 6(1).

95 Case C-13/05 *Chacon Navas* (n 91), para 38.

96 In the spirit of the EU approach, although bound by the broader EU definition, the EAT held that a worker's promotion exams were a normal day-to-day activity under the UK definition: *Paterson v Commissioner of Police for the Metropolis* [2007] IRLR 763. See also, *Chief Constable of Dumfries and Galloway v Adams* [2009] ICR 1034 (EAT, Sc), where nightshift work was held to be a normal day-to-day activity.

97 *Chief Constable of Norfolk Constabulary v Coffey* [2019] UKCA 1061 [35] citing [2018] ICR 812 (EAT) [51] (Judge Richardson).

jobs, an employer perceiving that a person could not do the job is likely to have thought also that the inability was long-term, or even permanent, and thus exceeding the 12-month threshold. However, where job is short-term, further evidence would be required to show that the employer considered the effects exceeded 12 months. This would prove difficult only where the job was intended to be short-term, rather than one with a general expectation of successive renewals.

Besides this partial solution, problems remain, even in employment cases. First, a post-Brexit definition may not stretch to many specialist occupations. Second, in any case, this does not account for those acting upon the impairment alone, rather than knowledge of the job description. This could arise out of bigotry, fear, or perhaps, a blanket unreasoned resistance to making reasonable adjustments.[98] Here, a perception of an impairment alone is enough to trigger the less favourable treatment. Yet, without the other section 6 features, there is no perceived discrimination. This is in contrast to actual disability cases. Take this example, suggested by the Government when introducing a conventional model of direct discrimination into disability law:

> [A]n employer, on learning that a job applicant has diabetes, summarily rejects the application without giving any consideration of the applicant's circumstances or whether the person concerned would be competent to do the job (with or without a reasonable adjustment).[99]

In a parallel case of perceived discrimination, where the employer misperceives that an applicant has diabetes, and similarly disregards the application at that point, there is no coincidental perception of the other three 'features which are set out in the legislation'.[100] *This* employer cares not about job performance, but has acted upon prejudice, phobia, or fear. Whichever way, a defendant here has not perceived anything about the applicant's job performance or abilities. Likewise, landlords, service-providers, and employers could well discriminate because they fear negative reactions from residents or neighbours, customers, or co-workers, as the case may be. Such reactions straddle the border between bigotry and stereotyping. It seems anomalous that 'perception theory', being underpinned with notions of dignity and stereotyping, when realised in law cannot address bigotry, phobias, or even some 'duty dodging'.

Severe disfigurements

In addition to the comparison and the complex definition of disability, a third problem not addressed, even by the revised requirement, relates to perceived

98 A conclusion of the ET in *Chief Constable of Norfolk Constabulary v Coffey* cited with approval [2019] UKCA 1061 [78] and [76].

99 Explanatory Notes to the *pre-consultation draft* DDA 1995 (Amendment) Regulations (SI 2003/1673), para 32; see also the previous Code of Practice Employment and Occupation (2004) London: TSO (ISBN 0 11 703419 3), para 6.7.

100 See n 97 and accompanying text.

disfigurements. The Equality Act deems that a 'severe disfigurement' has substantial long-term effects on day-to-day activities.[101] In effect, this means that a severe disfigurement is deemed to be a disability for the purposes of the legislation. Examples suggested are 'scars, birthmarks, limb or postural deformation (including restricted bodily development), or diseases of the skin'.[102] Tattoos or decorative or other (non-medical) piercings are excluded.[103]

For actual discrimination, the statutory Guidance advises that 'Assessing severity will be mainly a matter of the degree of the disfigurement which may involve taking into account factors such as the nature, size, and prominence of the disfigurement'. It may be necessary to take account of the disfigurement's location (e.g. on the back as opposed to the face),[104] although a disguised disfigurement, say with makeup, still qualifies.[105]

For perceived discrimination, there will be no actual disfigurement, or (more likely) one that is not 'severe'.

Perceived disfigurement

In rare cases there might be no disfigurement. For example:

> An employer searching social media for details of a job applicant finds a photograph showing a severe facial disfigurement. The disfigurement was caused by a motoring accident, and has since healed to the point where it is invisible. The employer discards the application because of the disfigurement which he misperceives is present-day.

Assuming that the photograph displayed a disfigurement that was severe (in the legal sense), it would not be difficult to endow the employer with that perception.[106]

Perceived severity

For most cases though, liability is likely to turn on whether a defendant perceived an actual non-severe disfigurement to be 'severe'. Ordinarily, perceived

101 EA 2010, sch 1, Part 1, para 3. See generally, H Saunders, 'The invisible law of visible difference: Disfigurement in the workplace' (2019) 48(4) *ILJ* 487.

102 'Guidance on matters to be taken into account in determining questions relating to the definition of disability'. Made under EA 2010, s.6(5), revised version, with effect from 1 May 2011 (SI 2011/1159), para B25 http://odi.dwp.gov.uk/docs/law/ea/ea-guide-2.pdf accessed 30 December 2020.

103 Equality Act (Disability) Regulations 2010, SI 2010/2128, reg.5. EA 2010, sch 1, para 3(3) also empowers the Minister to exclude, 'in particular', deliberately acquired disfigurements, although, at the time of writing, this had not been done.

104 Guidance (n 102) para B25.

105 Guidance (n 102) para B24.

106 There can be liability for discriminating because of a past disability (EA 2010, s 6(4) and sch.1, para 9), but here, the treatment is because the employer perceived to disfigurement to be present-day.

discrimination is a mistake of fact. Not so here. A danger is that if a defendant, fully appraised of the facts, thinks that a disfigurement is severe when it is not, the dispute descends into one of opinion. Moreover, this would be an opinion attributed to, but denied by, the defendant. Confined to direct evidence of the severity, most cases would fail. Take this example:

> A retail employer rejects an applicant with a minor birthmark on her neck, because he considers it would deter customers.

Assuming that the defendant denies that he considered the birthmark to be severe, some evidence that he was lying would be required. Unless there is such evidence, say, absurd comments that all visible birthmarks were unnatural and are abominable, the claim would fail. Of course, it is unlikely in such an employer gave any thought to the severity question. His consideration centred on the reaction of his customers rather than whether the severity of the birthmark crossed some legally-derived threshold. In addition to most (if not all) claims necessarily failing, this logic flies in the face of two policy objectives. With impunity, employers, landlords, and service providers (including some educationalists), can pander to customer preferences or even announce their prejudices regarding minor disfigurements (and by implication, with all the more force, severe disfigurements). It must surely have been a policy objective of disability equality law to address such unedifying conduct.

It has been suggested, though, that evidence of these 'customer reaction' fears provides a solution.[107] Such considerations are circumstantial evidence that a defendant perceived a minor disfigurement to be severe. This could 'bridge the gap'[108] between the law's assessment, and the defendant's opinion, of the severity. This certainly recognises the reality of most situations and may prove attractive to tribunals, otherwise faced with closing down a meritorious claim. It has the attraction of simplicity and justice, but carries technical shortcomings.

The question is not the perception of how others would respond to the disfigurement, but the perception of the severity of the disfigurement. This is not a mere quibble. There are fundamental and practical objections. First, the underlying purpose of the exceptional disfigurement provision is to assume the *effects* of a disfigurement. This gives it its unique 'social barrier' quality.[109] The purpose and drafting of this provision is clear. To claim disfigurement discrimination, there is no need to prove the effects, that is, other people's reactions. If the effects of a disfigurement are not relevant to proving actual discrimination, why should they become relevant to a perceived case? Not only

107 H Saunders, 'The invisible law of visible difference: Disfigurement in the workplace' (2019) 48(4) *ILJ* 487, 505–506.

108 Ibid.

109 Most disability discrimination law identifies persons for protection on a functional basis, i.e. what the person cannot do. The 'severe disfigurement' provision assumes persons can function normally and that the barrier to equality is other person's reactions.

does it place an extra burden upon claimants, it is a fundamental departure from the underlying purpose of the provision.

On a more practical level, a 'customer reaction' fear could be *evidence* that a defendant perceived the disfigurement to be severe, as it was, in his mind, severe enough to deter customers. But this cannot be presumed. Much could turn on the context, including the defendant's own values. An employer, for example, might consider that an applicant fell short of a standard appearance in a particular job, such as a beauty parlour. Another might reject anyone whose appearance he considered to carry an imperfection. In sum, attractive as it may be, 'reaction' evidence cannot be an automatic route to proving a perceived severity. It is, at best, a partial solution.

A second suggested solution[110] relies on the logic of *English v Sanderson Blinds*.[111] In this harassment case, in may be recalled, Mr English was harassed by colleagues using homophobic sexual innuendo, suggesting he was homosexual, knowing full well that he was not. The Court of Appeal found that this conduct could amount to unlawful *harassment* (on the ground of sexual orientation). In other words, what mattered was the nature of the conduct (discriminatory) and not the protected characteristic of the victim.[112] This logic could be applied to perceived disfigurement claims, it is suggested. If a defendant displays prejudice towards a disfigurement, then whether or not there is one is irrelevant. The first thing to note here is that although the Court of Appeal considered the difference between this case and perceived discrimination was 'barely perceptible',[113] perceived disfigurement discrimination is somewhat further away in principle. Once this is realised, the analogy with *Sanderson* breaks down. In *Sanderson* the conduct was inherently discriminatory. This is so in normal perception cases also. The treatment is less favourable because of *a* protected characteristic. The analogy may hold true where the only issue is treatment because of a disfigurement that does not in fact exist (see the photograph example, above). But where liability is to turn on the 'severity' element, the analogy breaks down. The treatment here is *not* because of a protected characteristic. It is not unlawful to treat less favourably someone because of a non-severe disfigurement, a characteristic deliberately excluded from the provision. If *Sanderson* were applied here, the issue would remain whether the treatment was on the basis of a severe disfigurement.

Most cases are likely to relate to a disfigurement's severity, rather than its existence. The problem here is that there will rarely be direct evidence of a (mis)perception of the severity. In rare cases, evidence of 'customer reaction' may be probative. But this must be admitted with great caution, so as not to signal that evidence of public reaction becomes the norm for disfigurement

110 H Saunders (n 107) 506–507.
111 [2008] EWCA 1421.
112 This 'discrimination per se' theory is discussed in 'The associative discrimination fiction: Part 1' (2021) 72(1) NILQ 29.
113 [2008] EWCA 1421 [38] (Sedley LJ).

discrimination claims. Otherwise, most cases should fail under the current statutory formula.

Rather perversely, a better solution exists if a claim were couched under the standard 'functional' formula for direct disability discrimination. This idea has roots in the passing of the Disability Discrimination Bill 1995. An amendment was tabled – and rejected[114] – to drop the 'severe' element. For the Government, Lord Mackay[115] assumed that those with a non-severe disfigurement could use the functional definition, with its lower threshold of 'substantial'. At the time, 'substantial' had yet to be interpreted as meaning 'more than minor or trivial',[116] and so this solution may have been inadvertent, and not particularly helpful at the time. Nevertheless, assuming a non-severe disfigurement is (or is perceived to be) an impairment, a claim could succeed where it had a *more than minor or trivial* 'long-term effect on day-to-day activities'. Many (if not most) disfigurements are likely to be permanent, and unlike many other disabilities, this is likely to be obvious, and thus readily perceived. Here, Underhill's LJ caution regarding a defendant being unlikely to have considered this 'long-term' element will have little traction. Indeed, under this solution, *perceived* disfigurement discrimination could be pleaded as *actual* functional discrimination.

Although this might mean including public reaction in disfigurement claims, there are two factors that mitigate the impact of this. First, the evidence here is more likely to focus on how the claimant felt about the disfigurement, with such factors as to how a consequent lack of confidence prevented them from participating in many day-to-day activities, including social, personal, and work activities. Where this included public reaction, it would only be a partial matter. It would be a largely subjective enquiry,[117] and more dignified than an objective analysis of whether the disfigurement was severe enough to warrant public disgust.[118] Second, the threshold, *more than minor or trivial*, being much lower than 'severe', means that there is likely to be much less emphasis on the public reaction and undignified discussions as to the severity of the disfigurement.

114 HL Deb, 13 June 1995, vol 564, col 1650 (Lord Mackay of Ardbrecknish) https://api.parliament.uk/historic-hansard/lords/1995/jun/13/disability-discrimination-bill accessed 30 December 2020.

115 Lord Mackay of Ardbrecknish, i.e. *not* the Lord Chancellor, Lord Mackay of Clashfern.

116 EA 2010, s 212(1) codifying *Goodwin v The Patent Office* [1999] ICR 302 (EAT) 310 (Morison J).

117 In an actual disability case, Eady J confirmed that in some cases, notably where the deformity is hidden but apparent, the impact upon the claimant could be taken into account when deciding the 'severity' question. *Hutchinson 3G v Edwards* (EAT, 29 April 2014) UKEAT/0467/13/DM, [54]–[56] and [36] www.gov.uk/employment-appeal-tribunal-decisions/hutchison-3g-uk-ltd-v-mr-c-edwards-ukeat-0467-13-dm accessed 30 December 2020.

118 H Saunders labelled this process 'gruelling and personally invasive': 'The Invisible Law of Visible Difference: Disfigurement in the Workplace' (2019) 48(4) ILJ 487, 507, citing A Lawson, 'Disability and employment in the Equality Act 2010: Opportunities seized, lost and generated' (2011) 40 *ILJ* 359, 361.

Another drawback is that this might require the claimant to reveal otherwise private feelings, an influential factor in the decision in *English v Sanderson Blinds*,[119] based on the 'dignity' matter of a person not being required to reveal their sexual orientation in order to bring a claim. This is a powerful point, although here is a difference between one's protected characteristic and how one feels about one which is likely to be visible. This is a makeshift solution, with advantages over the dedicated formula, but, as these drawbacks demonstrate, it is not an ideal one.

Relaxing the burden in disability cases

Thus, there remains a problem of perceived disability discrimination being harder to prove than for most other grounds and unable to address the principal mischiefs of prejudice and stereotyping. The question then, is whether it is possible to ease the burden further and bring it into line with (or closer to) the other grounds. There are several possibilities. The highest burden, as portrayed in Underhill's J 2010 statement, is that the defendant should perceive that the claimant meets the legal requirements for disability. That would be too high. Not only would it bar nearly every claim, it is more than required in actual disability cases, where,

> provided the employer has actual or constructive knowledge of the facts constituting the employee's disability, the employer does not also need to know that, as a matter of law, the consequence of such facts is that the employee is a 'disabled person' as defined in [the legislation].[120]

This suggests that the requirement for perceived discrimination should be no higher, which is in line with Underhill's LJ apparent revision (the 'features benchmark'). Nonetheless, as noted above, this still presents considerable barriers exceeding those faced by other claimants.

While it is true that bringing perceived disability discrimination closer to other grounds would make it *out of line* with cases of actual disability, this is palatable when viewed in a broader context. Those with an actual disability are afforded a wider range of protections than available to the victim of perceived discrimination, including indirect discrimination, discrimination arising from disability, and the reasonable adjustments duty.[121]

Assuming this neutralises that objection, it is open to consider how to ease the burden, or find alternatives. The focus here is on scenarios where the defendant does not hold in his mind all four 'features' defining a person with a disability, yet misperceives that the victim has a disability.

119 [2008] EWCA 1421 [39] (Sedley LJ).
120 *Gallop v Newport City Council* [2013] EWCA 1583 [36] (Rimer LJ).
121 EA 2010, ss 19, 15, and 20–21 respectively. This point was made in *Fortt v Chief Constable of South Wales Police* (ET, 18 May 2015) Case No: 1601986/2014, [50] (Judge S Davies).

Two possibilities are considered here. The first considers reducing the elements required in the perception. The second finds a solution via the 'reason why' question.

Easing the standard: the functional requirement

The first possibility is to reduce the number of features required in the defendant's mind. This is the position in the United States, where since 1974, the requirement is that the defendant perceived only an impairment.[122] Nowadays, the Americans with Disabilities Act 1990 provides for perceived discrimination where the claimant was 'regarded as having … an impairment … whether or not the impairment limits or is perceived to limit a major life activity'. This does not apply to impairments that are 'minor and transitory'. (A transient impairment is one 'with an actual or expected duration of 6 months or less'.[123]) The Congressional history of this 'regarded as' aspect, draws upon the more general theories underpinning perception discrimination, but is telling as to the specific problem to be addressed. For example, 'Discrimination against people with disabilities … often results from false presumptions, generalizations, misperceptions, patronizing attitudes, ignorance, irrational fears, and pernicious mythologies'[124] as well as 'stereotypical assumptions, fears and myths not truly indicative of the ability of such individuals'.[125] The result is, 'that unfounded concerns, mistaken beliefs, fear, myths, or prejudice about disabilities are often just as disabling as actual impairments, and its corresponding desire to prohibit discrimination founded on such perceptions'.[126] The inclusion of the 'minor and transitory' rider excludes 'common ailments like the cold or flu'.[127] It is a response to

122 Rehabilitation Act 1973: s 505 (29 USC § 706(7)(B)(iii)): This 'Perceived disability' prong was introduced into the Act in 1974. See now, EEOC 29 CFR appendix, para 1630.2(l) (2008) at 'Section 1630.2(l) Regarded as Substantially Limited in a Major Life Activity' www.govinfo.gov/content/pkg/CFR-2018-title29-vol4/xml/CFR-2018-title29-vol4-part1630.xml accessed 30 December 2020.

123 42 USC s 12102(3)(B). The Act was amended in 2008. ADA 1990, s 3(1), 42 USCA s 12102: '(1) … The term "disability" means, with respect to an individual … (C) being regarded as having such an impairment … (3)(A) An individual meets the requirement of "being regarded as having such an impairment" if the individual establishes that he or she has been subjected to an action prohibited under this chapter because of an actual or perceived physical or mental impairment whether or not the impairment limits or is perceived to limit a major life activity'. See, e.g. *Mercado v Puerto Rico* 814 F.3d 581, 588 (1st Cir, 2016).

124 Committee for Education and Labor, HR Rep No 101–485(II) (1989–1990) at 30. Congress has yet to supply transcripts online www.congress.gov/congressional-report/101st-congress/house-report/485/2 accessed 5 December 2020.

125 Ibid., at 40.

126 Committee for Education and Labor, HR Rep No 110–730 (I) (2007–2008) at 13. Here, Congress was reversing the Supreme Court's restrictive interpretation, using a drafting ambiguity (*Sutton v United Airlines* 527 US 471 (1999)), to restore

'concerns raised by members of the employer community regarding potential abuse of the Act and the misapplication of resources on individuals with minor ailments that last only a short period of time'.[128]

In addition to the policy concerns of the US Congress, there is another reason to ease the burden. A demanding burden can only discourage those bound by the legislation *not* to acquire knowledge of disability and their related legal obligations. Employers, service providers, landlords, and the like would be better off turning a blind eye to the law, the Codes of Practice, Guidance, and all the extra-legal advice available. Ignorance here becomes an advantage.

An attempt to introduce something similar to this American model in the UK was rejected by the Government during the passage of the Equality Bill, on the basis that, 'it would be most inequitable for somebody who did not have a disability to have a lighter test to gain protection than somebody who did, and that is the logical fault in the proposal'.[129] As noted above, this objection can be met because someone with an actual disability is afforded a wider range of protections.[130] As well as addressing the difficulty of proving a case otherwise, such an amendment can address the policy concerns underlying the legislation, as explained by the US Congress and neglected in the UK Parliament.

Easing the standard: severe disfigurements

As noted above, a similar amendment was tabled – and rejected[131] – for severe disfigurements. This occurred under the passing of the Disability Discrimination Bill 1995. The proposal was to drop the 'severe' element on the basis that the size or severity of a disfigurement does not dictate the person's ability to cope; it is other people's perceptions that matter.[132] This would apply to actual and perceived discrimination. Given that the underlying purpose of this exceptional provision is to address 'social barriers',[133] rather than functional ones, this is a

the lower 'regarded as' standard www.congress.gov/congressional-report/110th-congress/house-report/730/1 accessed 5 December 2020.

127 Ibid., HR Rep No. 110–730, pt. 1 (2008) at 14.

128 Ibid.

129 Equality Bill Deb 16 June 2009 *Cols 195–197* (Solicitor-General) https://publications.parliament.uk/pa/cm200809/cmpublic/equality/090616/am/90616s02.htm accessed 30 December 2020. This reason was given in two ET judgments when rejecting a lower standard: *Estlin v Central Manchester University Hospitals NHS Foundation Trust* 2412374/2011 (ET, 20 November 2014); *Balakumar v Imperial College of Health Care NHS Trust* 2201372/15 (ET (London Central) 22 January 2016). Both reported R Crasow, '"Perceived disability discrimination": Achieving a fair outcome for the non-disabled' (2016) 133 *Emp LB* 2–4.

130 Text to n 121 and accompanying text.

131 HL Deb, 13 June 1995, vol 564, col 1650 (Lord Mackay of Ardbrecknish) https://api.parliament.uk/historic-hansard/lords/1995/jun/13/disability-discrimination-bill accessed 30 December 2020.

132 Ibid., col 1642 (Baroness Hollis).

133 See above, n 109.

powerful argument. In addition to this, the 'severe' requirement exceeds that for other disabilities where the functional requirement (the substantial effect on day-to-day activities) needs only to be 'more than minor or trivial'.[134] Hence, despite the absence of a functional requirement, the severe disfigurements provision imposes higher threshold on victims of disfigurement discrimination.[135]

A solution via the 'because of' (or 'reason why') question

Rather than a rigid reduction in the features required for the perception, a less formal possibility is to require that the defendant acted on 'a generalised concept of disability'.[136] This provides tribunals with some leeway in particular cases, but is exposed to accusations that it provides a vague and unpredictable standard. However, much the same thing can be achieved with a careful approach to statutory interpretation.

The premise here is that requiring the misperception to align with all four features of section 6 of the Equality Act 2010 is asking the wrong question. Section 6 merely defines a *person* with an actual disability, not disability per se. The mistake is assuming that a perception that a person has a disability must be through the lens of section 6. This need not be so. The definition of direct discrimination (perceived or otherwise) lies in section 13, not section 6.

The starting point for this premise is an example of perceived discrimination on one of the other protected characteristics. A shopkeeper refuses to serve a turbaned Sikh man, misperceiving him to be a Muslim. The shopkeeper associated the turbaned man with media pictures of al-Qaeda terrorists, and in particular, Osama bin Laden.[137] There is no doubt that this would be perceived direct discrimination.[138] Yet, no proof would be required to show that the defendant shopkeeper had in mind a working knowledge of religions to have made the mistake. He would not be asked to recite the five pillars of Islam, for example. Nonetheless, he perceived the customer as a Muslim, which falls within the legal protected characteristic of 'religion'.

Now suppose an employer rejecting an applicant, misperceiving him to have a mental disability. This was because of the applicant's facial tic. The employer could not name the impairment he perceived, nor could he specify its effects;

134 EA 2010, s 212(1) codifying *Goodwin v The Patent Office* [1999] ICR 302 (EAT) 310 (Morison J).

135 This point was made by H Saunders, 'The invisible law of visible difference: Disfigurement in the workplace' (2019) 48(4) *ILJ* 487, 503.

136 *Fortt v Chief Constable of South Wales Police* (ET, 18 May 2015) Case No: 1601986/2014, [56] (Judge S Davies).

137 Human Rights Watch, '"We are not the enemy" hate crimes against Arabs, Muslims, and those perceived to be Arabs or Muslims after September 11', Vol 14 no G November 2002, p. 15 www.hrw.org/reports/2002/usahate/ accessed 30 December 2020.

138 See e.g. the US EEOC, *Religious Garb and Grooming in the Workplace: Rights and Responsibilities,* para 5 www.eeoc.gov/eeoc/publications/qa_religious_garb_grooming.cfm accessed 30 December 2020.

he just feared having to deal with unconventional behaviour in his workplace. Just as the shopkeeper need not be aware of the details of religion, this employer need not know of the details of mental or physical illnesses. The difference is that Islam readily falls under the legal term 'religion' (section 10) while a mental impairment requires the three additional functional features to fall under the legal term 'disability' (section 6).

Thus, it appears that the root of the problem is the legal requirement for a disabled person to have functional characteristics. This is in contrast to most other protected characteristics, where the Act defines the characteristic, rather than the *person* with the characteristic.[139] For example, the legislation makes no demand that a 'religious person' practices their faith, nor that a homosexual person has had a same-sex relationship, nor (more ridiculously) that a woman wears feminine clothing or an older person exhibits stereotypical geriatric behaviour.

For perceived discrimination though, the distinction between disability and these other protected characteristics is illusory. This is best understood with a revisit to the legislative framework. As a reminder, the Equality Act 2010 provides, by section 6, that 'a person has a disability' if he or she has the four 'features' (impairment, substantial, long-term, day-to-day activities).[140] Meanwhile, the definition of direct discrimination (section 13) requires less favourable treatment *because of* disability (the 'reason' for the treatment). As is well known, the absence of a possessive adjective (*his* or *her* protected characteristic) was a deliberate piece of drafting. It does not necessarily apply to the victim's, or indeed anyone else's,[141] protected characteristic, but has a more generalised meaning. Thus, the word 'disability' when attached to section 13 has a different, somewhat generalised, connotation than when defining a person who has a disability. This was apparent in the *Coleman* dictum that influenced this drafting.[142] The conclusion must be that the definition of disability in section 6 does not necessarily control its meaning in section 13.

This is shown by focussing on the mistake. The shopkeeper banning the Sikh man has made a mistake over the (factual) definition of religion. He mistook the significance of a turban. The employer rejecting an applicant made a mistake over the (factual) definition of mental illness. He mistook the significance of the tic. The shopkeeper made an entirely subjective mistake. In

139 Along with disability, exceptions are gender reassignment (EA 2010, s 7), marriage (s 8), and pregnancy (ss 17 and 18).

140 EA 2010, s 6.

141 *Showboat Entertainment Centre v Owens* [1984] ICR 65 (EAT), 73, focussing on the (white) victim's *attitude* to race; see also the harassment case, *English v Sanderson Blinds* [2008] EWCA 1421, where nobody's protected characteristic was involved, the focus being on the discriminatory nature of the conduct complained of.

142 'The principle of equal treatment enshrined in the directive in that area applies not to a particular category of person but by reference to the grounds mentioned in Art 1': Case C-303/06 *Coleman v Attridge Law* [2008] 3 CMLR 27, paras 38 (and 50). See above, text to n 12.

this context, he did not understand the meaning of 'religion'. It had nothing to do with the legal definition of religion as a protected characteristic other than the coincidence of the word 'religion'. He chose *his own* definition of religion as the reason to eject the Sikh man. Likewise, the employer chose *his own* definition of disability to reject the applicant. His reason had nothing to do with the legal definition of a disabled person other than the coincidence of the word 'disability'. The central feature of these cases is the defendant's mistake. It is not primarily a mistake as to the identity of the victim, but of the *reason* for the conduct. This is a subtle distinction, but one easily drawn from the legislative framework. Given that this is a section 13 question, if a defendant can be liable for perceived discrimination for making a mistake about a 'generalised concept' of religion, then why not so for making a mistake about a 'generalised concept' of disability?

This may jar with the notion of perceived discrimination as it is normally presented, which is a mistake as to the victim's protected characteristic, as legally defined (for disability in section 6). But section 13 was drafted more broadly than that, and deliberately so.[143] The section 13 'because' question is about the reason for the treatment, which could be the defendant's mistaken understanding of the meaning of, say, mental illness. Nonetheless, it should be actionable under section 13. It may well be that this form of discrimination is detached from the notion of 'perceived discrimination'. As such, just as with associative discrimination,[144] the notion of 'perceived discrimination' can take the reasoning down a blind alley, losing sight of the broader tenet of section 13.

The subtlety is more starkly exposed by reverting the logic back to cases of *actual* disability. If the four features of disability were required for the *reason* for the treatment (under section 13), the most blatant examples of actual-disability discrimination would be immune from discrimination law and a broader legislative purpose would be wrecked. Suppose an employer includes in a job advertisement, 'no disabled need apply'.[145] As it appears, this exclusion does

143 Equality Bill Deb 17 June 2009, col 254: 'The "because of" turn of phrase in clause 13 is broad enough and is intended to be broad enough to cover much more than just cases in which the less favourable treatment is due to the victim's association with someone who has the characteristic or because the victim is wrongly thought to have that characteristic. The formulation is intended to and does cover cases, for instance, of less favourable treatment because of a refusal to comply with instructions to discriminate. It is also intended and does cover a case in which someone is treated as if they had a protected characteristic that they neither have *nor are perceived to have* at the time' (Solicitor-General). Emphasis supplied.
https://publications.parliament.uk/pa/cm200809/cmpublic/equality/090616/pm/90616s04.htm accessed 30 December 2020.

144 See above, 'Perceived discrimination as associative discrimination' pp. 114.

145 See the previous Code: 'An employer may advertise internally for a promotion, stating that the post is not suitable for anyone with a history of mental illness, and exclude, unknowingly, a member of staff with a history of schizophrenia'. 'Disability Discrimination Act 1995 Code of Practice on Employment and Occupation' TSO (ISBN 0 11 703419 3).

not meet the section 6 requirements, and this shortfall means that the advertisement is not directly discriminatory against anyone either rejected or deterred. While it is arguable that the term 'disabled' equates to an 'impairment', the advertisement does not express the other features (substantial, long-term, day-to-day activities), or anything resembling them. As such, this advertisement could be distinguished from one expressed to exclude women, Muslims, Asians, Homosexuals, and so on. Yet, it would likewise be an affront to the equality legislation if it were lawful for employers to deploy an expressed generalised 'no disabled' policy. In addition to harmonising the policy goals of the equality law, there are doctrinal reasons to interpret section 13 in this way. This can be appreciated from the legislative history on discriminatory advertising. As the above policy argument implies, discriminatory advertising can be addressed by individuals under section 13 as direct discrimination. Prior to the Equality Act 2010, however, equality legislation specifically outlawed discriminatory advertising, reserving enforcement to the relevant enforcement body. For example, the Disability Discrimination Act 1995 (DDA 1995), s 11, outlawed advertisements that 'might reasonably be understood to have indicated' that a job was open only to persons not having a disability, or that no reasonable adjustments would be made.[146] There was no expectation that an advertisement should fulfil the four 'features of disability' to be unlawful, just as there was none requiring a specific racial description. Furthermore, under the Race Relations Act 1976, an advertisement remained unlawful even if the activity or conduct suggested was in fact lawful in practice (say, under an exception).[147] The Act's White Paper explained 'the public display of racial prejudices and preferences is inherently offensive and likely to encourage the spread of discriminatory attitudes and prejudices'.[148] The original DDA 1995 was expressed in terms open enough to follow this line, there being no qualification to advertisements that 'might be reasonably understood' to be discriminatory. However, a rider was added in 2004 limiting liability to when the advertised practice would be unlawful.[149] These provision have two relevant features. First, for liability, it is not necessary for an advertisement to express the protected characteristic according to a definition elsewhere in the same legislation. It is enough that it 'might reasonably be understood' to refer to the protected characteristic in question. Second, for race (and at one time disability), even if the apparently discriminatory activity or conduct suggested by the advertisement were lawful, the advertisement remained *un*lawful.

146 See also DDA 2005, s 10. See also, SDA 1975, s 38; RRA 1976, s 29.

147 RRA 1976, s 29: 'indicates, or might reasonably be understood as indicating, an intention by a person to do an act of discrimination, whether the doing of that act by him would be lawful'.

148 Racial Discrimination Cmnd 6234, p. 19.

149 DDA 1995, s 16B(2), inserted by DDA 1995 (Amendment) Regulations 2003/1673 Part 2 reg 15(1) (1 October 2004). This followed the line taken with the rider in the SDA 1975, 38(2).

These specific provisions were repealed by the Equality Act 2010, and incorporated into the Act's general edict against direct discrimination under section 13, which, the Explanatory Note declared, covered advertisements.[150] This was in response to the ECJ case, *Feryn*, holding that a person merely deterred from applying for a job by discriminatory pronouncements and advertisements could sue for direct discrimination.[151] Given the non-regression principle,[152] and the short title of the Act, declaring that it was to 'reform and harmonise equality law' and 'increase equality of opportunity', the most logical interpretation of section 13 is that its interpretation must be levelled up to the standard required for racially discriminatory advertisements. In the context of this discussion, it means that in relation to section 13, 'disability' has a looser meaning than that provided in section 6. It also means that 'inherently offensive' advertisements which are 'likely to encourage the spread of discriminatory attitudes and prejudices' applies to all protected characteristics, and especially one particularly susceptible to misunderstanding and stereotypes, disability.

For both policy and interpretive reasons, it follows that if section 13 should apply to discriminatory advertisements that fall short of a precise description of the protected characteristic in question, then it should apply to other conduct in the same way. Assuming a claimant has an actual disability, her claim would centre on the section 13 'because' question. This employer's reason for the treatment is its own 'generalised concept' of disability, and *not* the section 6 formula. If cases of actual disability need not rely on section 6 for the section 13 question, then there needs to be a very good reason to depart from this for perceived cases. This can occur when the actual issue was that the treatment was because the defendant wrongly thought that the victim fulfilled the *legal* definition. (A consequent rejection may have been a reluctance to make reasonable adjustments.) In such cases, a reference to the section 6 definition could inform this section 13 question, but it remains a section 13 question. Otherwise, there is no need to refer to section 6 to decide the s 13 question.

Conclusion

A general social construct theory has sometimes been cited as underpinning the notion of perceived discrimination. More regularly, notions of dignity are cited, especially in cases of disability. In the UK and EU, policy dictates that perceived discrimination is a form of direct discrimination. Realised in law, the standard definition(s) of direct discrimination are not particularly bespoke for

150 Explanatory Notes to the EA 2010, para 63. See Joint Committee on Human Rights, Legislative Scrutiny: Equality Bill; (26th Report, 12 November 2009) (2008–9, HL 169, HC 736) Part 8, para 56.

151 Case C-54/07 *Feryn* [2008] ECR I-05187 (ECJ). The EAT has held that a person with no interest in post cannot sue: *Keane v Invstigo* (11 December 2009); *Berry v Recruitment Revolution* (EAT, 6 October 2010).

152 Member States cannot use the implementation of EU law to reduce the rights concerned. See e.g. Race Directive 2000/43/EC, Preamble, para (25).

the task. The 'because' or 'reason why' element can be drafted 'openly' so that the claimant need not possess the protected characteristic in question. This removes one barrier to perceived direct discrimination. This has been done in the EU and UK, but not in United States, save for disability. Under the US 'closed' definition, there are some imaginative, but only partial, solutions, depending on a separate protected characteristic of the claimant.

The comparative element however, still integral to the UK jurisprudence, remains an obstacle for the fundamental reason that a comparator's circumstances cannot be materially different. Given that the claimant has no actual protected characteristic, a comparison can test nothing. Various methods of circumnavigating this obstacle are suggested, from changing the defendant's perception, the claimant's attributes, treating the case as akin to associative discrimination, or bypassing the comparison altogether. None of these techniques is entirely satisfactory.

There is a distinct problem with disability discrimination, where the exceptionally complex (functional) definition of disability is said to prevent most claims, as a defendant would be unlikely to have these complex elements in mind when acting. The most prevalent proposal is to reduce the elements required in perception cases to just one, the impairment. This was in the United States, but there has been legislative and judicial resistance to this, for fear of making it easier to claim for perceived than actual discrimination. It is suggested that this is the wrong debate, and a proper solution lies in a more detailed approach to statutory interpretation, and detaching the definition of disability from the definition for direct discrimination. A parallel problem exists for the exceptional severe disfigurement provision. Again, the most prevalent proposal is to drop the 'severe' requirement. Until then, the best solution in perceived cases is to ignore them and utilise the functional provisions instead, and claim actual discrimination.

Further reading

A Broderick and D Ferri, *International and European Disability Law and Policy: Text, Cases and Materials (Law in Context)* (2019, CUP).

A Lawson, 'Disability and employment in the Equality Act 2010: Opportunities seized, lost and generated' (2011) 40*ILJ* 359.

H Saunders, 'The invisible law of visible difference: Disfigurement in the workplace' (2019) 48(4) *ILJ* 487.

For the United States

DF Flake, 'Religious discrimination based on employer misperception' (2016) *Wisconsin Law Review* 87.

DW Greene, 'Categorically black, white, or wrong: "Misperception discrimination" and the State of Title VII protection' (2013) 47(1) *University of Michigan Journal of Law Reform* 131.

AB Mayerson, 'Restoring regard for the "regarded as" prong: Giving effect to Congressional intent' (1997) 42 *Villanova Law Review* 587.

A Onwuachi-Willig and ML Barnes, 'By any other name?: On being "regarded as" black, and why Title VII should apply even if Lakisha and Jamal are white' (2005) *Wisconsin Law Review* 1283.

CR Senn, 'perception over reality: Extending the Ada's concept of "regarded as" protection under federal employment discrimination law' (2009) 36 *Florida State University Law Review* 827.

7 Sexual orientation, marriage, and discrimination

Introduction

Two areas of controversy accompany many cases of discrimination and sexual orientation. One is the clash with the Human Rights of freedom of religion and free expression. These cases tend to centre on objectively justifying indirect discrimination, or squaring the discrimination provisions with these human rights. They do not raise issues over the fidelity of the definitions themselves and are not discussed here. The second controversy arises where (heterosexual) marriage becomes a proxy for (homosexual) discrimination. The UK definition of discrimination comes with a proviso for these circumstances, levelling the status of gay and straight formal relationships. The original main purpose of this was to prevent marriage being used as a proxy for sexual orientation discrimination against a same-sex couple in a civil partnership, a particular issue in the days before same-sex marriage was introduced. But it has not supplied the certainty intended. With or without the proviso, determining whether such discrimination is direct or indirect has proved difficult, once again exposing the 'fuzzy border' between the two. In addition, this issue *does* raise questions over the fidelity of the direct discrimination provisions, with the comparative and 'reason why' elements seemingly at odds. The problems were played out in full in the *Bull v Hall* litigation.[1]

The case of *Bull v Hall*

A small hotel advertised:

> Here at Chymorvah we have few rules, but please note, that out of a deep regard for marriage we prefer to let double accommodation to heterosexual married couples only – thank you.

The claimants, a couple in a same-sex civil partnership, were refused accommodation in a double room and consequently complained of discrimination on

1 sub nom *Preddy v Hall, Hall v Bull* [2011] Eq LR 283 (C Ct); [2012] EWCA 83; [2013] UKSC 73.

DOI: 10.4324/9781003187547-7

the ground of sexual orientation. The Supreme Court unanimously found for the claimants, but with a mixture of reasoning. Two of the five Justices found that the discrimination was *indirect* (but not justified), while three found it to be direct, but divided, over their reasoning. Divergences of opinion on the precise definitions of direct and indirect discrimination emerged in three areas: first, the significance of a proviso specific to sexual orientation (that marriage and civil partnerships were not to be treated as materially different); second, the minority's finding of indirect discrimination; and third, the attempted reconciliation of domestic and EU law, especially the 'Indissociable' and 'Exact Coincidence' Rubrics.

The proviso

For sexual orientation only, there is a proviso for making a comparison. The relevant legislation at the time was the Equality Act (Sexual Orientation) Regulations 2007.[2] Regulation 3(1) provided:

> (1) For the purposes of these Regulations, a person ('A') discriminates against another ('B') if, on grounds of the sexual orientation of B or any other person except A, A treats B less favourably than he treats or would treat others (in cases where there is no material difference in the relevant circumstances).

The proviso came with regulation 3(4):

> (4) For the purposes of paragraphs (1) and (3), the fact that one of the persons (whether or not B) is a civil partner while the other is married shall not be treated as a material difference in the relevant circumstances.

For the purposes of any comparison, paragraph (4) equalises the status of marriage and civil partnerships. (Bear in mind, the case arose before same-sex marriage was introduced;[3] the Equality Act 2010 brings same-sex marriage into this class.[4]) Thus, a defendant stipulating 'heterosexual marriage' could not argue that no comparison was possible on the basis that a couple in a civil partnership was 'materially different' from a married couple.[5]

2 SI 2007/1263, applying to the provision of goods, facilities and services, education, disposal and management of premises and exercise of public functions. At the time, employment was covered by the Employment Equality (Sexual Orientation) Regulations 2003, SI 2003/1661. All is now consolidated in the Equality Act 2010, with a generic proviso at s 23. See n 4, below.
3 By the Marriage (Same Sex Couples) Act 2013.
4 For the purposes of direct and indirect discrimination, Equality Act 2010, s 23(3) provides that where the protected characteristic is sexual orientation, being a civil partner or married is not a material difference between the circumstances relating to each case.
5 Ibid. The Explanatory Note (92) states that the proviso 'enables a civil partner who is treated less favourably than a married person in similar circumstances to bring a claim for sexual orientation discrimination'.

To complicate matters beyond the three-two split in their reasoning, two of the majority (Lady Hale and Lord Toulson) held that there was direct discrimination even without this proviso,[6] while for Lord Kerr, it was essential to his finding of direct discrimination.[7] Lady Hale explained that civil partnerships and (heterosexual) marriage were generally accepted as equivalents, a point merely 'emphasised' by the proviso: 'Civil partnership is not called marriage but in almost every other respect it is indistinguishable from the status of marriage in United Kingdom law'.[8] The key word here is 'almost'. Thus, *legally*, heterosexual marriage and same-sex civil partnerships *are* different,[9] hence the proviso stating that they should be treated as 'equivalents' in certain circumstances. Lady Hale's conclusion here is to render the proviso redundant without explaining why its inclusion was erroneous. If Lady Hale were correct, the drafter, by tradition, would have begun the proviso with the phrase 'For the avoidance of doubt …', which is common practice in statutory drafting.[10]

On the other side of the table, the dissenting Justices Neuberger and Hughes actually shared the opinion that the proviso made no difference to the outcome, only this time, in support of their finding of *indirect* discrimination. For Lord Neuberger,

> It is merely concerned to establish that, for the purpose of establishing whether there has been direct or indirect discrimination, it must be assumed that there is no 'material difference' between a person in a civil partnership and a married person.[11]

Lord Neuberger also agreed with Lord Hughes on this point, who held that the proviso did not apply to the separate question of identifying the ground of the treatment.[12] Lord Neuberger then reasoned that,

> [T]he suggestion that this interpretation … is contrary to the purpose of the Regulations seems … to be circular or self-fulfilling: it assumes that the purpose of regulation 3 [as a whole] is to render discrimination in a case such as this direct, when that is the very question at issue.[13]

6 [2013] UKSC 73, respectively [29]; and [67] and [70]. Lord Toulson was a touch ambiguous here, stating that reg 3(4) 'reinforced' this view, agreeing with Lady Hale's reasoning, while (at [70]) stating he agreed with Lord Kerr's point (at [57]): 'By virtue of reg 3(4) [the claimants] are to be treated as being not materially different from a married couple'.
7 Ibid., [62].
8 Ibid., [26]. Lord Toulson appeared to agree, ibid., [70].
9 See e.g. Matrimonial Causes Act 1973, s 12(2), voidability for non-consummation does not apply to same sex marriage.
10 A Westlaw search of this phrase under 'Legislation' produced 1467 results (July 2021).
11 [2013] UKSC 73 [78].
12 Ibid., [92] (Lord Hughes).
13 Ibid., [78].

This goes a step further than Lady Hale's reasoning and attempts to ascribe a concrete purpose to the proviso, but, with respect, it does no more to support such an interpretation beyond saying it is confined to the comparison. No examples were given to demonstrate how this might work, or where the proviso *could* make a difference, save it be redundant. Lord Neuberger's secondary view that the proviso cannot convert discrimination from indirect to direct is rooted in the case before him, and fails to look beyond that. Suppose, as Lady Hale had,[14] that the claimants were not in a civil partnership. Analysed as direct discrimination, the victims' comparator would be an unmarried heterosexual couple, who would also be refused a double room. Without the proviso, it would be at least arguable that there is no difference between this couple and one in a (same-sex) civil partnership, with the resulting rather awkward comparison between *any* same-sex couple (be they in a civil partnership or not), and a heterosexual married couple (who would be admitted). This points to a finding of *direct* discrimination. The proviso ensures that the comparator would be an *un*married heterosexual couple (who would also be rejected), which defeats a direct discrimination claim at that stage. In turn, this comparison suggests *indirect* discrimination, because (for the time being anyway) homosexuals are less likely than heterosexuals to be in a civil partnership/marriage. As this example demonstrates, Lord Neuberger's fear of a proviso converting every case of discrimination from indirect to direct is misplaced. It has the potential to do quite the reverse, depending on the particular facts. It will point towards direct discrimination only in certain cases, such as the one before him; this is, notably, where the victims were in a civil partnership.

In another sense, the minority's reasoning on this point is effectively no different to Lady Hale's (and Lord Toulson's). Both sides of this debate render the proviso redundant (and without explanation as to why they thought its inclusion superfluous), a 'cardinal sin' of statutory interpretation.[15] Only Lord Kerr gave the proviso some relevance. Moreover, there is a clear difference of opinion as the meaning of direct and indirect discrimination in the context of sexual orientation and marriage requirements.

The minority's rejection of direct discrimination

Lord Neuberger and Lord Hughes agreed that this case should be treated as one of indirect discrimination. Lord Hughes reasoned that as, 'being married is a condition which same sex couples cannot fulfil, the practice of the defendants amounted … to indirect discrimination on grounds of sexual orientation'.[16] Lord Hughes said this conclusion applied to same-sex couples not in a civil partnership, as well as to same-sex couples in a civil partnership. Lord

14 Ibid., [19]–[24].
15 *Re Florence Land Co* (1878) 10 Ch D 530 (CA), 544 (James LJ). See also *Hill v William Hill (Park Lane) Ltd* [1949] AC 530 (HL) 546–547 (Viscount Simon).
16 [2013] UKSC 73 [93].

Neuberger took a similar line, on the basis that being in a civil partnership made no difference.[17] But most of their focus was on why this was not direct discrimination.

Both found that by applying the legislative formula (including the proviso) to the comparison, the question remained as to the 'ground' of the treatment. At this point, the focus should move away from the characteristics of the victims, and towards the hoteliers' reason(s) for the treatment.[18] Here, Lord Neuberger said that isolating sexual orientation as the ground presented 'only a partial description of the discrimination being practised in this case'.[19] Meanwhile, Lord Hughes held that ground for the treatment was simply and wholly 'marriage', as unmarried heterosexual couples, along with same-sex couples not in a civil partnership, as well as the claimants, would all be rejected.

While it may be correct (although rarely necessary) to separate the elements of the comparison and the ground(s) for the treatment,[20] this must be undertaken with some care. Lord Neuberger's answer ignores the additional qualification that the protected characteristic (in this case, sexual orientation) need only be one of the reasons for the treatment for a finding of direct discrimination.[21] Lord Hughes merely exchanges the basis of the rejection for another: a benign reason. Such a reason is a heresy for the domestic jurisprudence, which emphatically forbids the use of a 'benign motive defence' in direct discrimination.[22] Thus, the application of the formula here by both Justices flies in the face of long-established orthodoxy. Moreover, it blurs the boundary between direct and indirect discrimination.

17 Ibid., [75]–[76].

18 The mistake, according to Lord Hughes, of finding direct discriminating from the comparison was that, 'It concentrates on the characteristics of these claimants rather than on the defendants' reasons for treating them as they did': ibid., [88].

19 Ibid., [77].

20 This may occur where statistics suggest latent direct discrimination, and circumstantial evidence goes to prove the 'ground'. See e.g. *King v Great Britain-China Centre* [1992] ICR 513 (CA), and in the US, *International Brotherhood of Teamsters v United States* 431 US 324 (Sup Ct, 1977). In *Shamoon v Chief Constable of the RUC* [2003] ICR 337 (HL) [11], Lord Nicholls suggested the reverse approach, that in some cases the comparison cannot be made without first identifying the ground of the treatment, and further, if the ground of the treatment is based on a prohibited characteristic, then a tribunal can 'avoid arid and confusing disputes about the identification of the appropriate comparator'. See also *Macdonald v Advocate General for Scotland* [2003] UKHL 34 [5]–[7] (Lord Nicholls); *Islington LBC v Ladele* [2009] ICR 387 (EAT) [37]–[39] (Elias J).

21 *Owen and Briggs v James* [1982] ICR 618 (CA). See further below, text to n 59.

22 *R v Birmingham City Council, ex parte Equal Opportunities Commission* [1989] 1 AC 1156 (HL) 1194; R *v Commission for Racial Equality ex parte Westminster CC* [1985] ICR 827 (CA); *James v Eastleigh BC* [1990] 2 AC 751 (HL); *R (E) v Governing Body of JFS* [2009] UKSC 15. A number of examples are given in n 51.

The 'indissociable' and 'exact coincidence' rubrics

It should be noted, first of all, that these rubrics are discussed in detail in Chapter 2.[23] Here, they are discussed only in the context of the *Bull v Hall* judgment.

For Lady Hale, it seemed, both of these rubrics had to be satisfied for a finding of direct discrimination where the challenged criterion is not the protected characteristic in question. This can be described as a direct discrimination by a proxy. At the time of the case, this could be a requirement to be 'married'. Each rubric derives from Opinions of Advocates General in the European Court of Justice (ECJ). In *Bressol*, AG Jacobs advised that there could be direct discrimination if a criterion was 'necessarily linked' or 'indissociable' from the protected characteristic in question.[24] In *Schnorbus*, AG Sharpston added that there was direct discrimination where there was an exact coincidence between those advantaged and disadvantaged by the criterion and a protected characteristic.[25] According to Lady Hale, the outcome turned on the circumstances of the victim: that is whether or not the victim was in a civil partnership (the case predated same-sex marriage). Where the victim was *not* in a civil partnership (unlike the case before her), only the first rubric was satisfied: the criterion of 'heterosexual marriage' *was* 'indissociable' from sexual orientation.[26] But there was not an exact coincidence – between those suffering the disadvantage of being denied a double room, and those enjoying the correlative advantage of being allowed one – with the protected characteristic.[27] In other words, as well as barring all homosexual couples, the criterion barred also some heterosexual couples (the 'advantaged group'). In support, Lady Hale cited the facts and decisions from the two ECJ cases that provided the rubrics. She noted that in *Schnorbus*, the challenged criterion favoured all men and no women, and in *Bressol*[28] it favoured all Belgian nationals, but disfavoured most, *but not all*, non-Belgians.[29]

In *Schnorbus*, the challenged criterion was a requirement of 'military service', in circumstances where only men could undertake military service. In *Bressol* (a claim of nationality discrimination), the challenged criterion was the 'right of residence'. Belgium nationals enjoyed an automatic right of residence, while non-nationals could qualify via a number of other (narrowly drafted) criteria.

23 See Chapter 2, 'The incorporated and cumulative cases: Direct or indirect', pp. 7.
24 Case C-79/99 *Schnorbus v Land Hessen* [2000] ECR I-10997, Opinion of AG Jacobs, para AG33.
25 Case C-73/08 *Bressol v Gouvernement de la Communauté Française* [2010] 3 CMLR 559, Opinion of AG Sharpston, paras AG53 ('indissociable') and AG56–57 ('exact coincidence').
26 Because 'at present persons of heterosexual orientation can marry and persons of homosexual orientation cannot': [2013] UKSC 73 [20].
27 Ibid., [21].
28 Respectively, Case C-79/99 [2000] ECR I-10997; Case C-73/08 [2010] 3 CMLR 559.
29 [2013] UKSC 73 [21].

These were held to be instances of *indirect*, rather than direct, discrimination. Lady Hale employed these EU materials because it was 'highly desirable' the definitions should be 'both internally consistent and consistent with EU law'.[30]

For Lady Hale, this approach tallied with a conventional reading of the statutory formula, notably the comparison. Where the homosexual victim is not in a civil partnership, as Lady Hale's example postulates, the comparator (with no material differences) is a heterosexual person, not in a marriage.[31] And so, the element of less favourable treatment could be tested by asking, 'How would the hotel have treated a heterosexual unmarried couple?' The answer, of course, is in exactly the same way. Both victim and comparator would be refused, and so the refusal to accommodate the victim was not less favourable. For Lady Hale, what made 'all the difference', was the victims' status as civil partners, which she found (as noted above) was generally accepted as equivalent to (heterosexual) marriage.[32] These circumstances now dictate that this is a case of direct discrimination. The criterion now imports a term, 'not in a civil partnership', which was indissociable from sexual orientation. Further, there was an exact coincidence – between those disfavoured (those in a civil partnership) and those favoured (married heterosexuals) – with the protected characteristic. This was because only homosexuals could be in a civil partnership and only heterosexuals could be in a 'heterosexual marriage'. This aligns also with the legislative formula. Comparators are now drawn from a narrower class of persons, married heterosexual couples, any of which would have been treated more favourably.

Another way to digest this remorseless but, perhaps, disorienting logic, is to envisage a two-stage test to qualify for the hotel's double room. First, couples must be 'married', which at the time meant 'married or in a civil partnership'. This disqualified some homosexuals and some heterosexuals, and so did not directly discriminate because of sexual orientation. The second stage applied only to those who passed the first stage, that is heterosexuals who were married and homosexuals in a civil partnership. The ban on those in a civil partnership can only disadvantage homosexuals while the admission to married couples could only advantage heterosexuals. Hence, this is direct discrimination because of sexual orientation.

This is neat and tidy, but it papers over some cracks. First of all, *Bressol* and *Schnorbus* present a more nuanced picture than Lady Hale suggested. The 'indissociable' and 'exact coincidence' rubrics were proffered by Advocates General in separate cases; but neither were repeated by their respective judgments.[33] Indeed, in *Bressol*, the Court of Justice disregarded Advocate General

30 Ibid., [22].
31 Nowadays, the status of the respective formal relationships has levelled out considerably, with the introduction of same-sex marriage and opposite sex civil partnerships: respectively, the Marriage (Same Sex Couples) Act 2013 and SI 2019/1458. For Northern Ireland, both are covered in SR 2019/514.
32 [2013] UKSC 73 [25], [26] and [29].
33 In *Schnorbus*, [2000] ECR I-10997, para 33, the Court's sole reasoning was: 'According to the criteria established by the case law of the Court, only provisions

Sharpston's advice that the nationality discrimination was direct.[34] It did so without giving reasons,[35] leaving the meaning and status of AG Sharpston's test somewhat vague. It is therefore somewhat isolated and could well be slowly forgotten (despite Lady Hale's efforts). It also leaves Lady Hale's association between the rubrics and the Court of Justice's decision as somewhat shaky. After all, the author of the 'exact coincidence' test considered that its application identified direct discrimination, and yet Lady Hale is citing with approval both the test and the Court of Justice's (contrary) decision. The relevance of the indissociable rubric was also misplaced. AG Jacobs expressly limited it to a physical nexus, excluding any legal nexus,[36] as was the case in *Bull v Hall*. Presenting the tests as authoritative is affording them a higher status than they were given by the Court of Justice.

Second, when discussing the circumstance where the victim was *not* in a civil partnership, Lady Hale implied that the facts of *Bressol* and *Schnorbus* represented this scenario. As noted above, Lady Hale's starting point was that the criterion (not yet including 'not in a civil partnership') bars *all* homosexuals but also *some* heterosexuals and therefore failed the 'exact coincidence' test: none of the disadvantaged group qualified, while *some* of the advantaged group (married heterosexuals) did so. *Bressol* presented a reverse image of this scenario, where *all* of the *advantaged* group (Belgian nationals) qualified, but *some* (albeit very few) of the disadvantaged group could do so as well. This has fidelity to the exact coincidence rubric, albeit with the advantaged and disadvantaged profiles reversed. However, *Schnorbus* was presented by Lady Hale as a case where a criterion advantaged *all* men and disadvantaged *all* women. On this basis, it would pass the exact coincidence test. Bear in mind that AG Jacobs' explanation for *Schnorbus* not being direct discrimination was the absence of indissociability, there being only a legal nexus.[37] This picture appears even more complex (or 'fuzzy') when put into a wider context, which is discussed next.

which apply differently according to the sex of the persons concerned can be regarded as constituting discrimination directly based on sex'. (Citing Case C-249/96 *Grant v South-West Trains* [1998] ECR I-621, para 28.) In *Bressol*, [2010] 3 CMLR 20, para 45, the Court merely reasoned that 'A residence condition … is more easily satisfied by Belgian nationals, who more often than not reside in Belgium'. At the time of writing (April 2019), no ECJ Judgments have repeated either 'test'.

34 Case C-73/08; [2010] 3 CMLR 559, paras 40–46.

35 In *Patmalniece v Secretary of State for Work and Pensions* [2011] UKSC 11 [33] Lord Hope suggested it because AG Sharpston's approach was 'too analytical' and that the ECJ preferred to look at the 'conditions as a whole'. See also [69] (Lord Walker).

36 Case C-79/99 *Schnorbus v Land Hessen* [2000] ECR I-10997, Opinion of AG Jacobs, para AG 40.

37 For a criticism of this particular reason, see Chapter 2, 'The incorporated and cumulative cases: Direct or indirect', p. 7.

The fuzzy border

To appreciate the fuzzy border between direct and indirect discrimination in 'Bull v Hall' type cases, consider the case's history and surrounding precedents. The county court held that the decision on direct discrimination was confined to those in a civil partnership, with the proviso being pivotal. The Court of Appeal upheld the decision, but did so on the wider basis that the challenged requirement directly discriminated whether or not the claimants were in a civil partnership; here the proviso made no difference. It relied on *James v Eastleigh.*[38] And, as seen above,[39] the Supreme Court had a three-way division over the matter, with one Justice finding direct discrimination because of the proviso, two without it, and two others holding that the discrimination was *indirect*. And within that, two of the majority confined the decision to those within a civil partnership. In the meantime, the Court of Appeal had heard a similar case, *Black v Wilkinson.*[40] The essential difference was that the claimants were *not* in a civil partnership. Here the Court of Appeal found direct discrimination, but only because it felt bound by its own decision in *Bull v Hall*. Otherwise, the Court of Appeal thought this (and indeed *Bull v Hall*) to be *indirect* discrimination, holding that such cases *were* distinguishable from *James v Eastleigh.*[41] As if to highlight the uncertainty here, the senior judges'[42] *opinions* (in *Bull v Hall* and *Black v Wilkinson*) were divided six–five in favour of this type of case[43] amounting to direct discrimination.

Lady Hale addressed the matter when making a point of demarcation (which coincidently supports the 'mutually exclusive' doctrine).[44] She noted that a case such as this would be 'much harder' to analyse as indirect discrimination, because the criteria, now including 'not in a civil partnership' was not facially neutral: it did not apply to all irrespective of sexual orientation.[45] In other words, the 'second test' applying only to a sub-group of those married or in a civil partnership, barred all homosexuals and admitted all heterosexuals. This is inconsistent with the statutory formula for indirect discrimination, which required a 'provision, criterion or practice' that the defendant 'applies or would apply equally to persons not of B's sexual orientation'.[46] On its face (and again at the time), a criterion of 'heterosexual marriage (not in a civil partnership)',

38 [2012] EWCA Civ 83 [61] (Rafferty LJ), [40] (Sir Andrew Morritt C).
39 See text accompanying n 6.
40 [2013] EWCA Civ 820.
41 Ibid., [21]–[23] (Lord Dyson MR, with whom Arden LJ and McCombe LJ agreed).
42 Those of the Court of Appeal and Supreme Court.
43 That is where the couple are in a civil partnership. The 'six' were Lady Hale, Lords Kerr and Toulson, and the *Bull v Hall* Court of Appeal. The 'five' were Lords Neuberger and Hughes, and the *Black v Wilkinson* Court of Appeal.
44 See Chapter 2, 'The incorporated and cumulative cases: Direct or indirect', pp. 21–27.
45 [2013] UKSC 73 [32].
46 SI 2007/1263, reg 3(3). See now Equality Act 2010, s 19.

did not apply 'equally' to the sub-group of heterosexual and homosexual persons who were married or in a civil partnership; it applied exclusively to homosexual persons and inclusively to heterosexual persons.

This logic of course relies on the 'exact coincidence' between the criterion and sexual orientation. This is detected by the criterion's effects: only heterosexuals (married) are advantaged and only homosexuals (in a civil partnership) are disadvantaged. A feature of the 'exact coincidence' rubric is its focus on the *effect* of a challenged criterion upon a *group*. This tends to eclipse the elements in the legislative formula and its individualist nature. In support of his finding of direct discrimination in *JFS*,[47] Lord Mance maintained, '[A]n organisation which admitted all men but only women graduates would be engaged in direct discrimination on the grounds of sex'.[48] This example is not a proxy case. Women are expressly disadvantaged and so the criterion is facially discriminatory, and thus directly discriminatory. This accords with policy and can be squared with the legislative formula, despite the formula's symmetrical nature. For instance, an employer may dismiss a female worker stating 'You're a typical unreliable woman', without dismissing other female employees. The employer may have similarly dismissed a man stating 'You're a typical arrogant man'. In part, at least,[49] the reason for the treatment in each case is sex. In *JFS*, under a school's entrance requirements for Orthodox Jews, *all* of the *advantaged* group ('Racially Jewish'[50]) qualified, but some of the disadvantaged group did so as well (matrilineal descendants of Converts). It is quite arguable that *JFS* is a 'proxy' case (the school incorporating the Office of Chief Rabbi's definition a Jew). So it is arguable that Lord Mance supposed this example to apply generally (including proxy cases). We can see that, ordinarily, direct discrimination can occur where only *some* of the victim's group is disfavoured, or, presumably, vice versa (where some of the advantaged group are disfavoured: 'male graduates, no women'). Hence, the 'exact coincidence' rubric applied so meticulously by Lady Hale in *Bull v Hall* seems to be at odds with Lord Mance's dictum, *unless* this dictum has no application to proxy cases.

This raises the question of whether the logic of the dictum should apply also to proxy cases. Policy suggests that it should; after all, the effect is the same. The problem is that such cases also resemble *indirect* discrimination, suggesting the fuzzy border. This might explain Lady Hale's attempt to demarcate the case of a couple in a civil partnership from one where they are not. But this relied heavily on the *effects* of the criterion rather than the criterion itself. Hence, Lady Hale re-wrote the hotelier's criterion and created a sub-group (those

47 *R (E) v Governing Body of JFS* [2009] UKSC 15, discussed in Chapter 2, 'The incorporated and cumulative cases: Direct or indirect', pp. 8–12.
48 [2010] 2 AC 728 [89] (Lord Mance, citing counsel Dinah Rose QC, ibid., 738.)
49 This is sufficient for a finding of discrimination: *Owen and Briggs v James* [1982] ICR 618 (CA). See further below, text to n 59.
50 That is the Jewish people whose ancestor was the patriarch Jacob (Israel) and with whom the covenant of Mount Sinai was made through Moses upon the Exodus from Egypt. See e.g. *JFS* [2009] UKSC 15 [86] (Lord Mance).

married or in a civil partnership) to demonstrate the distinction between direct and indirect discrimination. This technique focuses on the potential victims rather than the criterion itself and is somewhat artificial in that it supposes that the hotel's policy was directed only at those in a civil partnership, when patently it was broader than that. The difficulty here is that the criterion could be re-written in many ways with a particular purpose in mind, such as demonstrating the effect of the challenged practice, or to fulfil a particular judge's desired result. For instance:

'Double Rooms Policy. No homosexuals. Heterosexual couples welcome if married'. Or perhaps:

> Our devout Christian belief means that in this small dwelling which we share with our guests, our double room is available only to couples married according to Biblical teaching. We would consider it sinful if we facilitated in our own home relationship outside of such a marriage.

One appears more palatable than the other perhaps, but they add up to the same thing, as do *both* of Lady Hale's versions: homosexuals are not welcome in our double rooms. Should it make a difference that heterosexuals were welcome only if married, or barred if not, or that the rule is 'because of' religion and not sexual orientation, or (as Lady Hale postulated) that the victims were not in a civil partnership? (Bear in mind here that Lady Hale's – and Lord Toulson's – theory was not based on the proviso, so this is not an isolated theory driven by a statutory quirk, or exception.) If these add up to the same thing, should the way they are expressed, or their *group* effect, dictate whether this is direct or indirect discrimination? If we take the legislative formula (as we should) to focus on the reason for the treatment, and exclude from this analysis (as we should) benign motive defences,[51] the only remaining factor in the hotel's requirements is sexual orientation. This applies however the criterion is expressed. It includes Lady Hale's demarcated variety where the victims are not in a civil partnership. These supposed victims would be refused accommodation

51 Although, the legislative provision itself may be read down, or held incompatible, in deference to the defendant's freedoms of religion and/or expression under the European Convention of Human Rights, incorporated into UK by the Human Rights Act 1998. See *Lee v Ashers* [2018] UKSC 49. 'Benign motive defences' are not recognised in cases of direct discrimination: *James v Eastleigh BC* [1990] 2 AC 751 (HL) (policy to help pensioners); *R (E) v Governing Body of JFS* [2010] 2 AC 728 (SC) (to accord with religious doctrine); *Ministry of Defence v Jeremiah* [1980] QB 87 (CA)*Ministry of Defence v Jeremiah* (women not required to work in dirty part of factory); *Amnesty International v Ahmed* [2009] ICR 1450 (EAT) (preference for neutrality excluded Sudanese nationals, as did safety concerns); *Grieg v Community Industry* [1979] ICR 356 (EAT) (woman rejected to protect them from harassment). In the US, see, *Diaz v Pan Am* 442 F 2d 385 (5th Cir 1971) certiorari denied, 404 US 950 (1971) *Diaz v Pan Am* (customer preference for (female) cabin crew); and *Chaney v Plainfield Healthcare* 612 F 3d 908 (7th Cir 2010) *Chaney v Plainfield Healthcare* (care home acceded to patient's preference for a white nurse).

because they are unmarried *and* homosexual. As noted above, just because they could have been refused for either reason, the sexual orientation element does not become irrelevant.[52] But as Lady Hale reasoned, it is feasible to conclude that the criterion of 'being married', was *applied* equally to hetero- and homosexual couples (but adversely affecting homosexuals), thus resembling *indirect* discrimination; it only became direct when the hotelier had to choose between two couples in legal relationships, thus eliminating 'being married' from the analysis, leaving only sexual orientation. Lady Hale's meticulous analysis holds the line between direct and indirect discrimination. But it is rooted in a nuanced variation of the scenario. Without this, the distinction between direct and indirect discrimination would blur, if not dissolve. In truth, as these arguments demonstrate, scenarios such as *Bull v Hall* readily straddle the definitions of direct and indirect discrimination. As such, in these scenarios, the law cannot distinguish between notions of direct and indirect discrimination. There is a fuzzy border.

Further interpretations

The opinions so far discussed bring a wide range of interpretations of the same challenged practice. Some considered the case indistinguishable from *James v Eastleigh*.[53] For them, the discrimination was direct irrespective of whether the victims were in a civil partnership (and nowadays, a same sex marriage). For others, this was a critical factor, and so the hotel policy was directly discriminatory *only if* the victims were in a civil partnership.[54] (Although for one out of three of these judges, the proviso was critical.) Otherwise the policy indirectly discriminated. At the other extreme, some considered the discrimination indirect in any case.[55]

If this were not enough to illustrate the fuzzy border, the hotel policy is in fact capable of two further interpretations under the direct/indirect dichotomy. The policy, it may be recalled, was expressed thus:

> Here at Chymorvah we have few rules, but please note, that out of a deep regard for marriage we prefer to let double accommodation to heterosexual married couples only – thank you.

The criteria to qualify for a double room were 'heterosexual' and 'married', with the rider that this only applied to 'couples'. The first interpretation presumes that the word 'heterosexual' qualifies the requirement of *marriage* (and is thus an adjective rather than a noun). It thus assumes that 'heterosexual

52 See *Owen and Briggs v James* [1982] ICR 618 (CA). See further below, text to n 59.
53 [2012] EWCA Civ 83 [61] (Rafferty LJ), [40] (Sir Andrew Morritt C), [58] (Hooper LJ, agreement with both judgments).
54 [2013] UKSC 73 (Lady Hale, Lord Kerr and Lord Toulson).
55 [2013] UKSC 73 (Lord Hughes and Lord Neuberger).

marriage' is a proxy; this was the apparent basis of the judgments in both the Court of Appeal and Supreme Court, although not expressed as such. Read this way, the criteria ensure that even those in a same-sex marriage conducted in another jurisdiction would not be admitted.[56] This was the view Lady Hale and Lord Toulson and evidence that the policy directly discriminated because of sexual orientation.[57] Viewed as a proxy, these persons would be barred not because of their sexual orientation, but because their *marriage* was not a 'heterosexual' one. This interpretation differs from those above which do not take into consideration persons from the disadvantaged group who qualify. These are homosexuals in an opposite-sex marriage,[58] along with lone homosexual persons (willing to pay the premium for a double room). It now becomes arguable that these two possibilities convert, or dilute, the policy from direct, to *indirect*, discrimination, simply because these persons are not barred by the policy, if treated as a proxy case.

The second interpretation turns on the criterion, 'heterosexual', which (as noun) is facially discriminatory. As such, this prompts the question of why Lady Hale analysed the scenario of a couple not in a civil partnership as a 'proxy' case. Was it not enough for direct discrimination that the hotel very clearly will not admit *any* homosexual couples to its double rooms? In such a case, should a bar on unmarried heterosexual couples make any difference? Lady Hale's solution, in effect, was in the comparison, which did not include the circumstance of marriage/civil partnership. This disclosed that some heterosexuals (those not married) would be barred, and so the policy could only indirectly discriminate. Where the victims were in a civil partnership, a more refined comparison retained the factors of 'married/civil partnership' and 'couple'. The only difference now between the applicants and their comparator couple was sexual orientation, which disclosed direct discrimination, as a homosexual couple who were married or in a civil partnership would be barred while any heterosexual counterpart would be admitted. Such a finding tends to jar with the well-established principle from *Owen and Briggs v James*.[59] Here, it might be recalled, a job applicant was rejected for three reasons: her record of unemployment, interview demeanour, and race.[60] The Court of Appeal had little trouble in defeating the argument that she would have been rejected for either of the first two reasons; a white candidate with a poor work record or unsatisfactory interview demeanour would have been similarly rejected.[61] There was a racial factor and so this discrimination was direct.

Owen and Briggs was not cited in the *Bull v Hall* litigation, and so there was no attempt at reconciliation. The differences can be explained (if not

56 Along with those married under the more recent British Marriage (Same Sex Couples) Act 2013. For Northern Ireland, SR 2019/514.
57 [2013] UKSC 73, respectively [30] and [65].
58 Lady Hale chose to 'leave aside' such a consideration, ibid., [20].
59 [1982] ICR 618 (CA).
60 Ibid., 621.
61 Ibid., 623.

reconciled) by the respective weight afforded to the statutory elements of direct discrimination. While Lady Hale was led by the comparison, *Owen and Briggs* began and ended with the 'because' element. Had it adhered to the comparison, according to Lady Hale's reasoning, it would have concluded that the discrimination was *indirect*: to be selected, a candidate had to have a satisfactory demeanour, work record, and be white. That barred all of the disadvantaged group (those of colour), but also *some* of the advantaged group (whites with an unsatisfactory demeanour/poor work record). Thus, it could be argued, Lady Hale's comparison 'obscured any analysis of the relative weight to be given' to the protected characteristic as a cause of the refusal.[62] Further, *Owen and Briggs* suggests that there was no need for the Court of Appeal in *Bull v Hall* to start with criterion to be married, and associate that with sexual orientation (and thus with *James v Eastleigh*). There is some support for the *Owen and Briggs* interpretation from Lord Nicholls, who maintained that, in some cases a comparison cannot be made without first deciding the 'reason why' the claimant was treated so. And if this reason is based on a prohibited characteristic, then a tribunal can 'avoid arid and confusing disputes about the identification of the appropriate comparator'.[63]

In the UK, the focus is on form. Thus, anything facially discriminatory ought to amount to direct discrimination. This removes any benign motive (such as religion) from the analysis, but the logic of this is that a proxy *cannot* amount to direct discrimination: if we cannot look behind the form to appreciate a benign reason, then likewise we cannot look behind an apparently benign proxy to appreciate a discriminatory reason. So, hiding the protected characteristic behind some proxy, such as marriage, ought to reclassify the conduct as apt for an indirect discrimination analysis. This in turn jars with *James v Eastleigh* (and perhaps *JFS*), of course. And it shows, among other things, that the formula for direct discrimination can be self-contradictory. First, the comparison and 'because' elements are not always in harmony, notably here, in mixed ground cases. And second, if the formula is taken as one of form, then no proxy cases should be recognised; this second feature especially is exposed in the variety of opinions in the *Bull v Hall* litigation.

Conclusion

Although focussed on direct discrimination, the *Bull v Hall* litigation exposes (at least) five interpretations of the universal notions of both direct and indirect discrimination, with indirect discrimination generally used as the residual

62 *Woodhouse v West North West Homes Leeds Ltd* [2013] IRLR 773 (EAT) [59] (Judge Hand QC), citing *Owen and Briggs v James* in support.

63 *Shamoon v Chief Constable of the RUC* [2003] ICR 337 (HL) [7]–[12]. See also *Islington LBC v Ladele* [2009] ICR. 387 (EAT), [37]–[39] (Elias J). Lord Nicholls repeated this point in *Pearce & McDonald* [2003] ICR 937 (HL) [5]–[7]. In *Chief Constable of Norfolk Constabulary v Coffey* [2019] UKCA 1061 [76], Underhill LJ said that this was now 'very well established'.

category. This is because, of course, most litigants will present their case as direct discrimination in order to minimise, or even eliminate, any defences. Put broadly, the five categories were: (1) Marriage was a proxy for direct discrimination; (2) Marriage was a proxy for direct discrimination *only* where the victims were in a civil partnership; (3) The criteria could only amount to *indirect* discrimination because one of the criteria was 'marriage'. The two additional categories were: (4) The criteria could only amount to *indirect* discrimination because some of the disadvantaged group could be admitted; (5) One of the criteria was facially discriminatory making this a 'mixed-ground' case of direct discrimination.

The discussions above included criticisms of these interpretations. The point here is not to suggest that they were all wrong, or to assemble them into some hierarchy, but to show the difficulty of applying the direct/indirect formulas to this type of case. The variety of interpretations show that the concepts of direct and indirect discrimination are not at all clear; there is a fuzzy border. They also show the problems raised by recognising both 'form' rather than a benign reason, and yet recognising a benign form as a proxy for discrimination, which is doing away with the form theory. Within that, the fifth interpretation shows a tension within the definition of direct discrimination, notably here, the need for *comparatively* poor treatment can be at odds with the cause of the treatment, with this definition not clear on which is more important.

Further reading

I Trispiotis, '"Alternative lifestyles" and unlawful discrimination: The limits of religious freedom in Bull v Hall' [2014] EHRLR 39.

8 Age discrimination and retirement

Introduction

Age is fundamentally different from other protected characteristics, yet it is required to be analysed under the conventional direct/indirect discrimination model with a counterintuitive adaption. Its uniqueness has been recognised in both the US and Irish Supreme Courts.[1] As one commentator observed, 'ageing is a process that will potentially touch all of us and yet age is also a characteristic that can attract discrimination whether on grounds of being too young or too old'.[2] Each person's age is constantly, and inevitably, changing. Lady Hale has observed, 'age is not "binary" in nature (man or woman, black or white, gay or straight) but a continuum which changes over time'.[3] Hence,

> [Y]ounger people will eventually benefit from a provision which favours older employees, such as an incremental pay scale; but older employees will already have benefitted from a provision which favours younger people, such as a mandatory retirement age.[4]

Thus, defining an age group in some cases is rather more nebulous than defining other protected characteristics. Much depends on the nature and/or the effect of the challenged practice. For instance, groups defined as 'over fifties' or simply '21-year-olds', are easily distinguished from 'people in their forties'. However, these last two groups belong to another group of those 'under fifty'.[5]

Although this fluid group-definition may produce some fuzzy boundaries, the notable (and counterintuitive) feature of the EU and UK legislation is that

1 Respectively, *Massachusetts Board of Retirement v Murgia* 427 US 307 at 312 and 313; and the Irish Supreme Court 118/97 In the Matter of Article 26 of the Constitution of Ireland and in the matter of the Irish Equality Bill, 1996 [1997] ELR 132.
2 H Meenan, 'Age equality after the Employment Directive' (2003) 10(1) *Maastricht Journal of European and Comparative Law* 9, 13.
3 *Seldon v Clarkson, Wright & Jakes* [2012] UKSC 16 [4], citing counsel, Dinah Rose.
4 Ibid [4].
5 Equality Act 2010, Explanatory Note 37.

DOI: 10.4324/9781003187547-8

direct age discrimination carries a broad quasi-generalised justification defence. This reduced protection reflects the policymaker's opinion that age discrimination is less of a social evil than discrimination related to other protected characteristics.[6]

The unfortunate consequence is that the defence has been applied inconsistently by both EU and UK courts. The technical difficulty for the courts is that the defence, having been borrowed from the concept of indirect discrimination, was designed for defences *not* based on the protected characteristic in question. To have a chance of success then, the defence must align with the facially neutral treatment that has been challenged. But the real issue for the courts, it seems, is the variety of policy attitudes towards the variety of age discrimination claims. Cases can be brought by teenagers or those nearing the end of their working life. Understanding the boundary between lawful and unlawful direct age discrimination requires an understanding of not only the age of the claimant, but the form of the treatment, ECJ jurisprudence, and, for the UK at least, the evolving (state) policy. The fuzzy border is not only inherent in the variety of cases brought. This seems to be little coherence regarding jurisprudence. For example, both sides of the divided Canadian Supreme Court cited 'dignity' in coming to their respective decisions on compulsory retirement as age discrimination.[7] And while the ECJ is content for individual refuseniks to be washed up with collective agreements on compulsory retirement, US legislation demands individual consent.[8]

There is also the rather bizarre matter of the UK courts ignoring ECJ guidance to follow *state* policy and instead following ECJ contrary 'precedents' arising from other Member States. This is discussed further below. In general, however, with the notable exception of UK state policy, policymakers, courts, and commentators are generally agreed that least protection should be provided for older workers when challenging compulsory retirement.[9]

To understand how these ingredients can influence judicial thinking and retirement, some understanding of the history is required.

6 Helen Meenan suggests that there is a hierarchy of protected characteristics with sex and race the most important, and age potentially afforded the least protection: (n 2), p. 10, citing, Sandra Fredman, 'Equality: A new generation?' (2001) 30 *ILJ*, 145 at 145 and 151; Ursula O'Hare, 'Enhancing European equality rights: A regional framework', 8 *Maastricht Journal of European and Comparative Law* 2 (2001), 133 at 158; G Rutherglen, 'From race to age: The expanding scope of employment discrimination law' (1995) 24 *Journal of Legal Studies* 491.

7 *McKinney v University of Guelph* [1990] 3 SCR 229*McKinney v University of Guelph*, [295], [297], [303], [314], [319], [391], [393], [410], [413], [424], [431], and [447].

8 See e.g. respectively, Case C-411/05 *Palacios de la Villa [*2007] IRLR 989; Age Discrimination in Employment Act 196729 USC s 626(f)(1). See further, EEOC 29 CFR s 1625.22, at https://www.eeoc.gov/laws-guidance-0,, click 'Regulations', scroll down to 1625. Accessed 16 October 2020.

9 See G Rutherglen (n 6), 495, noting that a study of age discrimination law in the United States revealed that the chief beneficiaries were middle-class white males.

History of the defences

Age discrimination was included in the Framework Directive 2000/78/EC, and implemented in the UK in October 2006 as the Age Regulations (SI 2006/1031), which was subsequently incorporated into the Equality Act 2010 as one of the 'protected characteristics' (s 4). Retirement is most likely to take the form of prima facie direct discrimination, as most retirements are directly linked to the age of the worker. In addition to the Genuine Occupational Requirement (GOR) defence, which is standard for direct discrimination on all protected characteristics, the legislation introduced two exceptional defences for age discrimination: a default retirement age, and a dedicated objective justification defence. The Framework Directive added a third, incorporating a defence common to all discrimination law. It provided that the Directive 'shall be without prejudice to measures laid down by national law which … are necessary … for the protection of health'.[10] Thus, depending on the circumstances of the particular case, any of these could have been used to defend compulsory retirement. Given that the default retirement age has since been repealed, nowadays the defences are reduced to the dedicated objective justification defence, a GOR, and the protection of health.

The Equality Act 2010 has no specific provision for the 'protection of health'. Although it does provide something that may accommodate some health-based defences. It exempts otherwise discriminatory conduct where it is done 'pursuant to … a requirement of an enactment'.[11] Thus, otherwise discriminatory conduct may be exonerated by legislation.[12] One must presume, or at least hope, that UK courts would sanction such a defence in line with the Directive, that is apply notions of legitimacy and proportionality.

Genuine Occupational Requirement (GOR)

By section 13, the Equality Act 2010, a person directly discriminates if A treats B less favourably than A treats or would treat others and does so because of a protected characteristic. For employment, this came with the usual Genuine Occupational Requirement exception (GOR), applicable to all protected characteristics.[13] Thus, the requirement for a person of a particular age is legitimate if it is necessary for the job in question. When introducing the original Age Regulations in 2006, the Government suggested that GOR exemptions would arise in 'very few cases'. One example given was for acting jobs.[14] However, where an employer seeks to retire workers for a reason related to job performance, the GOR defence may be the most appropriate.

10 Framework Directive 2000/78/EC, art 2(5).
11 Equality Act 2010, Sch 22, para 1.
12 See e.g. Case C-341/08 *Petersen* [2010] IRLR 254 (below, text to n 138).
13 EA 2010, Sch.9, para 1.
14 'Equality and diversity: Coming of age' (July 2005), at para 4.2.8. (DTI/Pub 7851/ 3k/07/05/NP. URN 05/1171).

Default retirement age

Upon its introduction in 2006, the UK legislation carried a widespread exception for compulsory retirement, the Default Retirement Age (DRA). It lasted until 6 April 2011, when the Coalition Government phased it out as part of a policy U-turn.[15] It provided a default retirement age for those aged 65[16] or over. This was an exemption for discrimination against those most vulnerable to it, and probably those who had had the highest expectation of the new age discrimination law. It permitted employers to dismiss workers who had reached 65 or the employee's normal retirement age, so long as they followed a complex procedure.

The exemption encompassed a narrower class of workers than those normally covered by discrimination legislation, applying only to 'employees' within the meaning of the Employment Rights Act 1996,[17] those in Crown employment, and House of Lords and House of Commons staff. To obtain the exemption, an employer had to comply potentially with two procedures.[18] The first was compulsory. The employer had to give the worker at least six months' notice of the retirement. However, the notice must have been within one year of the retirement. The second procedure would arise where a worker exercised a 'right to request' not to be retired. If this case, the employer had a corresponding 'duty to consider' the request. The employer must then have informed the worker of its decision, but there were no more demands than that: the employer need not have given reasons for its decision. Hence, an employer could sit through a meeting to discuss the retirement with a closed mind and simply confirm its decision at the end.

Compatibility

This sweeping exception to the general anti-discrimination principle was challenged for compatibility with the Framework Directive 2000/78/EC. The ECJ held merely that the Default Retirement Age fell within the scope of the Directive and as compulsory retirement amounted to direct discrimination, it

15 SI 2011/1069 reg 2(2). *Phasing Out the Default Retirement Age: Government Response to Consultation* URN 11/536. This and related documents are at www.bis.gov.uk/Consultations/retirement-age?cat=closedwithresponse accessed 30 December 2020. Where the employer had notified the employee of retirement before April 6, the exception applied, but no compulsory retirements could take place after 1 October 2011.

16 Or the employee's 'normal retirement age' if higher: ERA 1996, s 98ZC. The original default retirement age was provided in the age regulations 2006 SI 2006/1031, req 30. The exemption was adopted by the Equality Act 2010, Schedule 9, para 8.

17 An individual who 'works under … a contract of employment', ERA 1996, s 230 (1).

18 Employment Equality (Age) Regulations 2006 SI 2006/1031, Sch.6 (this part of the regulations remained in force after the Equality Act 2010).

would have to be justified under Article 6(1) and its particular guidelines (discussed below).[19] Upon return to the UK, the High Court held that it was justified, *but* had it been adopted in 2009 (instead of 2006) and had the Government not brought forward a review of it to 2010,[20] it would have found that the selection of age 65 would not have been proportionate.[21] This may have encouraged the Coalition Government in its change of policy and consequent repeal of this exception.

The 'objective justification' defence

The major inroad into the direct discrimination principle is provided by a rider in section 13(2): 'If the protected characteristic is age, A does not discriminate against B if A can show A's treatment of B to be a proportionate means of achieving a legitimate aim'. This rider, borrowed from the concept of indirect discrimination, is drafted openly and, if read literally, could apply to a non-exhaustive amount of aims. It was curtailed somewhat by the ECJ and the High Court as a result of compatibility litigation.

Compatibility with the Directive

The relevant litigation began with the ECJ in *Age Concern England*.[22] The Framework Directive's exception to the direct discrimination rubric is provided in Article 6(1), which permitted direct age discrimination defences 'including' those in pursuit of social policy objectives:

> Member States may provide that differences of treatment on grounds of age shall not constitute discrimination, if, within the context of national law, they are objectively and reasonably justified by a legitimate aim, including legitimate employment policy, labour market and vocational training objectives, and if the means of achieving that aim are appropriate and necessary.

Article 6(1) continued with some rather generalised examples relating to seniority of service, or the training of younger persons, or older persons with caring responsibilities, or those approaching retirement age.

19 Case C-388/07 *R (The Incorporated Trustees of the National Council on Ageing (Age Concern England)) v Secretary of State for Business, Enterprise and Regulatory Reform* [2009] E.C.R. I-1569, paras 21–30, 63.
20 The consultation for this was launched July 29, 2010, with a view of phasing it out from April 2011: *Phasing Out the Default Retirement Age* URN 10/1047 www.bis.gov.uk/Consultations/retirement-age?cat=closedwithresponse accessed 30 December 2020.
21 [2009] ICR 260 (HC Admin) [128].
22 Case C-388/07 *Age Concern* [2009] ECR I-1569.

The inclusion of those social policy objectives was not to the exclusion of others, suggesting again this was a completely open defence. However, the ECJ took those policy objectives expressed in Article 6 as a signal that the defence was limited to social policy objectives. As a consequence, the ECJ held that the UK legislation was compatible if it fulfilled social policy aims, which were 'distinguishable from purely individual reasons particular to the employer's situation, such as cost reduction or improving competitiveness'.[23] The aims may be identified from the 'general context' of the specific section.[24]

When the case returned to the High Court (now as *Age UK*),[25] Blake J explained the position thus:

a a social policy could be identified from the 'context' of the Explanatory Notes (to the Age Regulations 2006[26]) and Government's 'elaborate' and publicly available consultation process.[27]

b any defect in the defence as originally drafted could be cured by reading it down and in light of the emerging ECJ case law.[28]

c there was a 'clear distinction' between a government's social policy and 'individual business saying it is cheaper to discriminate than to address the issues that the Directive requires to be addressed'.[29]

So, it is clear. The defence can only be used in pursuit of a legitimate aim which itself must be in pursuit of a social policy. The social policy can be detected from government publications. The consequence of this is that legitimate aims may vary from Member State to Member State, as each pursues its particular social policies. This suggests the ECJ will decide cases according to a particular Member State's social policy. This will limit the influence of ECJ jurisprudence to particular, rather than general, application.

For the UK, the documents setting out (evolving) government policy are as follows:

The 'context' documents

- *Age UK* DTI Evidence [2009] IRLR 1017 (HC Admin) [72]–[77].
- Explanatory Notes to the 2006 Age Regulations (SI 2006/1031).
- 2003 Consultation: 'Age Matters – Consultation 2003' DTI, URN 03/920.

23 Ibid., para 46.
24 Ibid., paras 49–50.
25 *Age UK* [2010] ICR 260 (HC Admin).
26 SI 2006/1031, Explanatory Notes, paras 99–101.
27 *Age UK* [2010] ICR 260 [91]–[97].
28 Ibid., [96].
29 Ibid., [93].

- 2005 Consultation: 'Equality and diversity: coming of age. Consultation on the draft Employment Equality (Age) Regulations 2006' (July 2005) (DTI, URN 05/1171).
- 2010 Consultation: *Phasing Out the Default Retirement Age* URN 10/1047.[30]
- 2011 'Employment and Skills Guidebook. Employing Older Workers' (31 May 2011 – 'Business Link').[31]
- 2011 Consultation Response URN 11/536.[32]
- 2011 Explanatory Memorandum to the 2011 Regulations.[33]
- 2011 Age Positive: Workforce Management Without a Fixed Retirement Age (March 2011).[34]
- 2011 ACAS Guidance for Employers: Working Without the Default Retirement Age (March 2011).[35]
- 2014 ACAS 'Age and the workplace' (March 2014).[36]
- 2015 Altmann Report: 'A New Vision for Older Workers: Retain, Retrain, Recruit'.
- 2017 Government Response: 'Fuller Working Lives: A Partnership Approach'.[37]
- 2018 Women and Equalities Select Committee Report, *Older people and employment*.[38]

30 www.gov.uk/government/publications/phasing-out-the-default-retirement-age accessed 30 December 2020.

31 The Government's 'Business Link' archived at https://webarchive.nationalarchives.gov.uk/20121012150847/ www.businesslink.gov.uk/bdotg/action/detail?itemId=1086470993&r.i=1084590558&r.t=CAMPAIGN&type=RESOURCES both accessed 21 September 2020. The particular Skills Guidebook is available from the author.

32 https://assets.publishing.service.gov.uk/government/uploads/system/uploads/attachment_data/file/79303/11-536-phasing-out-default-retirement-age-government-response.pdf accessed 30 December 2020.

33 The Employment Equality (Repeal of Retirement Age Provisions) Regulations 2011, SI 2011/1069.

34 https://webarchive.nationalarchives.gov.uk/20120120070913/http:/www.dwp.gov.uk/docs/workforce-mgt-without-fixed-retirement-age.pdf accessed 30 December 2020. There are 8 Age Positive documents: https://webarchive.nationalarchives.gov.uk/20120823225659/ www.businesslink.gov.uk/bdotg/action/detail?itemId=1084590558&type=CAMPAIGN&furlname=agepositive&furlparam=agepositive&ref=&domain=www.businesslink.gov.uk both accessed 30 December 2020.

35 https://webarchive.nationalarchives.gov.uk/20190603111357/www.acas.org.uk/media/pdf/d/4/Working_wtihout_the_DRA_Employer_guidance_-_MARCH_2011.pdf both accessed 30 December 2020.

36 'Age and the workplace. Putting the Equality Act 2010 and the removal of the default retirement age (DRA) 2011 into practice' (ACAS, March 2014) https://archive.acas.org.uk/media/588/Age-and-the-workplace-a-guide-for-employers-and-employees/pdf/Age-and-the-workplace-guide.pdf accessed 30 December 2020.

37 DWP, ISBN: 978-1-78425-902-0 www.gov.uk/government/publications/fuller-working-lives-a-partnership-approach accessed 30 December 2020.

38 HC 2017–2018, HC 359 https://publications.parliament.uk/pa/cm201719/cmselect/cmwomeq/359/359.pdf accessed 30 December 2020. This report

- 2019 ACAS 'Age discrimination: key points for the workplace'[39]
- 2020 'Working past State Pension age'[40]

All of these (save for ACAS and the Select Committee Report) were produced by Government, although government documents have endorsed ACAS guidance on this matter.[41] A noticeable pivot in policy came in 2010 with the incoming Coalition Government. Alongside its forthcoming abolition of the default retirement age, the publications around 2010–2011 expressly rejected many assumptions previously made under the Labour Government, such as performance declining with age, and that compulsory retirement preserved 'dignity'. From 2015, the positive mood continued, although without direct reference to Labour's approach. Current policy towards older workers has evolved to 'Retain, Retrain, Recruit', with the Government response to the Altmann Report.

The approach of the UK courts

Case law in the UK will usually revert to the Supreme Court case of *Seldon v Clarkson, Wright & Jakes*.[42] The facts of *Seldon* arose before the abolition of the default retirement age, but centred on objectively justifying the retirement of a partner (in a firm of solicitors), to whom the default retirement age did not apply. The appeal thus gave the Supreme Court the opportunity to provide the exact meaning of this defence, and thus offer guidance as to when, and when not, a retirement policy is vulnerable to claims of direct age discrimination.

Under what is now Equality Act 2010, section 13(2), for a defence of objective justification to succeed, the employer must show (1) a legitimate aim, and that the means to achieve that aim is (2) appropriate and (3) necessary.[43] The issues for the Court were:

encourages working beyond any conventional retirement age, but says nothing about compulsory retirement and *Seldon v Clarkson*.

39 ACAS (February 2019) https://archive.acas.org.uk/media/6118/Age-discrimination-key-points-for-the-workplace/pdf/Age_discrimination_key_points_for_the_workplace.pdf accessed 30 December 2020.

40 www.gov.uk/plan-retirement-income/working-past-state-pension-age. For Northern Ireland guidance, see www.nidirect.gov.uk/articles/working-past-state-pension-age#toc-1 accessed 21 October 2020.

41 See, for example, 2011 Consultation Response, re Question C, p. 11; Explanatory Memorandum to the 2011 Regulations, para 9.1.

42 [2012] UKSC 16.

43 It is arguable that the phrase deployed in section 13(2) 'proportionate means to achieve a legitimate aim' imposes a lower burden on the defendant, such as *reasonably* necessary. This is a theme of Chapter 5 'Objective justification'. The parent Framework Directive deployed the usual EU 'appropriate and necessary' rubric (Article 6(1); see above, 'Compatibility with the Directive', and text following n 22.

1 what aims are 'legitimate aims'; and
2 whether an employer has to justify its retirement policy in general, or each individual retirement;
3 in the instant, whether the means was appropriate and necessary ('proportionality').

Before discussing those questions, there are two preliminary issues to note.

First, the objective justification defence is usually associated with indirect discrimination, where the employer must advance a legitimate *business* reason for the otherwise discriminatory action. However, as noted above, for direct age discrimination, an employer's aims must coincide with state social policy rather than be based on pure business reasons.[44] The Supreme Court adopted this,[45] although Lord Hope noted that the two are likely to be 'intimately linked'.[46] The aim also had to be legitimate 'in the particular circumstances of the employment concerned'.[47]

Second, although the employer's policy must accord with state social policy, there was no need for the employer to have the social policy in mind at the time the policy was adopted. It was enough, if after the event, the policy could be shown to *coincide* with state social policy.[48] The Supreme Court added weight to this opinion by citing ECJ authority from the normally highly protected area of sex discrimination.[49] This treats the word 'objective' with a good deal of respect. After all, everything about indirect discrimination is objective. This law is concerned with the *effect* of apparently neutral treatment, not its purpose. Therefore, the defence should not be concerned with the defendant's (subjective) motive or intention at the time of the challenged act.[50] This is consistent with the wording of the defences in the Framework Directive and the Equality Act 2010 (both set out above).

On the other hand, those legislative provisions do not *mandate* a purely objective approach. It could just as easily be said that the reasons given at the time the challenged practice was implemented had to be justified by objective standards. There is also authority edging towards this view. In a more recent case, on discrimination against part-time workers, the Supreme Court asserted:

> [I]n this as in any other human rights context, this court is likely to treat with greater respect a justification for a policy which was carefully thought

44 Framework Directive 2000/78/EC, Article 6(1), Case C-388/07 *Age Concern England* [2009] ECR I-1569 paras 46 and 49–50, and *Age UK* [2009] IRLR 1017 (HC Admin) [93].
45 *Seldon v Clarkson* [2012] UKSC 16 [28] (Lady Hale) [73] (Lord Hope).
46 Ibid., [73].
47 Ibid., [61] (Lady Hale).
48 Ibid., [59]–[60] (Lady Hale).
49 Joined Cases C-4/02 if and C-5/02 *Schönheit v Stadt Frankfurt am Main* [2004] IRLR 983, at para 12.
50 See Michael Rubenstein, 'Highlights' [2004] IRLR December.

> through by reference to the relevant principles at the time when it was adopted … it is difficult for the [employer] … to justify the proportionality of the means chosen to carry out their aims if they did not conduct the exercise of examining the alternatives or gather the necessary evidence to inform the choice at that time.[51]

This case involved perhaps the lesser-protected area of part-time work, and in particular part-time judges, who may elicit less sympathy. One would presume from this that the Court would take an equally strict view in areas apparently further up the hierarchy, such as race or sex. To add to the uncertainty, there is even an inconsistency within this statement. It begins with the relative term 'greater' respect, and concludes in absolute terms by suggesting justification is impossible without consideration of the alternatives at the time. The best that can be made of this is that the retrospective principle, applied in *Seldon*, should apply to other age discrimination cases, whatever was said in a case on discrimination against part-time workers. It may be argued, of course, that retrospective reasons should be given 'less' respect.

Moreover, this retrospective principle more clearly conflicts with a fundamental principle of Unfair Dismissal, which is that the facts discovered after the dismissal are irrelevant to liability. At first sight, it may seem that the two regimes are unconnected. But that is not always entirely so. It might be that an employer justifies the age-discriminatory element of a dismissal, but that does not in itself prevent the person bringing a parallel claim of unfair dismissal. Given that the employer in such a case has justified *direct* discrimination, the reason for the dismissal is 'age', which can be defended under the potentially fair reason of Some Other Substantial Reason.[52] (It cannot be explained as a matter of Capability, Qualifications, Conduct, Redundancy, or Legal Prohibition, the other potentially fair reasons provided by the Unfair Dismissal regime.[53]) Indeed, this was the Government view when repealing the default retirement age.[54]

In such circumstances an employer relying on the advice from the Supreme Court in *Seldon,* and not bothering to consider any social policy dimension when dismissing someone for retirement, may well find itself liable for unfair dismissal precisely for that reason. The anomaly would be confined to *liability*, because compensation could be reduced to nil in circumstances where the dismissal would have occurred in any case.[55] If the employer has defended successfully the age discrimination claim on the social policy basis, then that same

51 *O'Brien v Ministry of Justice* [2013] UKSC 6 [48] (Lady Hale and Lord Hope for the Court). The case concerned the Part-time Workers (Prevention of Less Favourable Treatment) Regulations 2000, SI 2000/1551.

52 Employment Rights Act 1996, s 98(1)(b).

53 Ibid., s 98(2).

54 2011 Consultation Response (n 32), p. 9; ACAS Guidance (n 35), p. 5.

55 *Devis v Atkins* [1977] ICR 662 (HL). This applies to discrimination claims as well: *Chagger v Abbey National* [2010] IRLR 47 (CA) [55]–[60].

defence should operate to reduce accordingly the compensation for unfair dismissal. And so, this need not be a complete disaster for the employer, but it is an anomaly that requires attention.

What aims are 'legitimate aims'?

A notable feature of Lady Hale's leading judgment in *Seldon* was her reference to ECJ caselaw to identify legitimate aims when objectively justifying direct age discrimination. This was notable because it was done without any reference whatsoever to the sometimes-contradictory UK social policy. This is discussed further below, as and when the issue arises. Nevertheless, it does mean that we should be aware of ECJ jurisprudence on the matter. Lady Hale assembled the following list of legitimate aims:

i promoting access to employment for younger people (Case C-411/05 *Palacios de la Villa* [2007] IRLR 989, Case C-88/08 *Hütter* [2009] All ER (EC) 1129, Case C-555/07 *Kucukdevici v Swedex GmbH* [2010] 2 CMLR 33);

ii the efficient planning of the departure and recruitment of staff (Case C-159/10 *Fuchs v Land Hessen*, [2011] Pens LR 335);

iii sharing out employment opportunities fairly between the generations (Case C-341/08 *Petersen* [2010] IRLR 254, Case C-45/09 *Rosenbladt* [2011] 1 CMLR 32, *Fuchs* (ibid.));

iv ensuring a mix of generations of staff so as to promote the exchange of experience and new ideas (Joined Cases C-250/09 & C-268/09 *Georgiev* [2011] 2 CMLR 7, *Fuchs* (ibid.));

v rewarding experience (*Hütter*, Joined Cases C-297/10 & C-298/10 *Hennigs* [2012] 1 CMLR 18);

vi cushioning the blow for long serving employees who may find it hard to find new employment if dismissed (C-499/08 *Ingeniørforeningen i Danmark*) [2011] 1 CMLR 1140[56];

vii facilitating the participation of older workers in the workforce (*Fuchs* (ibid.), see also Case C-144/04 *Mangold v Helm*, [2006] 1 CMLR 1132);

viii avoiding the need to dismiss employees on the ground that they are no longer capable of doing the job which may be humiliating for the employee concerned (*Rosenbladt*, ibid.); or

ix avoiding disputes about the employee's fitness for work over a certain age (*Fuchs*, ibid.).[57]

56 At paras 29–31. Although in this case, involving severance payments for experienced workers, those (over 59) with a pension entitlement were excluded. So, the exclusion discriminated against older workers. It was disproportionate because the exclusion related to entitlement rather than receipt.

57 [2012] UKSC 16 [50] (4).

These are somewhat overlapping, with the first three accommodating 'workforce planning' and in particular (i) and (ii) aimed at 'job-blocking', or 'intergenerational fairness'. The final two relate to what has become known as 'dignity'. Aim (iv) can cut both ways depending on the balance required between old and young. Aims (v) and (vi) relate to more favourable treatment of older workers, although as will be seen below the court seem to take a much stricter attitude here.

Workforce planning

In general, workforce planning is a legitimate aim. The aim itself can be subdivided into *attrition profile, job-blocking,* and *encouraging pension provision.*

On the attrition profile, the Explanatory Notes to the Age Regulations 2006 explained that 'for employers, being able to rely on a set retirement age allows the recruitment, training and development of employees, and the planning of wage structures and occupational pensions, against a known attrition profile'.[58] This form of workforce planning, otherwise described as 'efficient planning of the departure and recruitment of staff',[59] was approved by the High Court in the *Age UK* case.[60] It was not addressed in *Seldon.* More recent documentation does not suggest a change of government policy on this form of workforce planning.

However, the matter of *job-blocking* was addressed in *Seldon.* Three aims were cited by the firm. The first was 'ensuring associates were given the opportunity of partnership after a reasonable period'. The second was 'facilitating the planning of the partnership and workforce across individual departments by having a realistic long-term expectation as to when vacancies will arise'.[61] These closely connected aims, labelled euphemistically as *intergenerational fairness,* or indelicately as *dead man's shoes,* were held by the Court of Appeal to coincide with the social policy that employers 'should have a retirement age providing great the likelihood of employment for young persons and reasonable prospects of promotion'.[62] The apparent source of this social policy was the defence itself, along with the default retirement age (in force at the time the facts arose).[63] This seems a little relaxed when the default retirement age expressly did not apply to partners, such as Mr Seldon, and the Court of Appeal cited no documents expressly in support of its view.

Nevertheless, the Supreme Court agreed, with Lady Hale calling on the ECJ authority confirming that the aims were not purely business aims, 'both of which are directly related to the legitimate social policy aim of sharing out professional employment opportunities fairly between the generations'.[64]

58 Age Regulations 2006, Explanatory Notes (100).
59 Case C-159/10 *Fuchs v Land Hessen* [2011] Pens LR 335, at para 47.
60 [2009] IRLR 1017 (HC Admin) [72].
61 The third aim was 'dignity', which is discussed below.
62 [2010] EWCA Civ 899 (CA) [this 18]. See also [20]–[22].
63 31 December 2006.
64 [2012] UKSC 16 [67], citing Case C-159/10 *Fuchs v Land Hessen* [2011] Pens LR 335, at para 60, see also para 47.

This may have been consistent with government policy (none was cited) at the time the facts arose, but not at the time the appeal was heard (January 2012). A year earlier, the Coalition Government pivoted to the opposite view:

> Older workers do not tend to block opportunities for younger workers. Evidence indicates that there was no positive effect on youth employment from measures which allowed older workers to retire early.[65]

This makes it clear that job-blocking may no longer be considered a public policy aim, and that this aspect of *Seldon* should no longer be good law.

That said, in substance, there may be little difference between the 'job-blocking' and 'attrition profile' policies. On this basis, it could be that the lawfulness of identical retirement practices depends on the label they are given. Employers would be advised to emphasize that the purpose of any retirement policy relates to matters such as recruitment, training, employee-development, wage structures, and occupational pensions, rather the than job and promotion prospects for younger people.

But this may not be relevant. Even though the government policy has changed, the law has not. In *Seldon,* Lady Hale cited Blake's J ruling that a defence coincide with the social policy of the state. The oddity was that she then omitted to cite any UK social policy, and instead cited ECJ authority concerning the social policies of Germany,[66] Spain,[67] Sweden[68] and Austria.[69] That could be overlooked on the basis that the facts arose before the date of the policy change, but it was odd that no reference at all was made to the change of policy. This is especially so in the Supreme Court, the forum for cases of public importance and guidance on the law for all interested parties. Instead, it provided a misleading picture for tribunals. It is not surprising then, that since *Seldon,* tribunals automatically have adopted the mantra that inter-generational fairness is a legitimate aim.[70] This automatic assumption has even

65 Age Positive: Workforce Management Without a Fixed Retirement Age (March 2011), p. 5; or 2011 Consultation Response, p. 2. Respectively https://webarchive.nationalarchives.gov.uk/20120120070913/http:/www.dwp.gov.uk/docs/workforce-mgt-without-fixed-retirement-age.pdfhttps://assets.publishing.service.gov.uk/government/uploads/system/uploads/attachment_data/file/79303/11-536-phasing-out-default-retirement-age-government-response.pdf both accessed 30 December 2020.

66 [2012] UKSC 16 [55]–[56], citing Case C-159/10 *Fuchs v Land Hessen* [2011] Pens LR 335 [60], see also [47].

67 Ibid., [33] citing Case C-411/05 *Palacios de la Villa [*2007] IRLR 989.

68 Ibid., [38] citing Case C-555/07 *Kucukdevici v Swedex GmbH* [2010] 2 CMLR 33.

69 Ibid., [35] citing, Case C-88/08 *Hütter* [2009] All ER (EC) 1129.

70 See e.g. *Ewart v Chancellor, Master and Scholars of the University of Oxford* [2019] 12 WLUK 565 20 Dec 2019 (ET) [235]; *National Union of Rail, Maritime and Transport Workers (RMT) v Lloyd* [2019] 3 WLUK 778 15 Mar 2019 (EAT) [50]; *Lord Chancellor and Secretary of State for Justice v McCloud* [2018] 3 All E.R. 208 29 Jan 2018 (EAT); *Warren v Royal Bank of Scotland* [2015] 5 WLUK 208 11 May 2015 (ET) [108]; *Dziubak v LX Engineering (North) Ltd* [2015] 3 WLUK 847 27 Mar

been made by the Court of Appeal. In *Air Products plc v Cockram*,[71] a challenged retirement age was adopted to align a payment scheme with a new pension plan. With no more reasoning than simply citing *Seldon*, the Court of Appeal held that this could be 'directly related' to the social policy of intergenerational fairness.[72]

In just one reported case, has a tribunal considered and referred to UK government social policy when ruling on the objective justification defence to age discrimination. This was the well-publicised incremental raising of the state retirement age, and thus undermined the employer's retirement age of 65.[73] The tribunal observed that an employer's social policy that conflicted with state social policy was not a legitimate aim.[74] It was ironic that none of this prevented the EAT from assuming that intergenerational fairness *was* a legitimate aim.[75]

The actual rationes decidendi *Seldon* on this issue are: a) legitimate aims must coincide with current UK social policy, and b) at the time the facts arose (31 December 2006) that policy favoured intergenerational fairness as a legitimate aim. Thus, it is possible for tribunals to sidestep the apparent guidance from *Seldon*.

Encouraging pension provision

With the DLA in place, the Government of the day saw this as a further aspect of workforce planning, and with it, a legitimate aim. This was because a definite retirement date would

> encourage employees to save now and make provision for their retirement, and avoid them putting off career and pension planning on the assumption that they will be able to continue working indefinitely.[76]

This was going to be hard to maintain with the repeal of the DLA. In line with the repeal Government policy pivoted. The emphasis shifted from a state-

2015 (ET) [5.8]; *John v Ministry of Justice* [2014] 12 WLUK 557 16 Dec 2014 (ET) [37] (retired/dismissed 7 December 2011); *White v Ministry of Justice* [2014] 11 WLUK 615 20 Nov 2014 (ET) [4] (6 December 2012); *de Castro Cerqueira v Embassy of Brazil* [2014] 11 WLUK 192 7 Nov 2014 (ET) [35] 31 January 2012; *Sharma v Lee (t/a TMM)* [2014] 6 WLUK 706 24 Jun 2014 (ET) [11.12] (30 April 2013); *Mathias v CRO Ports Sutton Bridge Ltd* [2014] 5 WLUK 948 28 May 2014 (ET) [8] (5 March 2012).

71 [2018] EWCA 346.

72 Ibid., [33].

73 *The National Union of Rail, Maritime and Transport Workers (RMT) v Lloyd* [2019] 3 WLUK 778 15 Mar 2019 (EAT).

74 Ibid., [47].

75 Ibid., [50].

76 Explanatory Notes 2006, para 100; see also DTI evidence, *Age UK* [2010] ICR 260 at [72].

imposed ceiling to individual choice and responsibility. For example, the 2010 Guidance noted that:

> The State Pension age is not a 'retirement age' – older workers can carry on working past their State Pension age, and continue to work while claiming their State Pension. Alternatively, they can defer claiming their State Pension for at least a year in return for either an enhanced pension, or a lump sum when they do decide to claim.[77]

A similar fluidity is envisaged for occupational pensions. Where they do not already cater for members working beyond the scheme's normal retirement age, employers are encouraged to review the terms with the scheme's managers.[78] The 2010 Guidebook observed that workers are notified by the state and/or workplace pension scheme as they approach the state/scheme retirement age; 'These notifications help to prompt older workers to consider their options for retirement or working on'.[79] ACAS guidance from 2014 provides examples of discussions between the employee and employer regarding the employee's retirement age and pension.[80]

Current Government advice (2020) takes the same line with an emphasis individual decision-making over generalised compulsory retirement. On its webpage, 'Working past State Pension age',[81] it advises that, 'There is no official retirement age and you usually have the right to work as long as you want to'. ACAS guidance published in 2019 makes much the same point under a section entitled 'The employees right to decide when to retire',[82] while its 2014 guidance gives an example of an employee wanting to remain working after his pension is due 'because he needs the money'.[83]

It appears that government policy has moved on from 'planning for a definite retirement date' to 'considering your options after a nominal retirement date'. Workers are now treated responsible enough to consider and plan their

77 2010 Employment and Skills Guidebook, p. 7.

78 Ibid.

79 2010 Employment and Skills Guidebook, p. 7. See also the Employment Equality (Repeal of Retirement Age Provisions) Regulations 2011, SI 2011/1069, para 7.1; and the Government 'Business Link' archived at https://webarchive.nationalarchives.gov.uk/20121012150847/www.businesslink.gov.uk/bdotg/action/detail?itemId=1086470993&r.i=1084590558&r.t=CAMPAIGN&type=RESOURCES both accessed 21 September 2020.

80 Ibid., pp. 24 and 25.

81 www.gov.uk/plan-retirement-income/working-past-state-pension-age. For even more emphasis see the Northern Ireland guidance www.nidirect.gov.uk/articles/working-past-state-pension-age#toc-1 accessed 21 October 2020.

82 ACAS, 'Age discrimination: key points for the workplace' (February 2019), p. 17 https://archive.acas.org.uk/media/6118/Age-discrimination-key-points-for-the-workplace/pdf/Age_discrimination_key_points_for_the_workplace.pdf accessed 30 December 2020.

83 ACAS 'Age and the workplace' (n 36), p. 26.

future without regulatory encouragement. This dilutes, if not extinguishes, any social policy associated with encouraging pension provision. This policy – reaffirmed after ten years – has been in place a good deal longer than the previous one. This should not disturb the legitimate aim of employers planning for pension provision against a known attrition profile (see above).

Stability of occupational pension

Where the employer's pension scheme is less amenable to flexible retirement dates, it might be that an individual employer wishes to 'preserve its stability' with a compulsory retirement age. Blake J recognised this as a social policy aim in *Age UK*.[84] This confirmed the view of the Government when contemplating the first Age Regulations. In a Written Statement to Parliament, the Government underpinned its policy thus:

> Furthermore … if all employers only had the option of individually justified retirement ages at the time the legislation was introduced, this could risk adverse consequences for occupational pension schemes and other work related benefits. Some employers would instead simply reduce or remove benefits they offer to employees to offset the increase in costs.[85]

This was all the defence of the default retirement age, but similar logic would seem to apply to an employer's compulsory retirement policy. Thus, there seems no reason to think that this has changed (There have been no subsequent cases nor government policy announcements since.[86]) Should 'pension stability' be pleaded as a legitimate aim in a retirement case, assuming that it is genuine the major issue is likely to be proportionality. See the Canadian case *McKinney v University of Guelph*, discussed below.[87]

'Dignity'

Is it more dignified for older workers to be tested for their performance or quietly retired? The law seems uncertain here. In *Age UK*, the Government presented 'dignity' as a social policy aim.[88] In January 2011, this view was reversed by the Coalition Government. The case of *Seldon* was squeezed somewhat between the two, with the facts arising in 2006 and the hearing in

84 *Age UK* [2010] ICR 260, Evidence [72], para 5, [90].

85 Hansard Written Ministerial Statements for 14 Dec 2004 (pt 4), Columns 127WS-130WS; or Lords Hansard Text for 14 Dec 2004 (241214–41), Columns WS78-WS81, Column 128WS.

86 For cases where the Government could not produce a legitimate aim for pension changes that discriminated against younger workers, see, *Lord Chancellor v McCloud* and *Secretary of State for the Home Department v Sargeant* [2019] ICR 1489 (CA).

87 [1990] 3 SCR 229. See below, text to n 192.

88 *Age UK* [2010] ICR 260, Evidence [71] and [74].

the Supreme Court beginning in January 2012, obliging the Court to decide the case on the old policy, but to offer guidance for tribunals and other interested parties on the new policy. It managed the first task, but completely failed the second, leaving the impression that the policy was a legitimate aim.

In *Seldon,* the 'dignity' aim was couched in these terms: 'limiting the need to expel partners by way of performance management, thus contributing to the congenial and supportive culture in the firm'.[89] The Court of Appeal accepted this wholesale, with Waller LJ reasoning that the policy was, 'intended to produce a happy work place'. He endorsed the policy thus: '[M]y experience would tell me that it is a justification for having a cut-off age that people will be allowed to retire with dignity'.[90] This was a surprisingly relaxed opinion, being based on the judge's own 'experience', rather than the legislative 'context' and ample documents available. One is reminded here of an observation made by Lady Hale just a few months previously. Dissenting in an employment case, she suggested that the majority were misled by their experience:

> But I should perhaps declare an interest, as the only member of this court to have spent a substantial proportion of her working life as an employee rather than as a self-employed barrister or tenured office holder.[91]

This could just have readily been a sideswipe at Waller's LJ reasoning. Nevertheless, in *Seldon*, Lady Hale led a unanimous Supreme Court accepting the 'dignity' aim, albeit with some discomfort. She noted the underlying assumptions which 'look suspiciously like stereotyping'. She likened it to an example of assumptions about women's physical strength. But Lady Hale considered herself bound by the 'Luxembourg court'.[92] Of course, this was not quite accurate. She was bound by the Luxembourg court to follow her own (UK) state social policy. In addition, the Luxembourg court has confirmed that the aim must pursue the public interest, and not merely an individual business interest.[93] On its face, this 'dignity' justification serves no purpose beyond the private relationship between employer and employee. In fact, there was evidence before the Court that performance did not decline until at least the age of 70 and that 'interpersonal skills' improved with age, suggesting that

89 [2012] UKSC 16, [9].

90 [2010] EWCA Civ 899 [22]–[24].

91 *Edwards v Chesterfield Royal Hospital NHS Foundation Trust, Botham v Ministry of Defence* [2012] 2 AC 22 (SC) [110] (14 December 2011) Seldon was decided 25 April 2012.

92 [2012] UKSC 16 [57]–[58]. At [67] Lady Hale cited Case C-45/09 *Rosenbladt v Ollerking Gebaudereinigungsges.mbH* [2011] 1 CMLR 32 (see para 43) and Cases C-159/10 and C-160/10 *Fuchs v Land Hessen* [2011] 3 CMLR 1299, para 47. See also, Case C-141/11 *Hörnfeldt v Meddelande* [2012] 3 C.M.L.R. 37, para 48 (decided after *Seldon*).

93 Framework Directive 2000/78/EC, Article 6(1), Case C-388/07 *Age Concern England* [2009] ECR I-1569 paras 46 and 49–50, and *Age UK* [2009] IRLR 1017 (HC Admin) [93].

collegiality could be improved by retaining older partners. This evidence was ignored.[94]

If it is to be justified as a social policy aim, a domestic court must be presented with evidence that it is a public interest policy. Indeed, the cases cited by Lady Hale were defended by the (German) state, the most authentic witness of social policy. No such evidence was apparent in *Seldon*. Indeed, had any evidence been presented, it would have revealed a U-turn in UK social policy.

As with the aim of intergenerational fairness, the new evidence would not have applied in Mr Seldon's case, the facts of which predated the change of policy. But the policy was first published in January 2011, some 12 months before the case was heard and 15 months before this judgment was handed down.[95] The change of direction announced by the Coalition Government included a rejection of the notion that performance management was somehow undignified. In fact, the policy now was quite the opposite. Employers should, 'Encourage an open culture of active performance management, formal or informal, throughout workers' careers to avoid unexpected announcements, confrontations or "loss of dignity"'.[96] Indeed, an ACAS guide on the new policy suggested that a failure to discuss poor performance with an older worker because this may seem undignified, may well be discriminatory.[97] Needless to say, subsequent tribunals ruling on cases arising after the change in policy have unthinkingly adopted 'dignity' as a legitimate aim.[98]

The current policy, 'Retain, Retrain, Recruit', obviously is consistent with this, notably the recommended retention and retraining, suggesting that instead of favouring retirement over performance management, employers should do quite the opposite. *Re*training without knowledge of a person's skills and performance could be a difficult, if not pointless and wasteful, task.[99] 'Dignity' is not expressed in the 'Retain, Retrain, Recruit' policy, so it cannot be concluded for certain that this policy endorses the Coalition Government's rejection of it. But what can be said is that 'dignity' cannot be allowed to get in the

94 Pamela Meadows 'Retirement Ages in the UK: A Review of the Literature' (Employment Relations Research Series No. 18, DTI, London, June 2003). For a summary see *Seldon v Clarkson (No 2)* 2013 WL 10924072 (ET, 28 May 2013) [46]–[47].

95 Respectively, 17–18 January 2012 and 25 April 2012.

96 2011 Age Positive: Workforce Management Without a Fixed Retirement Age (March 2011), p. 12.

97 'Age and the workplace (n 36). Putting the Equality Act 2010 and the removal of the default retirement age (DRA) 2011 into practice' (ACAS, March 2014), p. 26.

98 See, e.g. *Ewart v Chancellor, Master and Scholars of the University of Oxford* [2019] 12 WLUK 565 20 Dec 2019 (ET) [251]; *Warren v Royal Bank of Scotland* [2015] 5 WLUK 208 11 May 2015 (ET) [108]; *Dziubak v LX Engineering (North) Ltd* [2015] 3 WLUK 847 27 Mar 2015 (ET) [5.8]; *Hanley v Thomas Sagar Insurances* [2015] 7 WLUK 1031 31 Jul 2015; *Sharma v Lee (t/a TMM)* [2014] 6 WLUK 706 24 Jun 2014 (ET) [37] (30 April 2013).

99 'Fuller Working Lives: A Partnership Approach' (DWP 2017), esp pp. 20–22 and Annex 1, paras 5 and 10 (pp. 46–47).

way of retaining and retraining employees, and so as far as it can relate to performance management it cannot be a legitimate aim.

As a legitimate aim, 'dignity' is the most uncertain. When tied to performance management (as it usually is) and expressed social policy aim in some Member States, but not so in the UK. Whether expressed as a social policy or not it still has to satisfy the test of being in the public interest, rather than solely an individual interest of an employer. The uncertainty is compounded by the Supreme Court's omission to recognise the changing Government policy and offer appropriate guidance.

Reducing or redistributing unemployment

In *Palacios de la Villa,*[100] the ECJ accepted a goal of 'checking unemployment' as a legitimate basis for Spanish legislation permitting compulsory retirement to be negotiated into collective agreements.[101] Again, this shows a more relaxed judicial approach to age discrimination, or in particular towards older persons and retirement. 'Checking unemployment' is a triumph of form over substance; in fact, such policies merely redistribute it, from the young to the old. Redefining older unemployed people as 'retired' cannot change this. This criticism was neutered by the ECJ in *Petersen*, where the second aim cited for retiring dentists at 68 was 'the distribution of employment opportunities among the generations'.[102] The Court cited *Palacios de la Villa*, and held: 'Similarly, a measure intended to promote the access of young people to the profession of dentist in the panel system may be regarded as an employment policy measure'.[103]

Similarly, in *Rosenbladt*, the ECJ observed:

> The termination of the employment contracts of those [aged 65] directly benefits young workers by making it easier for them to find work, which is otherwise difficult at a time of chronic unemployment.[104]

Thus, it seems, 'redistributing employment' is a legitimate aim under the Framework Directive. However, it does not appear in any of the Consultation documents nor Explanatory Notes. Moreover, the 2011 Consultation Response expressed quite the opposite stance. In its forward, the Government declared:

100 Case C-411/05 *Palacios de la Villa* [2007] IRLR 989.
101 Ibid., at para 52.
102 Case C-341/08 *Petersen* [2010] IRLR 254, at para 38.
103 ibid at para 68. See also Case C-159/10 *Fuchs v Land Hessen*, [2011] Pens LR 335, paragraphs 47 and 60, observing that a balanced workforce 'helps to ensure that the experience of older staff is passed on to younger colleagues and that younger staff share recently acquired knowledge' (para 48).
104 Case C-45/09 *Rosenbladt* [2011] 1 CMLR 32, at para 43.

> Working longer is good for the economy, for society and for individuals. Evidence shows that keeping more people in work helps the economy grow.... We want employers to draw their workforces from the widest possible talent pool.... We believe strongly in the freedom of people to work on for as long as they want and are able to.

So, for reasons of economic growth and individual justice, the Coalition Government set itself dead against using retirement as a means to reduce unemployment or favouring employment of the young over the old. As noted above,[105] these aims fall under a broader umbrella term of 'intergenerational fairness', which having been repeated in *Seldon* was applied in UK tribunals.

This stance hints at a technical problem for the aim 'redistributing employment'. Favouring young persons over the old amounts to positive action, which normally requires a specific legislative sanction. Further, the concept of positive action has its roots in redressing historic disadvantage. The principal purpose of anti-age discrimination law is to address entrenched discrimination against the elderly. This aim does quite the opposite. It is akin to sanctioning positive action in favour of men, or whites. The Canadian Supreme Court has observed that such a redistributive aim

> should not be accorded much weight. If the values and principles essential to a free and democratic society include, according to *Oakes*, 'respect for the inherent dignity of the human person' and 'commitment to social justice and equality', then the objective of forcibly retiring older workers in order to make way for younger workers is in itself discriminatory since it assumes that the continued employment of some individuals is less important to those individuals, and of less value to society at large, than is the employment of other individuals, solely on the basis of age.[106]

Thus, the notion of redistributing unemployment faces two problems. First, as un-authorised positive discrimination it can amount to direct discrimination. Second, since 2011, it forms no part of UK state social policy.

Costs?

There could be many savings that come with an employer's compulsory retirement age. A rather obvious move by some employers, especially in hard times, is to retire 'expensive' older workers and replace them with younger, presumably cheaper, ones. This could arise where, say, the employer historically has rewarded long-service with an incremental pay scale (automatically

105 See p. 161, 'Workforce planning'.

106 *McKinney v University of Guelph* [1990] 3 SCR 229 (La Forest J, for the majority, giving more weight to pension stability and free collective bargaining), pp.302–303, citing *R v Oakes* [1986] SCR 103 [64].

promoting workers up a pay scale each year). Rather than upset this arrangement openly, an employer may preserve or manoeuvre its retirement policy to offset the expense.

Bearing in mind what was said in the *Age Concern* litigation, that an individual-business cost reduction or increase in competitiveness were not social policy aims,[107] it would appear that costs alone would not qualify as a legitimate aim. This occurred more general edicts on indirect discrimination law given by the ECJ. For example, in *De Weerd*, a case concerning indirect sex discrimination in social security the Court said,

> Although budgetary considerations may influence a member state's choice of social policy and affect the nature or scope of the social protection measures it wishes to adopt, they cannot in themselves constitute the aim pursued by that policy and cannot, therefore, justify discrimination.[108]

Such an absolutist edict has left the English Judiciary uncomfortable. There have been two distinctive attempts to mitigate its effect. A 'costs-plus principle', and second, what might be crudely labelled a 'disproportionate costs principle'.

In the context of justify discrimination, the costs-plus notion has its roots in the EAT case *Cross v* BA.[109] In *Redcar v Bainbridge*,[110] an equal pay case, Elias J said that 'an employer cannot defeat the right to equality by pointing to financial burdens alone, but he can pray the financial burdens in aid as some support for a decision which is objectively justified on other grounds'.[111] Similarly, in *Pulham v Barking & Dagenham LB*,[112] (a case of direct age discrimination) the EAT suggested that an 'exhausted' budget could be *a* factor (it would be 'unexceptional') in the proportionality analysis, but not, in itself, a reason to justify age discrimination, because the employer was responsible for allocating the budget in the first place.[113]

This in turn has been criticised elsewhere. In *O'Brien v Ministry of Justice*, the Supreme Court observed that 'it was a subtle point and which is not without difficulty'.[114] In *Woodcock v Cumbria Primary Care Trust*,[115] the EAT (Underhill

107 Case C-388/07, [2009] ECR I-1569, paras 46 and 49–50; *Age UK* [2010] ICR 260 [93]. See further above, text to n 23. See also *O'Brien v Ministry of Justice* [2013] UKSC 6 [69] (Lady Hale and Lord Hope for the Court).

108 Case C- 343/92 *De Weerd v Bestuur van de Bedrijfsvereniging voor de Gezondheit, Geestelijke en Maatschappelijke Belangen* [1994] ECR I-571 at para 35. See also, Case C-226/98 *Jorgensen v Foreningen af Speciallaeger* [2000] ECR I-2447, at para 42.

109 [2005] IRLR 423 (EAT).

110 [2008] ICR 249 (EAT).

111 Ibid., [92] citing *Cross v BA* [2005] IRLR 423 (EAT).

112 [2010] IRLR 184.

113 Ibid., [42]–[44] (Underhill J).

114 [2013] UKSC 6 [63] (Lady Hale and Lord Hope for the Court).

115 [2011] ICR 143 (EAT), affirmed [2012] ICR 1126 (CA). In *O'Brien v Ministry of Justice* [2013] UKSC 6 [70], the Supreme Court declined to express an opinion on *Woodcock*.

J) fired more precise ammunition at the suggestion. First, it was 'hard to see the principled basis for the rule' that required an 'admixture of some other element'. It would lead to 'artificial game-playing' by parties and tribunals to 'find the other factor', which itself would produce 'arbitrary and complicated reasoning', such as deciding where the cost stops and other factors start.[116]

These are valid points, but they were undermined somewhat by the reasoning and decision in the case itself. *Woodcock* concerned again a claim of direct age discrimination. Here, a chief executive was made redundant for two reasons:

1 to get him off the payroll before he reached 50, when he would have been entitled to early retirement, costing at least £500,000; and
2 he was redundant (and been kept on for one year doing very little).

It was held that the redundancy alone validated the dismissal. It is difficult to see how this apparently causative approach differs in substance from the 'costs-plus principle'. The case holds that where a determining reason (e.g. redundancy) exists, the accompanying reason of cost-savings will not undermine the legitimate aim. Indeed, when upholding the decision, the Court of Appeal said, 'it was obviously legitimate for the trust to have that [costs-saving] consideration in mind'.[117] This merely means that the existence of another reason legitimises cost savings as an aim. This carries the danger of allowing defendants to make discriminatory decisions purely on cost, and yet be exonerated where another reason conveniently exists. Identifying another reason for treatment complained of amounts to identifying two causes (costs plus one other). The only difference is that the causative approach labels just one of the reasons as a legitimate aim, while the costs-plus approach labels two (or more) of them as legitimate aims.

This approach also carries Underhill's J second and third objections. There could be just as many problems distinguishing one cause from another as there would be deciding where the cost stops and the other factors start, another of Underhill's J objections.

It would also lead to 'artificial game-playing'. For example, a subsidiary (non-costs) reason could be promoted and thus presented as the principal (and only) one, rendering it more palatable for a tribunal to uphold the justification. Indeed, the Court of Appeal made a point of this:

> The dismissal notice … was not served with the aim, pure and simple, of dismissing the claimant before his 49th birthday in order to save the trust the expense it would incur if was still in its employ at 50. It was served, and genuinely served, with the aim of giving effect to the trust's genuine decision to terminate his employment on the grounds of his redundancy.[118]

116 Ibid., [32].
117 [2012] ICR 1126 (CA) [67]–[68] (Rimer LJ, for the court).
118 Ibid., [67].

This is a gross misrepresentation of the case. The age discrimination claim does not relate to the redundancy per se. Mr Woodcock was not challenging the decision to dismiss him (indeed, he was claiming for an early retirement payment), he was challenging its timing, which was calculated to be for the timing of the dismissal was to save costs. A problem here is that in straining to find a non-costs aim, the judgment lost sight of the requirement that the legitimate aim must be one to fulfil a social policy, a requirement seemingly forgotten.

More generally, the Court of Appeal's factual analysis fuels a suspicion that an employer presenting a subsidiary reason as the primary one is more likely to have it recognised as *the* cause, and therefore the legitimate aim. This leaves the approach vulnerable to the question of deciding when a cause was the primary cause. It is well established that quite often there are many reasons behind the treatment complained of. For example, in *Owen v Briggs and James*,[119] a job applicant was rejected because of her unsatisfactory demeanour at the interview, her work record, and her race. She would have been rejected for any one of those reasons, yet it was held a claim for racial discrimination should succeed, as long as it was one of the reasons for her rejection. It might be asked whether Mr Woodcock would have been retired to save money even if he were not redundant, or whether he would have been retained (as he had been for a year) had it not been for the £500,000 costs. The point is that this approach has the danger of adopting the 'but for test' which fallen into disuse in the context of direct discrimination,[120] and in any case is undermined with a serious theoretical objection. In *Price Waterhouse v Hopkins*,[121] the US Supreme Court observed,

> Suppose two physical forces act upon and move an object, and suppose that either force acting alone would have moved the object. As the [*but for* test] would have it, *neither* physical force was a 'cause' of the motion unless we can show that but for one or both of them, the object would not have, moved; apparently both forces were simply 'in the air' unless we can identify at least one of them as a but-for cause of the object's movement. ... Events that are causally overdetermined, in other words, may not have any 'cause' at all. This cannot be so.[122]

Thus, it would seem that the reasoning underlying the decision in *Woodcock* is little different in substance from, and shares problems with, the costs-plus approach, while its causative method has the potential to run into other

119 [1982] ICR 618 (CA).
120 See e.g. Freedland, Deakin and Watt, 'Goodbye "but-for", hello "but-why?"' (1998) 27 *ILJ* 121; JFS [2010] 2 AC 728 (SC) [21]–[23] (Lord Phillips), [62]–[64] (Lady Hale), [78] (Lord Mance), [114]–[117] (Lord Kerr), [132] (Lord Clarke).
121 490 US 228 (1989).
122 490 US 228, at 241 (1989) (Brennan, J). This was a criticism of the conservative minority's dissent, who were using the but-for test to *restrict* the application of the legislation.

problems associated with the but-for test. It shares the features of the costs-plus approach, identified by the Supreme Court, of being 'subtle' and 'not without difficulty'.[123]

Moreover, this may be a lot of fuss about very little. The ECJ edicts on objective justification generally, as well as justification of direct age discrimination, are confined to measures whose *sole* aim is to save costs.[124] Therefore, where costs are not the sole reason for the treatment, or they are a subsidiary consideration behind a separate reason. The edict no longer applies. This can be seen in the case of *Petersen.*[125] A third aim (for compulsory retirement) was that in Germany there were too many dentists on the public panel, and this threatened the financial stability of the public health care system. It seems that this third aim - 'financial constraints' - was a legitimate aim, because it accorded with the 'public health' purpose. The point is, where there is more than one aim (as in the costs-plus scenarios, and as purported in *Woodcock*), the edict no longer applies.

Of course, *Pedersen* can be distinguished from *Woodcock* and the like, because it fell under the public health exception in Article 2(5).[126] Nonetheless, in cases of direct age discrimination, if the alternative aim could be couched as a social policy (even perhaps with a liberal interpretation), one might imagine that the financial stability of the public healthcare system could do so.

The desire to afford costs the status of a legitimate aim in itself has led to a different, perhaps less troublesome, principal. This 'disproportionate costs principle' is the second attempt to mitigate the absolutist effect of the ECJ edict. In *Woodcock,* speaking *obiter*, Underhill J went on to suggest that where the discriminatory impact was 'trivial' and the cost of the alternative 'enormous', costs alone ought to be able to justify discrimination, be it indirect discrimination generally, or, as in this case, direct age discrimination. This was 'common sense'.[127] While upholding Underhill's J decision, the Court of Appeal declined to comment on the suggestion.

This more general approach, led by the fact of disproportionality, has the benefit of defusing another problem identified elsewhere by Underhill J, which is the difficulty of distinguishing the legitimate aim from the means to achieve it. Elias J once wrote that the distinction was 'a matter of semantics'.[128] Underhill J has observed more than once that, 'the dichotomy of "aim" and "means" is not always clear cut and the two elements can sometimes reasonably

123 *O'Brien v Ministry of Justice* [2013] UKSC 6 [63] (Lady Hale and Lord Hope for the Court).

124 See above, text to n 23.

125 Case C-341/08 *Petersen* [2010] IRLR 254.

126 See above, text to n 138.

127 *Woodcock v Cumbria Primary Care Trust* [32], citing *Cross v BA* [2005] IRLR 423 (EAT) [63] (Burton J). Approved *Cherfi v G4s Security Services Ltd* (2011) UKEAT/0379/10/DM (EAT) [36], [45].

128 *Loxley v BAE Systems Land Systems (Munitions & Ordnance) Ltd* [2008] ICR 1348 [37].

be formulated in more than one way'.[129] Thus, he advised with a flourish, 'Tribunals need not cudgel their brains with metaphysical inquiries about what count as aims and what count as means as long as the underlying balancing exercise is carried out'.[130]

That said, this apparently palatable and practical solution (and certainly a more honest approach in Woodcock's case) runs into the ECJ edict. Like many 'common sense' solutions, it tends to be based on a hard case (making bad law), and/or the irony of a judge's subjective view of one party's meritorious position. Moreover, it runs against the more fundamental principles of the objective justification defence for direct age discrimination, which requires a social policy aim. As the *Age Concern* litigation made clear, cost reduction/improving competitiveness are not social policy aims.[131]

With these potential difficulties, the employer wishing to retire older expensive workers in order to replace them with younger ones would be well-advised to declare the apparently legitimate aim under the 'attrition profile' strand of the workforce planning policy (above), only mentioning the savings as part of its proportionality argument. This may not be possible in individual age discrimination cases (such as *Woodcock*). Here, the employer should consider any non-costs reasons for the treatment. If there are none, they may attract the sympathy of the tribunal by promoting subsidiary, or even fallacious, reasons as the primary ones (as in *Woodcock*). Combined with a disproportionate ('trivial') impact to the ('enormous') costs involved, this may prove convincing. Of course, fallacious or pretextual arguments proffered should be rejected. In *Petersen*, for example, the ECJ rejected the 'protection of the public' argument because the rule applied only to public sector dentists, and so lacked credibility.[132]

The needs of the business

Rather curiously, the Coalition Government has stated that in order to objectively justify a retirement 'an employer would need to show that they were acting to further a legitimate *aim of the business*'.[133] Taken at face value, this cannot be correct. A purely business aim was rejected by the ECJ and accordingly by the High Court in *Age UK*, as noted above.[134] Any business aim

129 *Land Registry v Benson* [2012] ICR 627 (EAT) [36], citing *Pulham v Barking and Dagenham LBC* [2010] ICR 133 (EAT) [15]. Cited with approval by Bean LJ, *Harrod v Chief Constable of West Midlands Police* [2017] EWCA 191, cited [26].

130 Ibid., *Pulham* [2010] ICR 133 (EAT) [15].

131 Case C-388/07 *Age Concern* [2009] ECR I-1569, paras 46 and 49–50; *Age UK* [2010] ICR 260 (HC Admin) [93].

132 Case C-341/08 *Petersen* [2010] IRLR 254, paragraphs 30, 38, 78. See further above, p. 168 and 173.

133 2011 Consultation Response, p. 4; Guidance 2010, p. 3, emphasis supplied.

134 Text to n 23.

would have to, at the least, coincide with a social policy aim (see *Seldon v Clarkson*, above).[135]

Aims beyond social policies

Employers have set aims of physical fitness, physical capabilities, or just 'ability'. Age discrimination law becomes engaged when the employer sets an age limit as a proxy for these aims. For certain types of work, this is the most obvious reason for employers to set a retirement age. Recital 18 of the Framework Directive, for example, identifies as a legitimate aim the 'operational capacity' of the armed forces, police, prison, or emergency services. Such aims are associated with job performance, and as such would not fall under the social policy exceptions available to the objective justification defence,[136] but under the Genuine Occupational Requirement (GOR) or health and safety exceptions.

In *Wolf*,[137] the challenged rule barred recruitment into the fire service of anyone over 30. This was to allow sufficient time for training, as fire fighters were retired from firefighting duties at age 45, and in itself recognised as a GOR. *Wolf* was a recruitment case, but much the same method has been used for retirement, as seen below in the next two cases, *Petersen* and *Prigge*.

In *Petersen*,[138] one of the aims of German legislation retiring dentists when they reached 68 was the protection of the health of patients under the statutory insurance scheme (it being 'thought that' performance declines after that age).[139] Under the Framework Directive, public safety and health falls under an exception in Article 2(5), which provides that the Directive 'shall be without prejudice to measures laid down by national law which … are necessary … for the protection of health'. The ECJ considered that the aim fell readily within Article 2(5), rather than the objective justification defence.[140] (Although this could have been a legitimate aim, it failed because the same rule did not apply to private health dentists.[141]) The ECJ took the same approach in *Prigge v Deutsche Lufthansa AG*, where airline pilots were retired at 60 under the aims of safety (of crew, passengers, and the public) and 'physical capabilities':[142]

135 Text to n 42.
136 Case 447/09 *Prigge v Deutsche Lufthansa AG* [2011] IRLR 1052, paras 79–82.
137 Case C-229/08, [2010] IRLR 244.
138 Case C-341/08, [2010] IRLR 254.
139 Ibid., at para 38.
140 Ibid., at para 50.
141 Ibid., respectively at para 45 and paras 57–62. There were two other aims. The first was to preserve the finances of the public system which also fell under Article 2(5) as this related to public health, and could be proportionate (at para 64). The second was intergenerational fairness and the excess of dentists in the public sector, which could be objectively justified (at para 77).
142 Case 447/09, [2011] IRLR 1052, paras 51, 58, 64 (safety) and 67, 75 (physical fitness).

> As regards airline pilots, it is essential that they possess, inter alia, particular physical capabilities in so far as physical defects in that profession may have significant consequences.[143]

Again, not being a labour market policy, the 'safety' aim was assessed under Article 2(5) rather than under the objective justification defence,[144] while the physical fitness requirement was assessed as a GOR. Once again, the 'safety' aim failed because of a discrepancy between the challenged retirement age (60) and that laid down in national and international rules (65).[145] Nonetheless, these cases confirm the fairly obvious exception which is provided in the Directive.

This presents a problem in the UK, as the Equality Act 2010 has no provision corresponding to Article 2(5).[146] This might be because it was seen as unnecessary. Although 'health and safety' did not appear as a social policy aim back in 2006, the Coalition Government assumed it was a legitimate aim under the objective justification defence.[147] Of course, *Petersen* and *Prigge* have set the law against this. The ECJ made it clear that health and safety was not a labour market policy and therefore could not fall under the objective justification defence.[148] Thus, if the UK tribunal or court wanted to entertain a public safety argument under the objective justification defence would have to disregard the hitherto over-respected ECJ jurisprudence in favour of the hitherto-ignored expressed UK social policy.

The other option is for the employer to argue that the aim of retirement is to satisfy an occupational requirement, or GOR (as in *Prigge* or *Wolf*[149]). One cannot imagine this would be too difficult given that if an employer's ability to do the job has a public safety dimension, such as dentists or pilots. This approach has the benefit of better alignment with both ECJ jurisprudence and UK social policy. But whichever approach is taken would present another problem. A tribunal or court would have to decide whether to accept the

143 Ibid., at para 67.
144 Ibid., paras 81–82.
145 Ibid., paras 75–76.
146 See EA 2010, Sch 9, Part 2 'Exceptions Relating to Age', paras 7–16, covering length of service benefits, minimum wage, redundancy, insurance, childcare, and contribution to personal pensions. In some limited circumstances it will be possible to argue that otherwise discriminatory conduct does not contravene the Act where it is done 'pursuant to… a requirement of an enactment': Sch 22, para 1, covering for age discrimination the areas of Services, Premises, Work, Education, and Associations.
147 Consultation: *Phasing Out the Default Retirement Age* (2010), pp. 11 and 31; Consultation Response (2011), p. 7; see also ACAS Guidance for Employers: Working Without the Default Retirement Age (March 2011), p. 5.
148 *Petersen* analysed the health and safety defence under art 2(5), and not 6(1) (paras 47–62), although art 6(1) was applied to the aim of 'sharing out employment opportunities' (paras 65–78). *Prigge* ruled that the ability to do the job was not a labour market policy under art 6(1) (paras 81–82).
149 Case C-229/08, [2010] IRLR 244. See above, p. 175.

generalisation of ability declining with age, something widely endorsed by the ECJ and expressly rejected by UK social policy (discussed further below[150]).

And so, it is conceivable that when presented with a public safety defence, a tribunal could ignore ECJ jurisprudence to entertain it, and then embrace the same jurisprudence when accepting a generalisation. The corresponding irony is that at one point UK social policy is followed, and at another it is ignored. It presents the potential for another fuzzy border.

Objective justification and proportionality

In sum, it seems that the most likely aims to be accepted are workforce planning ('attrition profile') and, where appropriate, pension stability, or health and safety (although in the UK, this would have to be expressed as a social policy aim, or being in compliance with the statutory requirement). Once the aim is established, the focus moves to proportionality: was the compulsory retirement an appropriate and necessary means to achieve the given aim? We will see that employers may find that tribunals afford them a degree of flexibility in choosing the means to achieve the aim.

Choice of age

The choice of a particular retirement age would seem the most vulnerable target for claimants. The question will be just how much proof an employer can be expected to produce to show that its chosen age is *necessary* to achieve the aim(s). In *Age UK*, the High Court criticised the Government for not choosing a default retirement age above 65, say 68, and but for the Government's forthcoming review (which led to the abolition of the DRA), it would have held that the age of 65 to be disproportionate to the twin aims of workforce planning and stability of pensions. In particular:

> It creates greater discriminatory effect than is necessary on a class of people who both are able to and want to continue in their employment. A higher age would not have any general detrimental labour market consequences or block access to high level jobs by future generations.[151]

Elsewhere, Blake J observed that employers would have 'a much more rigorous task' than the State when objectively justifying individual practices.[152]

However, the judicial indications elsewhere are that not much proof, if any, will be required, especially if employers align the retirement age with a norm, typically the state pension age. The ECJ, in *Palacios de la Villa, Petersen,*

150 2011 Consultation Response, p. 7. See below, p. 182, 'Job performance generalisations'.
151 [2009] IRLR 1017 [124]–[128].
152 Ibid., [97].

Rosenbladt, and *Georgiev*,[153] and the EAT and Court of Appeal in *Seldon*, displayed little scrutiny of the employer's chosen age.

The matter was explored in *Seldon*, notably by the Court of Appeal, and then upon its return via the Supreme Court to the employment tribunal and EAT. In this case, it may be recalled, an *employer* (not the State) was charged with justifying a chosen retirement age of 65. The Court of Appeal appeared notably relaxed about the choice of age. Waller, LJ reasoned:

> A rule which adopts 66 is less discriminatory to partners aged 65, but is now more discriminatory to partners aged 66. The selection of any age is going to be more discriminatory to that age. If that makes the rule unlawful, it would simply be impossible to justify a retirement age introduced with those aims.[154]

Inevitably, the Court of Appeal held that the age of 65 was proportionate, even after conceding that there was no evidence to show things would have been different if the chosen age were 68, 65, or 63. The decision was supported, Waller, LJ continued, by the Government's choice of 65 as the DRA.[155]

The Court's reasoning appears to be rooted in a head-to-head comparison between two workers, respectively aged 65 and 66, when the retirement age is *either* 66 or 65. The 66-year-old can complain he was treated less favourably than the 65-year-old or vice versa. This misses the point, which is achieving the *least* discriminatory means to achieve the aim. As such, any comparison should be (hypothetically) between 65 and 66 where *both* were retirement ages. This reveals it would be less discriminatory to retire the older worker because he would have one more year in employment and one year less unemployed or perhaps employed doing less desirable work. Nonetheless, the general point being made is that without evidence it is impossible for a tribunal to state what age would be the least discriminatory one.

On appeal, the Supreme Court merely returned the case to the employment tribunal to decide because in the first hearing it 'did not unpick the question of the age chosen and discuss in relation to each of the objectives'.[156] Although not expressed as such, this could be read as a tacit criticism of the Court of Appeal's less than germane reasoning.

Upon its return, the employment tribunal found that the choice of age was justified. This in turn was upheld in the EAT. Both afforded the matter some

153 Joined Cases C-250/09 and C-268/09 *Georgiev*, [54]–[55], where the compulsory retirement age (68) of university professors extended five years beyond pension entitlement and so 'did not unduly prejudice the legitimate claims of workers' who had reached 68.

154 [2010] EWCA Civ 899, [38].

155 Ibid., [39]. See also the Supreme Court appeal, [2012] UKSC 16 [68] where Lady Hale noted that at the time there was a 'designated retirement age of 65 for employees'.

156 Ibid., [68].

closer attention. A preliminary matter was whether the use of a particular age was an appropriate means to achieve the aims of workforce planning and intergenerational fairness (in this case, the retention of associates). Only the employment tribunal gave this some attention:

> In order to plan for the future of the firm there is a need for a realistic long-term expectation as to when and where vacancies will arise at all levels including partners and in all practice areas.... The Respondent produced a number of planning and strategy documents ... and needed to be aware of dates of retirement (in some cases possibly before the mandatory retirement *age)* and plan accordingly.[157]

It is notable here that the tribunal made its finding upon evidence that a certain date was required for the legitimate aims. The EAT apparently approved of this, but only in general terms. Instead of alluding to the evidence, Langstaff J cited only 'the judgments of the superior courts'.[158] This could be taken to suggest that this is not a fact sensitive matter, and that any employer stating that a certain date is required for these aims would clear this stage of the proportionality enquiry.

This left the matter of whether the choice of a particular age (in this case 65) was appropriate and necessary. Although conceding that a different age, such as 64 or 66 could achieve this employer's aims,[159] the employment tribunal called upon a number of factors justifying the choice of 65. These were the claimant's prior consent, the existing DRA and state retirement ages (both 65), ECJ authority, collegiality, and the avoidance of an anomaly of other workers having to retire at 65 (under the DRA) while partners (such as the claimant) would retire at a different age.[160] This last factor (the 'DRA anomaly') appears the most convincing. Indeed, the tribunal noted that a different age for partners would undermine the legitimate aim of retention of associates.[161] However, the logic relied on the employer's choice to invoke the DRA against its other workers. In other words, because the employer is allowed to discriminate against one group of workers, it should be allowed to discriminate against another. If the factor was weak then, it has diminished in two stages since. First, since the facts of *Seldon* arose, the High Court held that the DRA, if not abolished, should be raised to 68 as it would still achieve the policy aims of workforce planning and intergenerational fairness.[162] Claims arising after this case, but

157 (ET, 28 May 2013) [77]. Emphasis original. (The transcript is on Westlaw.)
158 [2014] ICR 1275 (EAT) [27] (Langstaff J), referring only to 'the judgments of the superior courts'. See also [2012] UKSC 16 [68] (Lady Hale).
159 (ET, 28 May 2013) [80].
160 Ibid., [82]–[87]. The DRA did not apply to partners.
161 Ibid., [84].
162 [2009] IRLR 1017 [119], [124]–[128]. The initial Seldon claim was decided on 4 December 2007, while *Age UK* was decided on 25 September 2009.

before the DRA's repeal,[163] would not face such an argument unless challenging a retirement age of over 68. Of course, *Seldon* was an unusual case where the claimant was exempt from the DRA. Second, since the abolition of the DRA, the employer has only the objective justification defence. If it were to align its retirement age for all workers, say, to the state retirement age, it would be difficult to argue against the claim by one group of workers that the particular age chosen should remain the same to prevent an anomaly with the other staff. This is saying simply that we can discriminate against one group because we discriminate against all the others. It is akin to defending an equal pay case on the basis that other women in the establishment receive less than equal pay.

Nevertheless, at least the employment tribunal looked to the circumstances of the case to narrow down the choice of age to the chosen one of 65. Not so Langstaff J in the EAT, who took a broader approach. While making it clear that the test was not one as broad as the 'range of reasonable responses',[164] he held that the proportionality test as one of *reasonable* necessity, the qualification being 'essential if one is looking for a particular age'.[165] This qualification has become rather fashionable in domestic courts, although not supported by EU jurisprudence.[166] Of course, it would have been sounder to cite the domestic authorities, rather than letting the facts dictate the law.

Whatever the merits of the qualification, Langstaff J had in mind when analysing the choice of age with a more theoretical approach,

> [a]s is obvious, if it were to be said that a day later than a given age would discriminate less, as it would if the interests of the retiree were to be considered, it would therefore be wrong in law not to take a day later as the date: and if a day later still, the same would apply—but then as a matter of principle it would seem that no date could be chosen lawfully because any date would be capable of being rendered unlawful by the argument that a slightly later date would serve just as well.[167]

As noted elsewhere,[168] a qualified test permits tribunals to depart from strict necessity test and balance the discriminatory effect of the challenged practice against the reasonable needs of the employer.[169] Consequently, for Langstaff J,

163 25 September 2009–6 April 2011.
164 [2014] ICR 1275 (EAT) [26]–[27], citing *Hardy & Hansons plc v Lax* [2005] ICR 1565 [32] (Pill LJ). For cases of Unfair Dismissal, the test is used to decide if a decision to dismiss was fair, that is within the range of reasonable responses.
165 Ibid., [26].
166 See Chapter 5 'Objective justification', p. 85.
167 [2014] ICR 1275 (EAT) [26].
168 See Chapter 5, p. 85
169 [2014] ICR 1275 (EAT) [27]. The test has its origins in the indirect sex discrimination case *Hampson v Department of Education* [1989] ICR 179 (CA) 196. See further Chapter 5 'Objective justification', p. 85.

'That balance, like any balance, will not necessarily show that a particular point can be identified as any more or less appropriate than another particular point'.[170]

This is a highly pragmatic approach, replacing the employment tribunal's fact-sensitive analysis with a principle. Langstaff's J principle dispenses with such details and suggests that irrespective of the facts of any particular case, employers have some leeway of a range of ages, centring, it seems, around the mid-60s. The principal seems to be based on the notion that it would always be impossible for an employer to choose the least discriminatory date. It must be presumed that Langstaff J envisaged a series of cases suggesting ever-increasing ages: a strict necessity test, which demands the least discriminatory means, would result in a tribunal suggesting that the age is raised to, say, 66. Then in a subsequent case with a different employer, whose retirement age is 66 will be told by a tribunal it should be raised to 67, for no better reason than is less discriminatory than 66. The perverse outcome with a strict test would be uncertainty.

This need not be so in every case. Take workforce planning. There will come a point where a much older age would detract from the required certainty because of the likelihood of unplanned departures, caused, say, by serious illness and/or a steep rise in mortality rates. Such evidence would be obtainable from the records of a medium to large business, or from the Office of National Statistics, or insurance actuaries, for example. For the retention of valuable workers, there may be more leeway. Evidence supporting a retirement age could come from records within the business, or within similar businesses, of younger workers quitting in favour of better prospects in a similar or rival, business. There might also be evidence of the harm caused, such as the cost of recruitment and retraining, and/or the loss of business. This might suggest a range, as the employment tribunal found in *Seldon*. Nevertheless, without the DRA anomaly, or other reason to maintain a general retirement age, the least discriminatory age at the top of that range should be the only lawful one. Just because an extra day or three will be just as capable of achieving the aim, the law should not maintain a year or three of discrimination.

It comes down to how seriously the law wishes to take age discrimination. UK policy suggests it should be taken seriously. Perhaps the closest analogy with other protected characteristics is with sex discrimination and equal pay, where a difference of treatment could be measured in numbers. As the ECJ have made abundantly clear, where there is a pay disparity between a predominantly female and predominately male occupation, the range of disparity is lawful only as far as supported by the *evidence*, and not by some broader 'range' based on notions of reasonableness or balance.[171]

170 Ibid.
171 Case C127/92 *Enderby v Frenchay HA* [1994] ICR 112.

Job performance generalisations

As noted above, aims of ability or physical fitness can fall under a GOR or Article 2(5), rather than the objective justification defence. In the cases cited (*Wolf, Petersen, Prigge*) a maximum age requirement was the means to achieve these aims. Even though they were not centred on the objective justification defence, and some concerned recruitment rather than retirement, they presented an opportunity for the courts to address generalisations about age, normally an antithesis of discrimination law.

The recruitment limit (30) in *Wolf*[172] was to allow sufficient time for training, as fire fighters were retired from firefighting duties at age 45. This was because, agreed the ECJ, 'very few officials over 45 years of age have sufficient physical capacity to perform the fire-fighting part of their activities'.[173] Accordingly, the ECJ concluded that the rule was justified as a GOR.

A notable feature of this case was that the job requirement in question was an age limit, not fitness per se. Nonetheless, the ECJ accepted *age* as the job requirement, noting 'scientific data deriving from studies in the field of industrial and sports medicine which show that respiratory capacity, musculature and endurance diminish with age'.[174] Hence, age was so closely related to job-performance it was a job requirement.

This acceptance of a generalisation regarding protected characteristic and physical fitness is out of step conventional jurisprudence. In a sex discrimination case, *Kalliri*,[175] the Greek police required officers to be at least 1.7m tall, because the job required 'physical attributes'. Predictably, the requirement put women at a disadvantage. The ECJ noted that not all tasks required physical attributes (e.g. traffic control), and in any case, height was not a necessary indicator of physical strength.[176] The decision has echoes of the classic American case, *Dothard v Rawlinson*,[177] where height and weight requirements for prison guards were not justified, as there were more accurate ways of measuring the physical strength required. It is notable also that these are cases of *indirect* discrimination, where one might expect the courts to provide defendants with a little more latitude than for direct discrimination, which is ordinarily perceived with less tolerance. Indeed, in *Seldon* itself, Lady Hale expressed doubts about this approach:

> The fact that most women are less physically strong than most men does not justify refusing a job requiring strength to a woman candidate just because she is a woman. … It would be consistent with this principle to hold that the fact that most people over a certain age have slower reactions

172 Case C-229/08, [2010] IRLR 244.
173 Ibid., at para 41.
174 Ibid.
175 C-409/16 *Kalliri* [2018] 2 CMLR 1.
176 Ibid., at paras 38–39.
177 433 US 321 (US Supreme Court 1977).

> than most people under that age does not justify sacking everyone who reaches that age irrespective of whether or not they still do have the necessary speed of reaction.[178]

Of course, as is clear by now, despite this reservation Lady Hale felt obliged by ECJ caselaw to reject this principle. Indeed, just a year before *Kalliri*, in *Sorondo*,[179] the Court considered it was a genuine occupational requirement that Basque police officers must be under 36 because 'from the age of 40 onwards, the operational performance of police officers … declines'.[180]

By contrast, Lady Hale's doubts were given substance by the Australian judiciary in *Commonwealth v Human Rights & Equal Opportunity Commission (Bradley).*[181] Here, the Army required trainee pilots to be aged between 19 and 28 because inter alia the job required 'an ability to maintain a high level of medical fitness for the duration of the six-year period of appointment'. It was held that the physical fitness requirement could not be allowed to 'have the effect of damning individuals over 28 years by reference to a stereotypical characteristic (less physical fitness) of their age group'.

It could be questioned whether the ECJ approach towards recruitment should be taken towards retirement of older workers. Employers at the recruitment stage have to predict the physical fitness of recruits over a considerable length of time, conceivably decades. This is less likely to be the case in retirement cases, which would undermine somewhat the use of age as a measure of fitness, especially where individual testing was available. None of these considerations troubled the ECJ when it eventually entertained a retirement case with physical fitness as the GOR and age as the means. In *Prigge*,[182] the 'physical capabilities' aim of retiring pilots at 60 was recognised as a GOR, upon the generalisation that it is 'undeniable that those capabilities diminish with age'.[183] The approach is similarly generous where something less specific, such as 'ability to do the job', is the aim. In *Petersen*, the ECJ accepted the proposition that there was a decline in performance of dentists once past 68. It rejected the defence, not because the retirement age was based on such a generalisation, but because it did not extend to private sector dentists.[184]

The Canadian Supreme Court agrees with the generalisation:

178 [2012] UKSC 16 [58].

179 Case C-285/15 *Sorondo* [2018] ICR 302.

180 Ibid., at para 42.

181 (1999) 95 FCR 218 (Federal Court of Australia). See also, *Commonwealth of Australia v Hamilton* (2000) 63 ALD 641.

182 Case 447/09 *Prigge v Deutsche Lufthansa AG* [2011] IRLR 1052.

183 Ibid., at para 67. The defence failed because a discrepancy between the challenged requirement (60) and national and international rules (65): ibid., paras 75–76.

184 Case C-341/08 *Petersen* [2010] IRLR 254, at paras 30, 38, 78. The argument failed because it applied only to public sector dentists, thus undermining its credibility.

> To begin with there is nothing inherent in most of the specified grounds of discrimination, e.g., race, colour, religion, national or ethnic origin, or sex that supports any general correlation between those characteristics and ability. But that is not the case with age. There is a general relationship between advancing age and declining ability.[185]

This has long been the view also of the United States Supreme Court. In *Massachusetts Board of Retirement v Murgia,*[186] for example, the Court, when sanctioning the retirement of uniformed police officers at 50, did so on the basis that 'there is a general relationship between advancing age and decreasing physical ability to respond to the demands of the job'.[187]

This generous acceptance of generalisations parallels that afforded to retirement for social policy reasons under the objective justification defence. But there is a fundamental difference. Given that these exceptions are pleaded as job performance requirements, they should be equated with the ability to do the job. This in turn renders the role of social policy especially that expressed by a particular government, rather uncertain. After all, job performance can be a purely individual matter, irrespective of government social policy. It will come as no surprise that the Coalition Government took the view that the notion of ability declining with age was a 'myth'.[188] This was consistent with its abolition of the default retirement age. Elsewhere, it asserted that 'productivity does not usually decline at least up to 70 years old - notably where older workers receive the same levels of training as younger workers'.[189] The current 'Retain, Retrain, Recruit' policy would appear to agree with this. Nonetheless, the question remains open as to whether this public policy, not expressed in the legislation, should influence the purely private matter of job performance and a GOR, which is provided for by the legislation. There are further areas of uncertainty. There are differences of opinion among policy-makers as to the efficacy of such generalisations. There are differences of opinion among the judiciary as to its legality under discrimination. Amongst that,

185 *McKinney v University of Guelph* [1990] 3 SCR 229, at 297, citing Note, 'The Age Discrimination in Employment Act of 1967' (1976), 90 *Harv L Rev* 380, at p. 384; Tarnopolsky and Pentney, *Discrimination and the Law* (1985), at pp. 7–5.

186 427 US 307 (1976).

187 Ibid., 310–311.

188 2011 Consultation Response, p. 7. But see the 2020 Government website which suggests that a 'good reason' for a retirement age is that 'the job requires certain physical abilities (e.g. in the construction industry)'. No reasoning is provided and this may be an inadvertent allusion to ECJ caselaw, as no reference is made to more explicit pre-existing Government policy. See 'Working after State Pension Age', www.gov.uk/working-retirement-pension-age. The parallel Guidance for Northern Ireland follows the pre-existing (Coalition) Government policy www.nidirect.gov.uk/articles/working-past-state-pension-age#toc-1 both accessed 21 October 2020.

189 Age Positive, pp. 5, 10, 14, and 20.

there is Lady Hale's doubts leaning one way and deference to the ECJ leaning another.

Link with pension

A factor in *Palacios de la Villa* was that workers could only be retired (aged 65) if they had sufficient pension contribution. This mitigated the discriminatory impact of the policy and so assisted the (successful) proportionality argument.[190] This suggests that tying a retirement policy to pension entitlement (be it state or otherwise) would help employers justify the policy.

Consent

Another factor for the ECJ in *Palacios de la Villa* was that the Spanish legislation permitted compulsory retirement only via a collective agreement. The evidence of the challenged law being made with the instigation, or cooperation, of trade unions and employers' groups clearly influenced the Court.[191]

Several interesting observations on this matter arose in the Canadian Supreme Court case, *McKinney v University of Guelph*.[192] Here, some university academics, aggrieved at a compulsory retirement age (65) in their collective agreement, claimed that the facilitating legislation, Ontario Human Rights Code 1981 (s 9(a)), which excluded those aged over 65 from protection under the Code's age discrimination prohibition, violated the non-discrimination tenet in section 15(1) of the Charter of Rights and Freedoms. In rejecting the claims (by a five–two majority), La Forest J proclaimed, 'The freedom of employers and employees to determine conditions of the workplace for themselves through a process of bargaining is a very desirable goal in a free society'.[193] It was noted also that the local union, as well as the labour movement generally, opposed McKinney's claim.[194]

In his concurrence, Sopinka J considered that were the claim to succeed, the Charter 'would be used to restrict the freedom of many in order to promote the interests of the few'.[195] Again, we see the dissonance with other protected characteristics. If, in deference to the majority of their customers, a number of retailers decided not to serve an unpopular minority, say, an indigenous tribe (in Canada), Romanies (across Europe), then the law would not hesitate to

190 Case C-411/05, [2007] IRLR 989, at para 73; see also Joined Cases C-250/09 and C-268/09 *Georgiev* [54]–[55], [63].

191 Ibid., paragraphs 53, 60, 74, and see Case C-45/09 *Rosenbladt* [2011] 1 CMLR 32, at para 39.

192 [1990] 3 SCR 229.

193 La Forest, J, delivering the judgment of Dickson C.J. and La Forest and Gonthier JJ, ibid., p. 313.

194 Ibid.

195 Ibid., p. 446.

hold that the exclusion was discriminatory, despite the unwritten pact between the retailers and the majority. Meanwhile, Cory J (concurring) observed,

> [b]argains struck whereby higher wages are paid at an earlier age in exchange for mandatory retirement at a fixed and certain age, may well confer a very real benefit upon the worker and not in any way affect his or her basic dignity or sense of worth. If such contracts should be found to be invalid, it would attack the very foundations of collective bargaining and might well put in jeopardy some of the hard won rights of labour.[196]

By contrast, the statutory exception under the United States federal Age Discrimination in Employment Act 1967 is based entirely on *individual* consent.[197]

A factor in *Seldon* was the individual consent given by an informed person when he signed the (law firm) partnership agreement. The Court of Appeal concluded that there are situations where 'it is legitimate to take into account the perception which the partner now challenging the clause had at one time'.[198] In the Supreme Court, Lady Hale echoed this sentiment, even though she acknowledged the age discrimination legislation was not on their minds when making the agreement. So, although Mr Seldon could not be said to have agreed to discrimination, is consent was evidence that he considered the retirement age to be fair.[199]

But there are various degrees of consent. The bargaining power of a job applicant can vary enormously. For most, there is no choice. Jobs are offered on a take-it-or-leave basis. This will be all the more so in times of chronic unemployment (ironically a situation the ECJ in *Rosenbladt* used to justify compulsory retirement of cleaners).[200] A trade union member may have a diluted influence over a collective agreement, whilst a non-member is likely to have none. There is all the difference between one of these workers, whose consent is largely illusory, and those represented by a powerful trade union, or an informed professional entering into a partnership agreement.

In practice, the overwhelming majority of a workforce may support a compulsory retirement age negotiated into a collective agreement, especially when it was linked to other benefits. Similarly, a highly skilled individual, with legal advice, may negotiate a detailed package, which included a retirement age. In either case, as long as the employer can produce an aim that coincides with social policy (most likely workforce planning), consent is likely prove a persuasive argument in justification.

196 Ibid., pp. 447–448.

197 29 USC s 626(f)(1). See further, EEOC 29 CFR s 1625.22, at https://www.eeoc.gov/laws-guidance-0, click 'Laws, Regulations', click 'Regulations', scroll down to 1625. Accessed 16 October 2020.

198 [2010] EWCA Civ 899 (CA), [30].

199 [2012] UKSC 16 [65]. See also *Seldon v Clarkson (No 2)* [2014] ICR 1275 (EAT) [34].

200 Case C-45/09, [2011] 1 CMLR 32, at para 43.

The cases show that the judiciary of Europe and North America are content to have the fundamental right to equality trumped by freedom of contract, majority rule, or bargained away with work-related benefits. This exposes something quite odd about compulsory retirement: for many workers (perhaps a majority of the nation's workforce) it is *desirable*. Its discriminatory nature is less important than the perceived benefits, making justification all the easier. This certainly encouraged the Canadian Supreme Court. That said, for other protected characteristics, such as race or sex, no such sympathy is likely to be shown for discrimination arising from agreement of any kind.[201]

Costs

It was noted above[202] that the EAT constantly has stated that employer's costs may form part of its proportionality argument as something in support of the aim, or even as a subsidiary aim. Thus, it seems, an employer retiring workers under any of the legitimate aims highlighted above, could deploy financial savings as a subsidiary aim and if not, re-label it as part of its proportionality argument. The point is it would seem, to elicit the sympathy of the tribunal.

Stability of pension scheme

Where the aim is the stability of pensions, the employer would have to show that compulsory retirement was an appropriate means to achieve the aim. This matter was discussed at length by the Canadian Supreme Court in *McKinney* (above). The majority's rejection of the claim was that a general retirement age of 65 was necessary to preserve the stability and integrity of pension schemes. They relied on the defendant's experts, who testified:

> In short, a number of issues regarding the design of occupational pension plans would have to be addressed if mandatory retirement were not permitted. So, too, would the wage policy followed by many employers, especially when the pension benefit is linked to the employee's earnings. The use of the occupational pension plan as a vehicle for deferring a portion of the employee's total compensation to the employee's later work years may be reduced. As before, not permitting mandatory retirement is likely to require compensating adjustments elsewhere in the compensation package and in the set of work rules that govern the workplace.[203]

The plaintiff's expert confined his evidence to effect upon pension plans of removing the Mandatory Retirement Age (MRA). He highlighted the experiences of Quebec and Manitoba, where the MRA was removed and no

201 See e.g. Case C127/92 *Enderby v Frenchay HA* [1994] ICR 112.
202 See text to n 58 et al.
203 [1990] 3 SCR 229, at 303 and 304.

'instability' was apparent in the pension plans as a result. He testified that deferred retirement would invoke some administrative costs for actuarial adjustments, which would 'pale into insignificance compared to administrative costs resulting from pension legislation'. He also noted EE that the removal of the MRA did not necessarily alter the normal retiring age in the pension plan. In Quebec and Manitoba, for example, legislation *required* that a normal retiring age be stated in the pension plan.[204] In other words, the pension matures at a certain date irrespective of whether the worker retires. The worker draws the pension, and may continue working with the option of contributing further to a pension plan.

The case demonstrates the judiciary's deference to legislation that derogates from the anti-discrimination principle when the treatment is ageist and related to retirement. Faced with divided expert evidence, the majority sided with the defendant. Given that the UK Coalition Government did not absolutely rule this out as an aim, the remaining issues would be whether compulsory retirement was an appropriate means, and whether the chosen age was necessary, or in the UK language 'reasonably necessary'.[205] It remains to be seen whether tribunals show the deference afforded by the Canadian Supreme Court.

The signs so far are double-edged. Attempts to stabilise pension provision which disfavour *younger* workers have failed because of the discriminatory impact. In a pair of related cases, involving a reduction in pension rights that ring-fenced the rights of those approaching retirement, the courts have held that social policy considerations did not preclude an apparently stricter proportionality test. In *Lord Chancellor v McCloud*, the EAT upheld the employment tribunal finding that reform of judicial pensions had an 'extremely severe impact … on the claimants [that] far outweighed the public benefit of applying the policy consistently across the whole public service pension sector'.[206] In the second case, *Sargeant v London Fire and Emergency Planning Authority*,[207] an employment tribunal had granted the Government a wide margin of discretion instead of assessing the reforms for proportionality. This was an error of law, the EAT found, and remitted the case. The Court of Appeal agreed, holding that although the state employers enjoyed a margin of discretion in public policy aims, the aims, and the means to achieve them, remained subject to objective justification, which was not apparent here.[208]

204 Affidavit of Peter C Hirst, Case on Appeal Vol 7, Tab 2, respectively paras 11 and 14. Available by request from the Supreme Court www.scc-csc.ca/case-dossier/info/dock-regi-eng.aspx?cas=20747. Hirst's evidence is summarised in the Appellants Factum, para 24: https://aspercentre.ca/wp-content/uploads/2017/06/McKinney-Appellants-David-Walter-McKinney-Jr-et-al-ilovepdf-compressed.pdf accessed 20 October 2020

205 See for example, *Seldon (No 2)* [2014] ICR 1275 [26] (EAT) (Langstaff J), above, text to n 164. The 'reasonably necessary' rubric is a theme of Chapter 5 'Objective justification'.

206 [2018] IRLR 284 (EAT) [167] (Sir Alan Wilkie).

207 [2018] IRLR 302 (EAT) [83] (Sir Alan Wilkie).

208 [2019] ICR 1489 (CA).

Conclusion

The obvious conclusion to draw from the legislation and its interpretation is that age discrimination is not treated as seriously as other recognised forms of discrimination. The 'social policy' exception for direct age discrimination provided by EU legislation is evidence of this. It seems to have been taken as a signal by the courts to take a much more generous approach to proportionality arguments, especially concerning older workers and retirement. This generous approach is not expressed in the legislation. 'Proportionality' is defined in the same way across all protected characteristics. The same can be said for retirement, where the legislation provides no particularly significant special treatment. Bear in mind here that the objective justification, 'health and safety', and GOR defences do not distinguish on their face older from younger workers, and certainly not retirement.

These uncertainties, or fuzzy borders, are exacerbated in the UK, where the Supreme Court has seemingly inadvertently departed from the guidance given by the ECJ and instead followed cases decided around respective Member State social policies, when the instruction was to follow its own (UK) social policy. Thus, there is a gap between EU and UK law. But this is not the usual failure to implement stricter standards provided by the ECJ. The irony is, given the relative freedom of the UK courts post-Brexit, they may depart from this practice and follow UK state policy.

Further reading

E Dewhurst, 'Are older workers past their sell-by-date? A view from UK age discrimination law' (2015) 78(2) *MLR* 189.

L Vickers, *Comparative Discrimination Law: Age as a Protected Ground* (Brill, 2018).

L Vickers and S Manfredi, 'Age equality and retirement: Squaring the circle' (2013) 42 (1) *ILJ* 61.

9 Victimisation and the unofficial defences

Introduction

In most western jurisdictions, discrimination law prohibits direct discrimination, indirect discrimination, and harassment, on protected grounds, such as race, sex, etc. Workers who use the legislation, or assist others to do so, need protection against retaliation by their employer. Accordingly, the legislation seeks to remove deterrents by creating a fourth cause of action, known in the UK as victimisation (and 'retaliation' in the US). The statutory formulas are sparse, apparently providing employers no defence. Yet in some cases, courts sympathetic to the employer have strained the formula to provide what amounts to a benign motive defence. The result is an incoherent body of case law. This chapter explores the problem in Britain, with some useful illustrations from the United States, highlighting the fuzzy borders created by the sympathetic courts.

It also suggests a new statutory formula that would provide certainty and clarity, as well as fulfilling the ambition of the anti-victimisation doctrine. Consider the following scenarios:

> Scenario 1: A worker issues discrimination proceedings against her employer and pending the outcome applies (unsuccessfully) for another job. Acting on standard legal advice, her employer refuses to provide a reference, as a precaution that anything said in it could prejudice the employer's defence. The reference would have been negative in any case and the refusal was not the cause of the worker failing to get the job. Nonetheless, the worker sues again, this time for victimisation.
>
> Scenario 2: A worker issues discrimination proceedings against her employer, who, following standard practice, suspends the worker's internal grievance process, pending the outcome of the proceedings. The worker now sues for victimisation.

In these scenarios, the employer has responded to legal proceedings in a predictable manner. It does not wish to create evidence that could prejudice its defence at the trial, for instance, by making informal concessions in a grievance process, or omitting minor faults (relevant to the claim) in a job reference.

DOI: 10.4324/9781003187547-9

Neither does it wish to state anything that could constrain its lawyers, in say, negotiation or tactics. In the second scenario, it may want to avoid the expense of duplicative proceedings. And at some stage in litigation, the employer will treat the claimant less favourably than it would treat a person who has brought no proceedings. No one would suggest, for instance, that a tribunal should excuse a claimant or her witnesses from rigorous cross-examination. If the employer must treat the complainant as it would treat a person who had not brought proceedings, the logical conclusion is that the employer cannot defend its case. By default, the employer would lose most, if not all, claims of victimisation.

Yet, in these scenarios, the worker is denied a reference or grievance process because she issued a discrimination claim, and even if she suffers no tangible harm by this (as suggested, perhaps, in Scenario 1), *other* workers, having seen that normal benefits of employment will be denied, would be deterred from making or supporting allegations of discrimination. Where the grievance process is suspended, the worker loses the chance of an informal resolution. Where the process is likely to exceed the statutory time limit, the worker faces a stark choice between the costs, time and stress of litigation, or dropping the litigation altogether. From this perspective, policy dictates that these employers should be liable for victimisation. The scenarios represent a universal 'victimisation dilemma'. In the United States, the dilemma was characterised thus:

> We recognize the countervailing concerns in this area of the law. On the one hand, we worry that employers will be paralyzed into inaction once an employee has lodged a complaint.... On the other hand, we are concerned about the chilling effect on employee complaints resulting from an employer's retaliatory actions.[1]

The dilemma is one of policy. However, the courts are hampered in solving it by the constrained statutory formula, which provides for liability simply where the employer invokes its general policy against a worker because the worker has been involved in a protected activity, such as bringing or supporting discrimination proceedings. There is no defence. On the face of it then, employers should automatically be liable in these scenarios. However, in a series of cases, British courts have sided *with* the employers, save where the employer has exceeded normal practice. In the United States, courts have vacillated, whilst the scant case law of the ECJ suggests that courts should take the workers' perspective. It follows that at least some of these decisions do not sit easily with the statutory formula and do not appear harmonious. This body of case law has produced a fuzzy border between a defendant's right to defend themself against litigation and the claimant's right not to be intimidated, deterred, or victimised for having made a complaint.

1 *Brooks v San Mateo* 229 F 3d 917 (9th Cir 2000) 928 (Judge Kozinski).

In addition to recognising this fuzzy border, the aim of this chapter is to resolve, as far as possible, this victimisation dilemma. Using the two scenarios, it investigates the problem exposed by the body of case law in both Britain and the United States. It will explore the dilemma and highlight any technical shortcomings or triumphs of the legislative formulas and case law. It will explore analogies with conventional discrimination and alternative theories of victimisation, and conclude that some victimisation cases are more analogous to the US doctrine of *discrimination by proxy*, or as it was once understood in the UK, *disability-related discrimination*. It concludes that although the victimisation dilemma cannot be entirely resolved, a new statutory formula with limited general and specific defences and guidelines would produce clearer boundaries and make this area of the law more predictable for employers and workers alike.

The legislation

The UK statutory formula for victimisation, originating in the Sex Discrimination Act 1975 and the Race Relations Act 1976 was revised in the Equality Act 2010, essentially to remove the comparative 'less favourable' element. For the purposes of the 'victimisation dilemma', little turned on this amendment. Most of the problematic case law was based on the old definition, which is set out here. The Race Relations Act 1976 provided:

> 2. Discrimination by way of victimisation[2]
> (1) A person ('the discriminator') discriminates against another person ('the person victimised') in any circumstances relevant for the purposes of any provision of this Act if he treats the person victimised less favourably than in those circumstances he treats or would treat other persons, and does so by reason that the person victimised has -
> (a) brought proceedings against the discriminator or any other person under this Act; or
> (b) given evidence or information in connection with proceedings brought by any person against the discriminator or any other person under this Act; or
> (c) otherwise done anything under or by reference to this Act in relation to the discriminator or any other person; or
> (d) alleged that the discriminator or any other person has committed an act which (whether or not the allegation so states) would amount to a contravention of this Act, or by reason that the discriminator knows

2 Similar definitions are provided in the parallel legislation: Sex Discrimination Act 1975, s 4; Employment Equality (Religion or Belief) Regulations 2003 SI 2003/1660 reg 4; Employment Equality (Sexual Orientation) Regulations 2003 SI 2003/1661 reg 4; Employment Equality (Age Regulations) 2006 SI 2006/1031, reg 4; Disability Discrimination Act 1995, s 55; Fair Employment and Treatment Order 1998 (Northern Ireland) SI 1998/3162, art 3.

that the person victimised intends to do any of those things, or suspects that the person victimised has done, or intends to do, any of them.

(2) Subsection (1) does not apply to treatment of a person by reason of any allegation made by him if the allegation was false and not made in good faith.

Paragraphs (a) to (d) define the 'protected acts'. The formula provides three elements: (1) the worker did a protected act; (2) the employer treated the worker less favourably than it treated (or would have treated) others; and (3) it did so *by reason that* the worker did the protected act. In addition, the treatment must have been employment-related.

The amended definition provided by the Equality Act 2010, section 27, draws together and largely replicates this version, save for one major change. It is no longer necessary to prove that the defendant treated the victim 'less favourably', only that the defendant *subjects him to a detriment.* This new phrase dispenses with the comparison, and so technically, victimisation is no longer a form of discrimination.[3] The EU directives provide a more general, but essentially similar, formula. For instance, the Race Directive provides that member States shall 'protect individuals from any adverse treatment or adverse consequence as a reaction to a complaint or to proceedings aimed at enforcing compliance with the principle of equal treatment'.[4]

The federal legislation in the United States is formulated in a broadly similar way to the UK version. Title VII of the Civil Rights Act 1964 outlaws employment discrimination 'because of' race, colour, sex, religion, and national origin. In addition, section 704(a) provides:

> It shall be an unlawful employment practice for an employer to discriminate against any of his employees or applicants for employment … because he has opposed any practice made an unlawful employment practice by this subchapter, or because he has made a charge, testified, assisted, or participated in any manner in an investigation, proceeding, or hearing under this subchapter.[5]

3 For problems with the comparison in victimisation, see *Aziz v Trinity Street Taxis Ltd* [1989] Q.B. 463 (CA), overruling *Kirby v Manpower Services Commission* [1980] ICR 420 (EAT).

4 Council Directive (EC) 2000/43 implementing the principle of equal treatment between persons irrespective of racial or ethnic origin [2000] OJ L 180, art 9. See also, Council Directive (EEC) 76/207 on the implementation of the principle of equal treatment for men and women as regards access to employment, vocational training and promotion, and working conditions [1976] OJ L 39, art 7; Council Directive (EC) 2000/78 establishing a general framework for equal treatment in employment and occupation [2000] OJ L 303, art 11.

5 Codified as 42 USC §2000e-3. Similar definitions are provided in Age Discrimination in Employment Act 1967 (29 USC § 623(d)) and the Americans with Disabilities Act 1990 (42 USC § 12203(a)).

The British formula covers a broad range of protected in acts. Note the 'catch-all' paragraph (1)(c). Sub-section (2) provides an exception only where an *allegation was false and not made in good faith.* Title VII's slightly looser formula simply protects those who have 'opposed' unlawful discrimination or 'participated' in proceedings.

Although the Equality Act 2010, and its predecessors, covers employment, services, public functions, housing, and education, the cases on the victimisation dilemma centre on employment. Unlike Title VII, which outlaws simply discriminatory 'employment practices', the British legislation specifies the employment practices where discrimination is unlawful. This includes recruitment, the terms of employment, access to opportunities for promotion, transfer or training, or to any other benefits, facilities or services, dismissal, or 'subjecting him to any other detriment'.[6]

For liability, the victimisation must relate to one of these rather specific practices or *any other detriment.* The obvious purpose of this last element is to catch any other unspecified employment-related treatment.

The scenarios

Scenario 1: Withholding a reference

This scenario has two noticeable features. First, the employer has not acted out of malice, but merely to defend itself in litigation. Second, the claimant apparently suffered no harm because the reference would have been negative in any case. This occurred in *Chief Constable of West Yorkshire v Khan.*[7] Sergeant Khan had issued discrimination proceedings against his employer, and pending the trial applied for a post with the Norfolk Constabulary. His employer refused to give a job reference. The reason given for this refusal was that it 'might compromise the chief constable and other respondents' handling of the case'.[8] Reversing all below, the House of Lords unanimously rejected Khan's victimisation claim, holding that the Chief Constable had not acted 'by reason that' Khan had brought proceedings, because the employer had acted 'honestly and reasonably' in accordance with 'perfectly understandable advice'.[9] In coming to this conclusion, the House relied on the distinction, made in *Cornelius v University College of Swansea,*[10] between a reaction to the *bringing* of proceedings (unlawful) and their *existence* (lawful).[11]

6 See RRA 1976, s 4(2); SDA 1975, s 6(2) (although *terms* predominantly are governed by the Equal Pay Act 1970, s 1); DDA 1995, s 4(4); Religion or Belief Regulations 2003, reg 6(2); Sexual Orientation Regulations 2003, reg 6(2), Age Regulations 2006, reg 6(2); Fair Employment and Treatment Order 1998 (NI), art 19. See now, Equality Act 2010, s 39(3), (4).

7 [2001] ICR 1065 (HL).

8 Ibid., [79].

9 Ibid., respectively [31], [44], reversing [2000] ICR 1169 (CA).

10 [1987] IRLR 141 (CA) 145–146. See text to n 14.

11 [2001] ICR 1065, [59], and [80].

In the US case, *Sparrow v Piedmont Health*, the claimant worked for a nursing agency, and after filing a complaint of sex discrimination, she requested a reference from her employer, who refused because while the complaint was pending: 'Mrs Sparrow may attempt to use the recommendation adversely against the Agency whether it be very favourable, favourable or not at all favourable'.[12] As in *Khan*, the reference was refused on legal advice that it could compromise the employer's defence. The advice differed slightly, because in *Khan* the employer was minded to provide a negative reference. In *Sparrow*, the lawyers feared a reference of any sort (be it negative, neutral, or positive) could be used against the employer. In the event, this refusal caused Sparrow no harm, as her prospective employer did not ask for a reference. And so, like *Khan*, this is a 'no reference-no harm' case. However, in this case a district court held employer liable for victimisation. The reasoning was sparse, stating simply that it 'sympathises' with the employer's position, but employers are liable if they refuse to provide a reference 'solely because' an employee has issued Title VII proceedings.[13]

Scenario 2: Suspending the grievance process

Suspending the grievance process and victimisation

The various approaches to this issue are represented by three cases. First, in *Cornelius v University College of Swansea*,[14] Ms Cornelius brought proceedings against her employer under the Sex Discrimination Act 1975 and, pending the outcome, she was refused a transfer request and access to the grievance process. Consequently, she brought a separate action of victimisation. The Court of Appeal rejected her claim for two reasons, the first centring on the causative element:

> The existence of the proceedings plainly did influence [the employer's] decisions. No doubt, like most experienced administrators, they recognised the risk of acting in a way which might embarrass the handling or be inconsistent with the outcome of current proceedings. They accordingly wished to defer action until the proceedings were over. But that had … nothing to do with the appellant's conduct in bringing proceedings under the Act.[15]

In other words, the Court distinguished between the *bringing* of proceedings and their *existence*. This enabled the Court to find that the protected act (the

12 593 F Supp 1107 (MDNC 1984), at para 12.
13 Ibid., 1118–1119.
14 [1987] IRLR 141.
15 Ibid., 145–146.

bringing of proceedings) was not the cause of the suspension of the grievance proceedings.

The second reason given was that Cornelius was not treated less favourably. The Court offered no reasoning for this decision, stating only, 'There is no finding that … [less favourable treatment] is made out, and it would certainly not be safe to infer that conclusion from the findings which have been made'.[16]

In the US case, *EEOC v Board of Governors of State Colleges and Universities and University Professionals of Illinois*,[17] the collective agreement provided a general policy to withdraw the grievance process from any worker who instigated legal proceedings against the employer. One Professor Lewis instigated the grievance process because he was not recommended for tenure. His complaint was that this decision breached University procedure. Lewis's grievance took more than a year to process. In the meantime, he issued proceedings for age discrimination in relation to his tenure claim, under the federal Age Discrimination in Employment Act 1967.[18] In accordance with its policy, the employer withdrew from the grievance process. On Lewis' behalf, the EEOC[19] brought these proceedings for victimisation. The employer argued first that the policy was invoked in good faith to save duplicative litigation. The Seventh Circuit wholly rejected this:

> [The legislation] is concerned with the effect of discrimination against employees who pursue their federal rights, not the motivation of the employer who discriminates.... The employer may not proffer a good faith reason for taking retaliatory action.[20]

The court bolstered its opinion using direct discrimination as an analogy, noting that 'an employer's alleged good faith is irrelevant, just as evidence of good faith has been held to be irrelevant in a case involving a discriminatory policy'.[21] On a point of statutory interpretation, the court noted that the legislation provided no exceptions to a retaliation claim, such as when retaliation would be rational or financially prudent, or in 'good faith', or otherwise. Instead, it advised, 'If the Board wants to lobby for a benign discrimination exception … its appeal would be appropriately directed to Congress rather than this Court'.[22]

The employer's second argument was that as the policy applied to all claims, whatever their nature, it did not treat Title VII claimants any less favourably than those who would sue for other reasons. The court rejected this argument

16 Ibid.
17 957 F 2d 424 (7th Cir 1992).
18 29 USC 621.
19 The Equal Employment Opportunity Commission, which is Federal enforcement body. See www.eeoc.gov.
20 957 F 2d 424, 427–428 (7th Cir 1992).
21 Ibid., 429.
22 Ibid., 428.

because workers' rights were just as 'effectively stifled' under the broadened policy.[23]

A third argument put forward was that the difference in treatment caused Lewis no harm. The court rejected this, largely on the facts. If Professor Lewis had waited for the year-long grievance process to conclude, his litigation would have been time-barred. In addition, his internal complaint related to the non-adherence to rules of tenure, rather than age discrimination, so different issues were to be decided.

The third case is *US v New York City Transit Authority*.[24] Here the employer operated a voluntary grievance process. However, if a complaint became formalised,[25] the employer would transfer it to its legal department and terminate the internal grievance process. The Second Circuit held that the policy did not amount to victimisation. It declared that 'ordinary' or 'reasonable defensive measures' were lawful, even though they result in adverse and differential treatment. A decision otherwise, the court stated, 'would impair the ability of an employer to place its defence in the hands of counsel', preventing 'the most basic precautions to defend against the claim' and the securing of attorney-client privilege to 'protect the fruits of investigation'. Further, findings by the grievance process may be used to prejudice the employer's defence at trial. Lastly, the policy is efficient and effective because it avoids parallel and duplicative proceedings. Overall, the employer should be 'free to choose to act in a benign and sympathetic way by satisfying grievances and settling disputes, or to proceed aggressively with litigation'.[26]

Time bars and the grievance process

There may be tactical reasons why a claimant launches legal action before the grievance process is complete. But one common reason will be to avoid being time-barred and losing any legal remedy. Where the employer's grievance process is likely to drag on beyond the three-month limitation period,[27] the worker has little option but to issue proceedings. Indeed, one reason the worker in the *Board of Governors* case launched his litigation was that the grievance process was likely to take a year to complete. Perhaps surprisingly, the courts will not normally extend the time limit because the claimant has waited for the outcome of the grievance process before issuing proceedings.[28] This procedural restriction is highly aggravating here, and militates against the

23 Ibid., 431.

24 97 F 3d 672 (2nd Cir 1996). Followed *Richardson v Commission on Human Rights* 2008 US App. LEXIS 15206 (2nd Cir 2008).

25 That is, either by litigation or by a discrimination charge filed with the EEOC.

26 97 F 3d 672, 677–678 (2nd Cir 1996).

27 Equality Act 2010, s 123. In the US, it is normally 180 days.

28 *Robinson v Post Office* [2000] IRLR 804 (EAT) [29]–[31] approved *Apelogun-Gabriels v Lambeth LBC* [2002] ICR 713 (CA), [16] and [24]. The position is similar in the US: *Delaware State College v Ricks* 449 US 250, 261 (Sup Ct 1980).

purpose of removing deterrents to invoking the anti-discrimination provisions. Effectively, the worker may choose either an informal (and presumably more amicable) solution *or* litigation.

Evaluation of the victimisation dilemma

To evaluate technically this apparent diversity of opinion, it is helpful to examine the cases element-by-element.

'By reason that', causation and motive

This element was discussed explicitly in *Cornelius, Board of Governors, Khan*, and *Sparrow* (briefly); and implicitly in *New York City Transit*. In essence, the arguments centre on a benign motive defence. This was expressed by the employer in *Board of Governors*, and roundly rejected.[29] It can also be detected in *Cornelius*, where the Court of Appeal compared the employer to 'most experienced administrators', when distinguishing the *bringing* from the *existence* of proceedings.[30] The House of Lords built on this logic in *Khan*, and ventured a step further, holding that an employer acting *honestly and reasonably* should not be liable for victimisation.[31] More recently, in *St Helens BC v Derbyshire*,[32] the House of Lords has rowed back from this position by 'reinterpreting' *Khan* as a case turning on the element in the employment provisions of *any other detriment*.

The distinction between the bringing and the existence of proceedings

This distinction is as artificial as it sounds. Its futility is realised by adding a second protected act to the claim, which could arise under the catch-all paragraph 1*(c)* if the claimant had 'otherwise done anything under or by reference to this Act'.[33] As well as having *brought* proceedings, the claimant was 'otherwise' *maintaining* them in existence. After all, on the court's logic, if maintaining proceedings is different from commencing them, paragraph 1*(c)* seems the appropriate place for such a claim.[34]

Further, this fine distinction between the *bringing* and *existing* of proceedings shows a drift away from the 'straightforward' approach adopted by the House

29 See text et al. to n 17.
30 See text to n 15.
31 See text to n 9. For the facts, see text to n 7.
32 [2007] ICR 841. For the facts, see text to n 72.
33 See e.g. RRA 1976, s 2(1)*(c)*. See section 2 above.
34 The distinction became even less credible when the employment tribunal in *St Helens v Derbyshire* made a third distinction: that the employer reacted not to the commencement or existence of proceedings, but to their 'continuance' (para 4(e) of the ET Decision, cited [2007] ICR 841 (HL) [55].) For the facts, see text to n 72.

of Lords in *Nagarajan v LRT*, where Lord Nicholls said: 'in the application of this legislation legalistic phrases, as well as subtle distinctions, are better avoided so far as possible'.[35] Finally, this distinction, which asks *why* the employer so acted, is rooted in the *employer's* perspective, which, according to the House of Lords, is contrary to EC law.[36] It is artificial, unduly legalistic, and contrary to EC law. As such it serves no useful purpose.

A benign motive defence?

Of course, what the courts were trying to achieve with this distinction (between the bringing and existence of proceedings) is exoneration for employers who defend litigation in the normal way. This is apparent from Lord Hoffman's observation in *Khan*:

> once proceedings have been commenced … the employer and employee become adversaries in litigation. That adversarial relationship … may reasonably cause the employer to [treat] … the employee less favourably than someone who had not commenced such proceedings. But the treatment need not be, consciously or unconsciously, a response to the commencement of proceedings. It may simply be a reasonable response to the need to protect the employer's interests as a party to the litigation.[37]

Here, in one piece of reasoning, Lord Hoffman combines the distinction with a 'reasonable' response 'to protect the employer's interests'.

This approach is also apparent in *New York City Transit*.[38] Although the causative element was conceded by the employer, the court's allusion to the employer's 'ordinary' and 'reasonable defensive measures'[39] indicates the employer's motive was the real reason for the decision. The judgment placed the reasonableness of the employer's conduct above any consequential adverse effect on the plaintiff. This suggests that this decision was based on the causative element, despite the employer's concession.

This sympathy for the 'reasonable' employer suggests that British and American judges have recognised a benign motive defence. The first suggestion of a benign motive defence in British victimisation cases arose in *Aziz v Trinity Street Taxis*.[40] Here, a taxi association expelled a member for making secret tape recordings to support a complaint of racial discrimination. Although the Court

35 [2001] AC 501, 513 (HL).

36 In Case C-185/97 *Coote v Granada* [1998] ECR-I 5199, [24], the ECJ focused on the deterrent effect of an employer's act on workers. In *St Helens Borough Council v Derbyshire* [2007] ICR 841[24]–[27], [66], the House of Lords held that this meant in victimisation cases the worker's perspective should prevail.

37 [2001] ICR 1065, [59].

38 97 F 3d 672 (2nd Cir 1996). See text to n 24.

39 Ibid.

40 [1989] QB 463.

of Appeal found he had been treated less favourably, it then went on to hold that this was not because of the protected act, but because of a breach of confidence.[41] On behalf of the court, Slade LJ explained that the victimisation provisions

> are concerned with the *motive* which caused the alleged discriminator to treat the complainant less favourably than other persons. In our judgment ... [it] contemplates a motive which is consciously connected with the race relations legislation.[42]

The House of Lords later disapproved of this quote, but not the decision.[43] Nonetheless, the theme returned in *Khan*, with Lord Scott stating that the statutory phrase *by reason that* suggested 'motive',[44] whilst Lord Nicholls said, 'Unlike causation, this is a subjective test',[45] implying the defendant's motive was the key. Elsewhere in *Khan*, the judges used different language to express the same thing, holding that an employer acting 'honestly and reasonably' should not be liable for victimisation.[46]

But, in *St Helens BC v Derbyshire,*[47] the House of Lords reinterpreted *Khan*, with a majority stating that the *honest and reasonable* 'defence' was simply another way of expressing that the worker had suffered no detriment: if the employer acted honestly and reasonably, it could not cause the worker a detriment.[48] Only Baroness Hale was more trenchant, stating, 'It would be better if the [honest and reasonable] "defence" were laid to rest and the language of the legislation, construed in the light of the requirements of the Directives, applied'.[49]

41 Ibid., 483–485.
42 Ibid., 485.
43 *Nagarajan v LRT* [2000] 1 AC 501, 512. The *decision* could be easily explained under US law, because it is unlikely that the breach of confidence would be regarded as a protected act, permitting a linguistically neater - if substantially the same - solution: see *Hochstadt v Worcester Foundation for Experimental Biology*, 545 F 2d 222, 228, 230 & 233 (1st Cir 1976). UK courts have less latitude, as an act is unprotected only if it is a false allegation and not made in good faith. This makes it more difficult to separate the breach of confidence from the collecting of evidence. See *Aziz* [1989] QB 463, 479 (holding that the secret recording was a protected act).
44 [2001] ICR 1065, [77].
45 Ibid., [29].
46 Ibid., [31] (Lord Nicholls); [44] The employer 'acted in accordance with perfectly understandable advice' (Lord Mackay); [80] The result allowed 'justice to be done to an employer who…would otherwise be placed…in an unacceptable Morton's fork'. (Lord Scott); [59] It was 'a reasonable response to the need to protect the employer's interests as a party to litigation'. (Lord Hoffman).
47 [2007] ICR 841. For the facts, see text to n 72.
48 Ibid., [68].
49 Ibid., [36].

The flaw in the majority's logic is that in most cases an employer defending litigation *will* cause a detriment, even though it acted just as 'honestly and reasonably' as Khan's employer.[50] This is the case normally with a denial of a grievance process or a job reference. If a case came before the House precisely the same as *Khan*, save that the denial of the reference *did* cause the claimant harm (e.g. because it would have been positive), a court either would have to find for the claimant, leaving *Khan* marooned and fit only to be distinguished to death, or find for the employer on the basis that it acted honestly and reasonably even though the claimant had been harmed. Thus, an honest and reasonable response by an employer normally cannot be equated with causing a worker no detriment.[51] Despite the opinions in *St Helens*, the deciding factor in *Khan* was the employer's reason, or motive, for acting, not the effect on the claimant, and the *honest and reasonable* defence survives.[52]

Once it is established that the decisions in *Cornelius* and *Khan* (and *New York City Transit*) turned on the employer's benign motive, it becomes easier to evaluate them. The first and most obvious problem for a benign motive defence is that it does not appear in the legislation.[53]

The legitimacy of such a defence has often been questioned using the meaning of the apparently parallel definition of direct discrimination. Here, there is discrimination if the employer treats the worker less favourably *on the ground of* sex, or race, etc. The phrase *on the ground of* is the supposed counterpart of the phrase *by reason that*, or more recently *because of*.[54] In the United States, Title VII of the Civil Rights Act 1964 more simply repeats the word *because* for this element.[55]

50 It also effectively overrules *Khan*, where a differently constituted House found that Khan *had* suffered a detriment. See M Connolly, 'Easy Case Makes Bad Law' (2007) 36 ILJ 364, 367–371.

51 For a discussion of whether harm or detriment should be necessary for liability, see 'Distinguishing the meaning of victimisation from the employment provisions' p. 0000.

52 It was applied, post-*St Helens*, in *Bird v Sylvester* [2008] ICR 208, [10], where the Court of Appeal also repeated the inaccurate equation that honest and reasonable conduct cause no detriment.

53 Noted in *EEOC v Board of Governors*, 957 F 2d 424, 428 (7th Cir 1992), text et al. to n 17.

54 Equality Act 2010, s 13. The Explanatory Note (61) to s 13, stated that this 'does not change the legal meaning of the definition'. It was merely 'designed to make it more accessible to the ordinary user of the Act'.

55 Sections 703(a) (discrimination) and 704(a) (victimisation) (42 USC § 2000e-2(a) and 42 USC § 2000e-3). See text to n 5. Note however, that s 703(a) provides only a general rubric against discrimination. The notions of direct and indirect discrimination (known as disparate treatment and disparate impact) were developed by the federal courts. For a summary, see e.g. *Teamsters v US* 431 US 324 335 n15 (Sup Ct 1977). For the *differences* between the discrimination and victimisation provisions, see *Burlington Northern v White* 126 S Ct 2405, 2411–2415 (Sup Ct 2006).

In both jurisdictions, a benign motive defence is not recognised for direct discrimination. This is to prevent employers citing 'customer preference' or 'appeasing the workforce' as motives for treating protected groups less favourably. For instance, in *Diaz v Pan American Airways*[56] a 'customer preference' for female cabin crew was rejected by a court of appeals as a defence to a direct discrimination claim brought by a male applicant. In *R v Commission for Racial Equality ex parte Westminster City Council*,[57] the council dismissed a newly-hired black worker to avoid industrial unrest from its white workforce. The Court of Appeal found the council liable for direct discrimination. Similarly, the US Supreme Court found an employer liable for refusing to hire fertile women on health grounds, stating that direct discrimination: 'does not depend on *why* the employer discriminates but rather on the explicit terms of the discrimination.... The beneficence of an employer's purpose does not undermine the conclusion that an explicit gender-based policy is sex discrimination'.[58]

This was the thinking behind the *but for* test decreed by Lord Goff in *James v Eastleigh*,[59] and adopted for the victimisation provisions in *Nagarajan*.[60] In the *Board of Governors* case, the court used the parallel with direct discrimination when rejecting the benign motive defence.[61] The point of the *but for* test, according to Lord Goff in *James*, was to avoid questions of motive.[62] But more recently, the House of Lords has drifted away from the *but for* test. Most notably, in *Shamoon v Chief Constable of the RUC*, a direct sex discrimination claim, the *but for* test was not mentioned. Instead, the Lords' speeches asked *why* the claimant was treated so.[63]

However, it is inconceivable on policy grounds that the House of Lords would decide any of the above *customer preference* or *appeasing the workforce* examples differently. The move could be explained by the House's perceived need to loosen the shackles of the *but for* test in victimisation cases, thus validating the decisions in *Cornelius* and *Khan*. The struggle with the *but for* test in victimisation cases is most evident in Lord Hoffman's speech in *Khan*. He first stated that the causal questions in the direct discrimination and victimisation provisions were 'not identical'.[64] This enabled him to distance the *but for* test

56 442 F 2d 385 (5th Cir 1971) certiorari denied 404 US 950 (Sup Ct 1971).

57 [1985] ICR 827 (CA). See also *Goodman v Lukens Steel* 482 US 656 (Sup Ct 1987).

58 *United Automobile Workers v Johnson Controls* 499 US 187, 199–200 (Sup Ct 1991) (Blackmun J), emphasis supplied. The Court held that decisions about the welfare of future children should be left to the parents.

59 [1990] AC 751 (HL), 774B-C.

60 [2001] AC 501 (HL). See section 2D above.

61 957 F 2d 424, 429 (7th Cir 1992), see text et al to n 7. Although the *but for* test is not used under Title VII: *Price Waterhouse v Hopkins* 490 US 228, 241 (1989 Sup Ct).

62 [1990] AC 751, 774 B-C.

63 [2003] ICR 337 (HL), [55] (Lord Hope), [116] (Lord Scott) and [134] (Lord Roger). For a technical objection to the *but for* test, see *Price Waterhouse v Hopkins* 490 US 228, at 241 (Sup Ct 1989) see above, p172, and more generally, M Connolly, *Discrimination Law* (Thomson: Sweet & Maxwell, 2011) p 90 et al.

64 [2001] ICR 1065, [56].

from the victimisation cases.[65] And this was because under the victimisation provisions, the reason for the treatment may be 'a reasonable response to the need to protect the employer's interests as a party to the litigation' which is not the same reason as the *commencement* of the proceedings.[66] By contrast, Lord Hoffman reasoned, 'Under section 1 [direct discrimination], one would have needed to go no further' than establish 'that an employee who had not commenced proceedings would not have been treated in the same way'.[67]

With respect, this is saying no more than that because the employers in these victimisation cases acted 'reasonably' the victimisation provisions are different and should accommodate a benign motive defence. The same could be said of direct discrimination where defendants have acted 'reasonably' by trying to help pensioners,[68] or protect women's fertility, or perhaps, avoid industrial unrest or accommodate customer preferences. The shortcoming of Lord Hoffman's reasoning is that it does not explain why 'reasonable' acts of victimisation should be defendable, whilst 'reasonable' acts of direct discrimination should not. This is in stark contrast to Lord Steyn's view in *Nagarajan* 'that victimisation is as serious a mischief as direct discrimination'.[69]

A more obvious difference between the formulas is that only direct discrimination carries specific *Genuine Occupational Requirement* or *Qualification* defences,[70] tempting a suggestion that courts should compensate for their absence victimisation cases. But, as the court in the *Board of Governors* case observed, if the legislature intended to validate victimisation where it would be rational, or financially prudent, or in 'good faith', or otherwise, it would have expressed this.[71] *Shamoon* removed one obstacle (the *but for* test) to a benign motive defence for victimisation cases, but it did not go so far as to validate such a defence.

This establishes the technical objection to a benign motive defence in victimisation cases. None appears in the legislation, and distinguishing the victimisation from the direct discrimination provisions cannot validate implying such a defence.

However, the practical benefit of a benign motive defence is that it provides a compromise of sorts to the victimisation dilemma. It permits employers to defend litigation, but confers to tribunals some control over their conduct. For example, in *St Helens BC v Derbyshire*,[72] the employer announced publicly that a minority of the workforce pursuing an equal pay claim were likely to cause redundancies. This effective threat was intimidating and likely to cause the claimants fear of public odium and reproaches by colleagues.[73]

65 Ibid., [57].
66 Ibid., [59].
67 Ibid., [59].
68 Rejected in *James v Eastleigh BC* [1990] AC 751.
69 [2000] 1 AC 501 (HL) 521.
70 See now Equality Act 2010, Sch 9, Part 1. Known in the US as *Bona Fide Occupational Qualifications*.
71 957 F 2d 424, 427–428 (7th Cir 1992). See text et al. to n 7.
72 [2007] ICR 841 (HL).
73 ET Reasons, para 4(d), cited ibid., [38].

The House of Lords found the employer liable for victimisation under the SDA 1975. Lord Neuberger (who gave the leading judgment) suggested that the employer should have set out privately 'in appropriately measured and accurate terms' the consequences of the claim succeeding.[74] This employer went beyond what was 'reasonable' by going public with the threat, and so could not rely on a benign motive in its defence. However, perhaps to escape accusations that it had created a benign motive defence, Lord Neuberger labelled the decision as turning on the element of 'detriment' in the employment provisions.[75] As such, in the context of victimisation, the element of *any other detriment* and the notion of harm require further consideration.

Harm, less *favourable, and detriment*

The requirement for *any other detriment* principally is the catch-all phrase to ensure that the treatment was employment-related. However, British courts have become preoccupied with the *standard* of harm required to meet this element. Given that most courts have assumed that the denial of a reference or a grievance process fell under *any other detriment*, the standard of harm required for this element can be critical. This also means that the issue of harm required for liability arises twice: once for less favourable treatment (or nowadays *subjects to a detriment*), and again for *any other detriment*.

Khan shows House of Lords following a consistent line of authority that the treatment is *less* favourable if the claimant perceived the treatment as less favourable, and that that perception was not unreasonable.[76] However, the standard of harm for *any other detriment* has varied somewhat. The general standard required was confirmed in the sex discrimination case *Shamoon v Chief Constable of the RUC*,[77] where the House of Lords asked if the treatment was such that 'a reasonable worker … might take the view … it was to his detriment?'[78] In *Shamoon*, one of the duties of a police inspector was the appraisal of officers. Following complaints by some of these officers, she was relieved of the appraisal duty. She brought a claim of sex discrimination.[79] The House of Lords held that the loss of the appraisal work was a detriment simply because it would reduce her standing amongst

74 Ibid., [68].

75 SDA 1975, s 6(2). See now Equality Act 2010, s 39(3), (4).

76 See, e.g. *EOC v Birmingham CC* [1989] 1 AC 1156 (HL); *Gill v El Vino* [1983] QB 425 (CA).

77 [2003] ICR 337.

78 Ibid., [35], citing *Ministry of Defence v Jeremiah* [1980] QB 87 (CA) 104. The same objective/subjective formula is used in the US. However, it is applied more robustly. In *Burlington Northern v White* 126 S Ct 2405, 2414–2415 (2006), the Supreme Court noted that 'personality conflicts at work that generate antipathy' and '"snubbing" by supervisors and co-workers' are not actionable.

79 Under the Sex Discrimination (Northern Ireland) Order 1976. Art 8(2)(b) is set out in identical terms to s 6(2)(b), SDA 1975.

colleagues.[80] Accordingly, in *Khan,*[81] Lord Nicholls reasoned that although Khan suffered no financial loss, he suffered a detriment because 'a reference is a normal feature of employment'.[82] Lord Hoffman held that given his state of mind at the time, Khan's view that he suffered a detriment 'was not unreasonable'.[83]

Specific limits to the meaning of detriment

On this element, *Shamoon* and *Khan* are consistent with each other and with the established meaning of what amounts to *less* favourable treatment. It is same mix of the subjective and objective and does not require some economic or physical consequence. However, case law has also provided one – or possibly two – limits specific to the element of *any other detriment* which could affect the victimisation cases.

First, there is long-standing Court of Appeal authority that the *de minimis* principle applies to the element of *any other detriment.*[84] In *Jiad v Byford*, May LJ observed *obiter* that 'Transitory hurt feelings may not (depending on the facts) suffice' for a detriment.[85] Ascribing the *de minimis* principle to the element of 'detriment' brings two problems. First, at the time, most of the European Directives mandated that there should be 'no discrimination *whatsoever*' on the protected grounds,[86] so it is questionable if the *de minimis* principle is compatible with EU law.[87] Second, as the legislation allows for damages for injury to feelings,[88] it would seem that even 'transitory hurt feelings' fall under this head. In *Vento v Chief Constable West Yorkshire Police,*[89] the Court of Appeal placed

80 [2003] ICR 337, [37], reversing [2001] IRLR 520 NICA. However, she lost her appeal because she was treated no less favourably than a male inspector would have been in the same circumstances.

81 [2001] ICR 1065.

82 Ibid., [14].

83 Ibid., [53].

84 *Peake v Automotive Products* [1978] QB 233, explained in *Ministry of Defence v Jeremiah* [1980] QB 87, 98.

85 [2003] IRLR 232 (CA) [21]. See also *Moyhing v Barts and London NHS Trust* [2006] IRLR 860 (EAT) [20].

86 Emphasis supplied. Equal Treatment Directive 76/207, art 2 (but not its successor, the 'Recast' Directive 2006/54/EC); Framework Directive 2000/78, art 2; but not the Race Directive 2000/43.

87 The only case law on the question is equivocal. See the Court of Appeal's opinion in the indirect sex discrimination case of *R v Secretary of State for Employment ex parte Seymour-Smith* [1995] ICR 889, 950, upheld [2000] ICR 244 (HL). At EU level, see the comment of AG Sharpston in C-400/08 *Re Shopping Centres Licensing: European Commission v Spain* [2011] 2 CMLR 50, para AG 63: 'The Court has never qualified that prohibition [on discrimination on the ground of nationality] by enunciating a *de minimis* criterion – a threshold of effect below which a measure is not caught'.

88 Noted by Lord Hoffman in *Khan* [2001] ICR 1065, [53]. See RRA 1976, s 57(4). See also SDA 1976. See now Equality Act 2010, ss 124(6) and 119(4).

89 [2002] ICR 318.

damages for *injury to feelings* into three bands. The lowest band, for 'less serious' cases, such as an 'isolated or one-off occurrence' should attract awards of between £500 and £5,000. In general, awards lower than this should not be made as they risk not showing a proper recognition of the injury to feelings.[90] The court did not mention if it envisaged a *de minimis* incident falling into this lowest band, but the reference to an isolated or one-off incident suggests that it could.

A possible second limit to the meaning of *detriment* could come about if the subjective/objective 'test' (see *Shamoon* and *Khan*, above) were reduced to a purely objective one, requiring tangible harm. This is the implication of the House of Lords' reinterpretation of *Khan* in *St Helens BC v Derbyshire*,[91] where Lord Neurberger (with whom the majority agreed on this point) explained *Khan* as turning on the element of *any other detriment*. Although he repeated the standard from *Shamoon*, he then stated that because the denial of the (negative) reference did not reduce Sergeant Khan's chances, the denial did *not* cause him a detriment.[92] This suggests, contrary to *Shamoon*, and indeed a differently constituted House in *Khan* itself, that the matter is purely objective and turns on whether the claimant actually suffered tangible harm. If this logic were taken up, all *no reference-no harm* cases will fail on this element, irrespective of any causative issue. This reinterpretation of *Khan* raises more questions than it solves. First, by suggesting that *Khan* was decided correctly because looked at objectively, Sergeant Khan had suffered no tangible harm, the House of Lords ignored its own opinion and ECJ authority that the matter should be judged from the worker's perspective.[93]

Second, the usefulness of *St Helens* analysis is reduced virtually to nil once it is appreciated that in most cases withholding a reference *will* harm the claimant. Normally, a reference would be positive or neutral, and so its withholding is very likely to damage the claimant's job prospects. There are less obvious possibilities as well, even where the reference would have been negative. For instance, an employer may damage the worker by informing the prospective employer of the reason for withholding the reference. Indeed, this occurred in *Khan*, a feature curiously overlooked in the speeches of both *Khan* and *St Helens*. In the US case *Rutherford v American Bank of Commerce*[94] an employer was held liable for victimisation after it 'eliminated' Ms Rutherford's chance of employment with another bank by informing it that she had brought a sex discrimination claim. This is enough to dissuade many employers from selecting a candidate. Even on a purely objective test, this alone would be detrimental to the worker. And even if it proved not detrimental to Khan, a reasonable worker would be entitled to fear so, which would lead to liability under the

90 Ibid., [65].
91 [2007] ICR 841. See further text to n 72.
92 [2007] ICR 841, [68].
93 See n 36.
94 565 F 2d 1162, 1164 (10th Cir 1977).

Khan or *Shamoon* 'reasonable worker' test. It is also the case that even where the employer does not provide a reason, the claimant could suffer a detriment simply because she would present an incomplete application, excluding her from any selection process.

Third, all these harmful outcomes could arise for exactly the same reason as the 'harmless' scenario in *Khan*: that the employer was acting on legal advice to protect its position in the principal proceedings. As such, the message sent out by *Cornelius* and *Khan* that employers may defend litigation in the normal way is highly misleading. The logic of *St Helens* places the employer's defence into the hands of fortune. The examples above show that only rarely will the claimant suffer no detriment, and where a reference is withheld, this normally will be beyond the control of the employer. Harm is even more likely when suspending a grievance process[95] (which suggests the House's tacit approval of *Cornelius* is suspect).[96] The irony of the House of Lords' analysis of *Khan* is that in trying to legitimise the reactions of 'reasonable' employers, it has reduced their defence virtually to nil.

Other issues with the harm principle

More generally, associating the element *any other detriment* with a harm principle raises four issues. First, it overlooks the deterrent effect on claimants. Second, it omits the deterrent effect on *other* workers. Third, it restricts tribunals' ability to order a remedy to *prevent* damage. Fourth, it could produce an anomaly.

First, the *St Helens* reinterpretation of *Khan* was described above as a *possible* limit to the element of *detriment* because on the facts before it the House of Lords found the employer liable. Yet, just as in *Khan*, the claimants were not physically or financially damaged by the council's public threat. The decision in *St Helens* is better explained by reverting to the purpose of the victimisation provisions. This was articulated by the ECJ in *Coote v Granada.*[97] Mrs Coote sued her employer following her dismissal for being pregnant. After those proceedings were settled, the employer refused to give her a reference and Coote sued for victimisation. The ECJ held that ex-workers must be protected from victimisation, otherwise

95 Save perhaps, in the unusual situation where a grievance process would have made no difference to the outcome; see ERA 1996, s 98A(2). For a robust view that suspending a grievance process will not cause harm, see *Lynch v Baylor* 2006 US Dist. LEXIS 62408, 31 (ND Tex 2006), affirmed 236 Fed Appx 918 (5th Cir 2007). 'Plaintiff suffered no harm from her inability to use Defendant's internal grievance procedure. By filing an EEOC complaint, Plaintiff could secure all the relief available from the internal grievance plus additional relief not available through Defendant's procedure'.

96 [2007] ICR 841, [4], [9], [15], [18], [21], [23].

97 Case C-185/97, [1999] ICR 100.

> [f]ear of such measures … might deter workers who considered themselves the victims of discrimination from pursuing their claims by judicial process … and would consequently be liable seriously to jeopardise implementation of the aim pursued by the [Equal Treatment] Directive.[98]

Similarly in the United States, in *Robinson v Shell*,[99] the Supreme Court stated that a primary purpose of the victimisation provisions is 'Maintaining unfettered access to statutory remedial mechanisms'. The Court held that providing a retaliatory negative reference for an ex-employee whilst discrimination proceedings were pending was unlawful. It noted that a decision otherwise would effectively vitiate much of the protection afforded by Title VII, by allowing the threat of post-employment retaliation to deter victims of discrimination from complaining, and providing a perverse incentive for employers to fire workers who might bring Title VII claims.[100] In both *Coote* and *Robinson,* the central issue was whether ex-workers were protected, but the underlying principle in each decision is that the purpose of the victimisation provisions is to outlaw deterrents to using the discrimination legislation.

Clearly, the claimants in *St Helens* could have been *deterred* from pursuing their equal pay claim, even though they were caused no tangible harm. This reasoning was not apparent in the speeches as the reinterpretation of *Khan* overshadowed the *ratio decidendi* of *St Helens*, which, logically, centred on the deterrent effect of the employer's action, rather than any notion of harm.

Second, a principle demanding that the *claimant* suffers harm, or is deterred, excludes conduct that could deter *others* from complaining about discrimination (or supporting such complaints). This has been characterised in some US courts as the 'chilling' effect of victimisation and is most apparent in job-reference cases. The 'fear of deterrent' purpose articulated in *Robinson* was presumed to cover third parties by the reputedly progressive Ninth Circuit in *Hashimoto v Dalton.*[101] Here Ms Hashimoto made a discrimination complaint whilst working for the Navy. After she was made redundant, but whilst her complaint was pending, she applied for a post with the Army. Her supervisor, Lowery, provided an undue negative job reference in retaliation for her discrimination complaint. However, Hashimoto's job application failed for other reasons. Nonetheless, she brought a claim of victimisation, which the court upheld. It was concerned with 'the chilling effect which Lowery's retaliatory conduct might have on the remaining employees under his supervision', even if the reference did not harm Hashimoto.[102]

98 Ibid., [24].

99 519 US 337 (1997).

100 Ibid., 345–346. Cited by the Supreme Court more recently in *Burlington Northern v White* 126 S Ct 2405, 2415 (Sup Ct 2006), where the majority stated that for liability the victimisation must have been such that it '*dissuaded* a reasonable worker from making or supporting a charge of discrimination'. (Emphasis supplied.)

101 118 F 3d 671 (9th Cir 1997) certiorari denied 523 US 1122 (Sup Ct 1998).

102 Ibid., 676. In *Carmona-Rivera v Commonwealth of Puerto Rico* 464 F 3d 14, 20 (2006), the 1st Circuit understood the 'reasonable worker' from *Burlington Northern*

Robinson and *Hashimoto* differ from *Khan* because references (albeit negative) were provided. *Hashimoto* and *Khan* stand out because the workers' job prospects were not damaged. *Coote* is distinguishable because although the claimant's job prospects were damaged (it was alleged), she could *not* have been deterred from pursuing her principal claim, as that had already been settled. Given that the ECJ expressed its judgment as based on the deterrent principle, their finding for Mrs Coote appears curious. An explanation is discernible in the US case *Smith v SEIU*.[103] Here, the plaintiff brought discrimination proceedings against his ex-employer, a trade union. After these proceedings were dead, the employer 'bad-mouthed' Smith in the industry, making it difficult for him to get further work. He sued for victimisation. The defendant employer argued that no reasonable person in Smith's position would be deterred by this retaliatory conduct; the principal proceedings were settled and Smith was no longer employed by the union. In other words, Smith 'had nothing to fear, and nothing to lose'. A district court rejected this argument. Citing *Hashimoto*, it stated, 'If defendants' interpretation were correct, a retaliation claim could never arise from conduct that occurs after protected activity. This is untenable'.[104]

This gets closer to the issue. It would be 'untenable' if it were lawful for employers simply to wait for the principal action to conclude, and *then* victimise the claimant. Indeed, this point was made by Lord Hoffman in *Khan*.[105] The effect would be two-fold. It would punish (or 'harm') the claimant for having complained about discrimination, and it would deter others from making such complaints. The only 'deterrent' here is to others, as the claimant's case has concluded. The same could be said of *Coote*. If – as the ECJ declared – the purpose of the law of victimisation is to allay fears of deterrents, and the claimant can no longer be deterred from pursuing her principal claim because it has been settled, the only persons who possibly could be deterred from making complaints are other workers. Thus, it could be said logically that the decision in *Coote* did not depend on whether Mrs Coote's job prospects actually were damaged; the deciding factor was that the employer's conduct could deter others from 'pursuing their claims by judicial process'.[106] Focussing on tangible harm to the claimant misses the broader purpose of victimisation law, which is to outlaw conduct that could deter the claimant or *other* workers from enforcing anti-discrimination law.

A third issue arising from the requirement of harm is that it restricts remedies preventing future damage. For instance, a worker in fear of her job prospects being damaged by the absence of a reference would have to wait until damage

(n 100) to include other workers. This is also the view of the Federal enforcement commission, the Equal Employment Opportunity Commission: 2 EEOC Compliance Manual §8, 8–12, 13 (1998).

103 153 Lab Cas (CCH) P35, 171 (ND Cal 2006).

104 Ibid., 12.

105 [2001] ICR 1065, [60].

106 Case C-185/97, [1999] ICR 100, [24].

was done before bringing an action for victimisation. In *Hashimoto*, damages were not awarded, but a remedial order preventing further retaliatory conduct, plus the plaintiff's costs, were ordered.[107] Thus, if liability depended on whether the refusal could deter the claimant *or* others from using the legislation, a tribunal could make a recommendation[108] (e.g. that the employer provides a reference), thus preventing damage to the claimant and dispelling the deterrent to others. If the problem were remedied at this early stage, damages would be minimal.

Fourth, demanding a certain degree of harm for the element *any other detriment* overlooks that this element is only one of many categories of employment-related conduct which is unlawful. Where, for instance, a case falls within *terms of employment* or *access to training, benefits etc.*,[109] there can be no workable *de minimis* principle: if the less favourable treatment relates to the terms of employment or training, benefits *etc*, the employment element is met. There is no question of degree.[110] The anomaly is that less favourable treatment that produced no tangible harm would be unlawful if it related to a term or benefit of employment, but lawful if it related only to *any other detriment*. Thus, had Khan couched his claim as a depravation of a benefit[111] (as Lord Mackay presumed)[112] no question of detriment would have arisen, leaving no scope for the House of Lords in *St Helens* to explain *Khan* as turning on the absence of a detriment.

British courts have taken the element *any other detriment* and ascribed to it various standards of harm required for liability. This focus on harm resembles the question of whether the treatment was *less* favourable, and tends to duplicate that question, save that the limits placed on what amounts to a detriment have produced an anomaly and thrown up a number of problems. These limits, especially as suggested in *St Helens*, will: (1) only apply to cases where the claim is pleaded under *any other detriment* and the claimant suffered no harm; (2) exclude from the provisions conduct that only deters the (unharmed) claimant

107 118 F 3d 671 (9th Cir 1997) 677–678.
108 SDA 1975, s 65(1)(c); see now Equality Act 2010, s 124(2)(c).
109 See n 6 and accompanying text.
110 See e.g. *Gill v El Vino* [1983] QB 425, where the less favourable treatment related to the parallel provisions for the supply of goods, facilities, or services under SDA 1975, s 29. These provisions outlaw discrimination by either *refusing* the service, or not providing it in the *like quality, manner, or terms*. The Court of Appeal, when upholding the plaintiff's claim, criticised the county court judge for confusing the simple question of whether the plaintiff was refused a service, with an inquiry into whether she suffered a 'detriment' and thus held that a refusal to serve women at the bar, offering table service instead, was *de minimis*. The judge should have then asked a separate question as to whether the refusal was 'less favourable'. See ibid., at 431 (Everleigh LJ), 432 (Brightman LJ), 432 (Sir Roger Ormrod).
111 Under RRA 1976, s 4(2)(b). See section 2B above.
112 [2001] ICR 1065, [38]. See also Lord Nicholls in *Rhys-Harper v Relaxion* [2003] ICR 867 (HL) [36], [45] (reference is a 'benefit'), and Lord Woolf in *Spring v Guardian Royal Exchange* [1994] ICR 596 (HL) 647 (reference is an implied contractual term).

or other workers; and (3) in some cases deny a remedy that would prevent an employer causing future damage to the claimant. Further, these limits enfeeble any so-called *honest and reasonable* defence because they render the employer's defence (of protecting its legal position) dependant on whether per chance the claimant suffered no harm, which in any event would be most unusual.

Distinguishing the meaning of victimisation from the employment provisions

At the root of these problems is the blurring of two distinct elements. The standard of treatment and harm (if any) required should belong to the element *treats less favourably/subjects to a detriment*, whilst the element *subjecting him to any other detriment* is concerned principally to ensure that the treatment is employment-related. The problem is the undue emphasis towards harm given to this second element and the differing standards ascribed to it.

A logical solution is to hold that establishing less favourable treatment is sufficient to establish a *detriment*. However, in *Khan*, Lord Hoffman observed, 'A person may be treated less favourably and yet suffer no detriment'.[113] He explained how the absence of a reference was *less* favourable (because of injury to feelings) but not detrimental because it caused Khan no economic loss.[114] But then curiously in the same paragraph he stated that the term *detriment* should be given a 'wide meaning' because of the availability of damages for injury to feelings. Upon this, Lord Hoffman held that Khan *had* suffered a detriment.[115] The matter was further confused by the analysis of *Khan* by a differently constituted House in *St Helens*, who considered that Sergeant Khan had *not* suffered a detriment.[116] This confusion alone is enough to support an equalising of standards. And with respect to Lord Hoffman, to layperson and lawyer alike, the notion that the same treatment is less favourable but not detrimental is anomalous, confusing,[117] and shows another drift away from the 'straightforward' approach urged by the House of Lords in *Nagarajan*.[118]

Although an equalising of standards is a logical solution, it is a distraction from the proper function of this element, which is ensuring that treatment was work-related.[119] For claims falling under *any other detriment*, liability should depend upon whether there was *work-related* less favourable treatment because of a prohibited ground (in this context a protected act). The practical solution

113 [2001] ICR 1065, [53].
114 Ibid., [52].
115 See n 50.
116 [2007] ICR 841, [68]. Lords Bingham [9], Carswell [43], and Baroness Hale [42] agreed with Lord Neuberger.
117 See e.g. *Jiad v Byford* [2003] IRLR 232, where the Court of Appeal and both tribunals below debated at length whether alleged workplace bullying was to the claimant's 'detriment' without questioning if it were *less* favourable. If the claimant had alleged that bullying related to his terms of employment (see e.g. *Reed v Stedman* [1999] IRLR 299 [19]), there would have been no such debate.
118 [2000] 1 AC 501, 513 (Lord Nicholls). See text to n 35.
119 *Cf* US approach: *Burlington Northern v White* 126 S Ct 2405 (2006), at 2414–2415.

for claimants is, where possible, to plead a case under one of the other 'employment-related' headings, such as *other benefits*, which readily covers grievance procedures and references.[120]

The new definition of victimisation, brought in with the Equality Act 2010, section 27,[121] appears to have endorsed, albeit inadvertently, the existing case law. The main purpose of this revision was to remove the comparative element (*less favourable treatment*), which had caused problems.[122] It was replaced with the phrase *subjects to a detriment*. This also brings the victimisation provisions into line with the growing number of victimisation provisions provided by Part V of the Employment Rights Act 1996, which cover areas such as whistle blowing, jury service, health and safety, Sunday working, family leave and working time rights.

The choice of wording brings problems. It means that the element of 'detriment' is no longer confined to one aspect of employment, but can now be applied legitimately to all cases of victimisation, thus endorsing the *Derbyshire* logic. Moreover, the phrase facilitates the misconceived notion, again from *Derbyshire*, that the focus should be on the *gravity*, and hence the *reasonableness*, of the defendant's conduct. As such, under section 27, courts could now consider the seriousness of the conduct irrespective of whether the conduct related to, say, 'opportunities for transfer' or 'any other benefits' of employment. If they conclude that pressure to compromise, or abandon, proceedings was 'fair and temperate', or that the withholding of a reference was a 'reasonable response', or that a suspension of a benefit or promotion opportunity was done upon 'reasonable' legal advice, or even just part of the general policy invoked against *all* litigants, the *Derbyshire* logic suggests they may conclude that the claimant had suffered no 'detriment'.

Such a misconceived notion of detriment not only jars with a literal reading of the statute, it is also at odds with the legislative history of section 27. In its response to its Consultation, the Government stated:

> We recommended ending the need for a comparator through aligning with the approach in employment law because this offers a more effective, workable system – not one in which it would necessarily be easier to win a case, but one where attention rightly focused on considering whether the 'victim' suffered an absolute harm, irrespective of how others were being treated in the same circumstances.[123]

120 See n 6 and accompanying text.
121 See above, text to n 3.
122 See *Kirby v Manpower Services Commission* [1980] ICR 420 (EAT), overruled, *Aziz v Trinity Street Taxis* [1989] QB 463 (CA).
123 Government Equalities Office, The Equality Bill – Government response to the Consultation (Cm 7454, 2008) para 735. See also, Department for Communities and Local Government, Discrimination Law Review. A Framework for Fairness: Proposals for a Single Equality Bill for Great Britain. A Consultation Paper (June 2007), para 161.

Subsequently, the Explanatory Notes to the Equality Bill, and the resulting Act, provided this example of victimisation: 'A woman makes a complaint of sex discrimination against her employer. As a result, she is denied promotion. The denial of promotion would amount to victimisation'.[124]

Assuming the 'complaint' amounts to proceedings, the facts of this example are on all fours with *Cornelius*, the only difference being the denial of a promotion rather than a transfer. More generally, it suggests that a 'normal', or 'reasonable', reaction to litigation does not necessarily exonerate the defendant. This is so, even where the reaction is one taken against all litigants, whether or not they are complaining of discrimination. We have yet to see whether the courts will defer to this legislative history or whether they continue to assess these 'litigation cases' by their pre-existing standards.

A better amendment would have been to replace the comparative element with the phrase *treats unfavourably*. This should be accompanied by a replacement of the phrase *any other detriment* with a 'catch-all' phrase *other employment-related treatment*,[125] thus signalling that its purpose merely is to ensure that the unfavourable treatment was employment-related. Of course, for the avoidance of doubt, it would be better if these purposes were spelt out. Unless otherwise expressed in the legislation, this will catch cases where the claimant is harmed or deterred, or where third parties are deterred.

Alternative formulas and theories

The consistent factor in *Khan* and *St Helens* is the House of Lords' sympathy with the 'reasonable' employer's dilemma. But the theories used for delivering this sympathy are technically unsound, capricious, and thus create another fuzzy border for equality law. If, as these decisions suggest, policy dictates that employers should have some scope to defend proceedings, an alternative theory and/or drafting of victimisation is required.

Parallels with direct and indirect discrimination

In both *Nagarajan* and *Board of Governors*, one reason for rejecting the benign motive defence was the analogy with the 'parallel' provision of direct

124 Explanatory Notes to the Equality Bill 2008, para 105. Explanatory Notes to the Equality Act 2010, para 106, and the Revised Explanatory Notes (October 2010) to the Equality 2010, para 103.

125 This should encompass work-related treatment delivered outside of work. See e.g. *Berry v Stevenson* 74 F 3d 980 (10th Cir 1996) and *Rochon v Gonzales* 438 F 3d 1211 (DC Cir 2006) (both digested in text et al accompanying n 143). Employment-related victimisation, harassment and discrimination against *ex-workers* is covered by a free-standing provision codifying Case C-185/97 *Coote v Granada* ECR-I 5199 (see text to n 97): Equality Act 2010, s 108 and *Rowstock Ltd v Jessemey* [2014] 1 WLR 3615 *Rowstock Ltd v Jessemey* (CA) 'correcting' an obvious drafting error.

discrimination, where such a defence strictly is outlawed.[126] It was noted above that only direct discrimination carries specific defences, which undermines the analogy, although this difference did not facilitate a benign motive defence in victimisation claims.[127]

However, the employer's predicament provides a clue to a more fundamental flaw in an analogy. The employer's argument in defence of its policy to deny a reference or grievance process is two-fold. First, it wants to defend its case properly. Second, it is a general policy that does not single out those who complain of discrimination. This second argument provides the clue. If the policy is of general application, then it is arguable that it is neutral on its face. This makes it more akin to *indirect* discrimination, which, of course, carries a general justification defence, which would accommodate an employer's benign motive. In the US case, *EEOC v Huber*,[128] a worker sued for discriminatory dismissal and in response her employer withheld her retirement benefits because she sought reinstatement. This was because if the employer paid benefits to persons who had a realistic possibility of being reinstated, the tax-exempt status of the plan could be lost for all participants. This was the policy for *all* dismissed workers who sought reinstatement, not just for those whose claims were based on discrimination. The court held that the policy was permissible because it 'appears to be significantly related to a legitimate business concern'.[129]

The court embraced the employer's 'benign motive' defence by treating the case as one of indirect discrimination. This was achieved by analysing the policy as a facially neutral one, which affected *any* dismissed worker seeking reinstatement.[130]

This is an attractive approach which equally could be applied to *Cornelius, Khan, Sparrow*,[131] *Board of Governors*, and *New York City Transit*, because, as in *Huber*, general policies to suspend a grievance process or withhold a reference would affect all workers who issued proceedings, not just those claiming discrimination. But this conclusion starkly contrasts with the analysis in *Board of Governors*, which reasoned that 'broadening' a policy made it no less effective against the plaintiff.

So, here are two apparently logical conclusions that conflict. Any reconciliation comes from understanding that each is half-right. *Huber* may appear to be an unconventional decision, but in fact it perpetuates the notion that discrimination and victimisation are parallel concepts, which facilitates the direct/indirect discrimination analysis for victimisation cases. The error with this analysis is that in most conventional discrimination cases there is a protected class identifiable by one single characteristic, be it sex, sexual orientation, religion, or

126 See text to n 57 (UK) and n 56 (US) respectively.
127 See text to n 70.
128 927 F 2d 1322 (5th Cir 1991).
129 Ibid., 1330.
130 Further explained in a rehearing 942 F 2d 930, 933–934 (5th Cir 1991).
131 See text to n 12.

race, etc. Normally, it is a straightforward task to distinguish a facially discriminatory practice from a facially neutral one.[132] The reason for this is that the protected class is easily identified by a single factor, be it the sex, sexual orientation, religion, or race, of the claimant. By contrast, the protected persons in victimisation cases are identified by what they have *done*: the protected activity. And in the instant cases, the protected activity requires two factors to be identified: (1) issuing proceedings and (2) for discrimination.[133] The challenged practice, triggered by just 'issuing proceedings', is *in part,* facially neutral and in part facially discriminatory, as in these cases the nature of the proceedings is discrimination. So *Huber* was half-right in identifying *claiming reinstatement* as the (facially neutral) ground of the retaliation, and *Board of Governors* was half right when identifying an *age discrimination* complaint (facially discriminatory) as the ground for the retaliation. The court in *Huber* omitted the facially discriminatory element whilst in *Board of Governors* the court omitted the facially neutral element. For victimisation, the distinction between direct and indirect discrimination becomes, once again, 'fuzzy at the border'[134] and analogies with direct *or* indirect discrimination theory are not particularly rational or helpful.

Parallels with victimisation by proxy

A more appropriate and useful analogy can be made with disability discrimination, which has its own solution to 'fuzzy border' scenarios. Disability discrimination is prone to 'fuzzy border' cases because frequently apparently neutral policies are directed at a manifestation of a disability, rather than the disability itself. Examples include a restaurant's *no dogs* rule,[135] or a *no wheelchairs* rule.[136] These examples compare with some victimisation cases, where the employer's apparently neutral policy is directed at a manifestation of the worker's protected act (proceedings) rather than the nature of the act (*discrimination* proceedings). These cases are also on the fuzzy border between direct and indirect discrimination.[137]

132 But see Lord Bridge in *James v Eastleigh BC* [1990] AC 751 (HL), 764, who held that as reference to 'pensionable age' was 'convenient shorthand' for sex discrimination. See also *International Union v Johnson Controls* 11 S Ct 1196, 1203–1204 (Sup Ct 1991).

133 Alternatively, this could be (1) reporting wrongdoing of (2) unlawful discrimination; or (1) giving evidence in support of a colleague (2) in that colleague's discrimination claim; and so on.

134 A phrase used by Cudahy J to describe the similar problem with disability discrimination law: *McWright v Alexander* 982 F 2d 222, 228 (7th Cir 1992).

135 Minister of State for Social Security and Disabled People, 253 HC Official Report (6th series) col 150, 24 Jan 1995. See also *Sullivan v Valllejo City Unified School District* 731 F Supp 947, 958 (ED Cal 1990) (school ban on service dogs).

136 *McWright v Alexander* 982 F 2d 222, 228 (7th Cir 1992).

137 In *Huber,* the manifestation was the claim for reinstatement.

The solution for disability law is provided by an additional model of discrimination. In the United States, under the federal Americans with Disabilities Act 1990, courts developed a hybrid model of discrimination: direct discrimination *by proxy*, aimed at treatment 'directed at an effect or manifestation of a handicap'.[138] It carries a justification defence.[139] In the UK, the Equality Act 2010, section 15 provides a similarly-worded hybrid theory known as *discrimination arising from disability*.

In a similar way, some victimisation cases are more accurately analysed as *victimisation by proxy*. The manifestation of the protected act is the issuing of legal proceedings, which is the target of the employer's retaliatory policy. But the policy is related to the protected act, and so should attract scrutiny under the victimisation laws. Although this theory provides a neater analysis of these victimisation cases, its chief attraction, and perhaps practical benefit, is its justification defence.

The justification defence

The next issue is defining the justification defence for this purpose. The standard justification formula – used in equal pay and indirect discrimination cases – requires the employer to show that the policy is genuine (legitimate aim), appropriate and necessary (proportionate). This is known as the '*Bilka* test'.[140] The formula requires the aim to be 'irrespective' of the protected ground, e.g. sex or race etc.[141] Here, because the prime facie victimisation is related to a protected act, the defence cannot necessarily be 'irrespective' of the protected act – by its nature, the defence must have more leeway than usual. Nevertheless, it should be able to be applied with some coherence, as the 'legitimate aim' should be related to the 'manifestation' of the protected act, such as legal proceedings, whatever their nature. If the aim were related to the nature of discrimination proceedings (e.g. sex or race etc.), then there should be liability under 'direct' victimisation, or even direct (e.g. sex or *race*) discrimination.

Take the scenarios where the employer has suspended a grievance process or denied a reference, with the stated aim of defending itself in the forthcoming trial. This response is likely to be genuine if it is no more than an invocation of a general policy that applies across a class of cases, not just discrimination ones. If it were invoked for the first time in a discrimination case, it would be suspicious.[142]

138 *McWright v Alexander* 982 F 2d 222, 228 (7th Cir 1992).
139 Under the ADA 1990, both indirect and direct discrimination are justifiable. See, EEOC 29 CFR § 1630.15 (available at www.eeoc.gov), and e.g. *Ethridge v State of Alabama* 860 F Supp 808, 817 (MD Ala 1993).
140 Case 170/84 *Bilka-Kaufhaus v Weber von Hartz* [1987] ECR 1607, [36].
141 Case 96/80 *Jenkins v Kingsgate* [1981] ECR 911, [11]; Case 170/84 *Bilka-Kaufhaus v Weber von Hartz* [1987] ECR 1607, [37].
142 It would also provide evidence of a discriminatory intent, suggesting a case of 'direct' victimisation, or even direct discrimination.

The response should be appropriate. This rules out underhand or even illegal tactics (and so in part coincides with the *honest and reasonable* test.) Two American cases illustrate this. In *Berry v Stevenson Chevrolet*,[143] a sales manager paid his sales staff their due bonuses out of his own pocket, and later, when the manufactures' cheque arrived, he forged a signature and cashed it for himself. His employer discovered the forgery and formed a reasonable suspicion that the manager had committed a fraud. Later, the manager sued for racial discrimination. The employer retaliated by reporting the suspected fraud to the police. The manager was acquitted of any criminal wrongdoing and his claim for victimisation succeeded. Similarly, in *Rochon v Gonzales*,[144] the FBI was held to have victimised an agent (who had previously complained of racial harassment) by refusing, contrary to policy, to investigate death threats a federal prisoner made against the agent and his wife. The conclusion reached by the House of Lords in *St Helens* also accords with this analysis, as the employer acted inappropriately by 'going public'.[145]

The response should also be necessary to achieve the aim. An employer cannot try to win at all costs. The indications from *Cornelius, Khan,* and *St Helens,* are that the employer is permitted to do what the courts consider is normal legal practice. A further consideration at the 'necessity' stage is weighing the employer's needs against the harm done, such as damage to the claimant, and/or the deterrent effect on the claimant and others.

This provides a neat, technically sound solution that restores some logic and certainty to the law. Its merit is that it would encompass *all* genuine and proportionate reactions to litigation, even those undreamt of, or not strictly related to defending the claim, such as in *Huber*.[146] This would allow the courts – legitimately – to evaluate each defence on its merits according to known and predictable criteria.

There would remain less predictable borderline cases, such as where issues other than those litigated were also part of the grievance (*Board of Governors*).[147] An employer may show that it is impossible to untangle the facts relating to both matters and so a grievance process for the unlitigated matter could compromise its defence of the litigated matter. Here, at least the parties would know by what criteria the case would be judged.

The demerit of this general justification defence is that it would hand to the courts formally a discretion over policy and could legitimise other undreamt-of or pernicious arguments that have nothing to do with defending litigation. Indeed the Court of Appeal in *St Helens* accepted that the employer had acted honestly and reasonably by making its 'effective threat' to the claimants.[148] This

143 74 F 3d 980, 986 (10th Cir. 1996).
144 438 F 3d 1211, 1213 (DC Cir 2006).
145 See text to n 72.
146 See text to n 128.
147 See text to n 17.
148 [2006] ICR 90, [49], [55], and [75]. See generally text to n 72. For an argument that the conduct amounted to contempt of court see M Connolly, 'Reinterpreting *Khan*: Easy case makes bad law' (2007) 36 *ILJ* 364, 372.

prompts a notion of a narrower justification defence, confined to defending the claimant's litigation. But this would exclude defences worthy of consideration, such as that in *Huber*, and so should be discarded. The optimum solution, it seems, is to combine the objective justification defence with some specified examples of what is and what is not permissible. This allows Parliament to dictate policy while leaving scope for unpredicted or innovative defences to be assessed by common criteria.

One or two causes of action?

If victimisation by proxy were the only cause of action, every defendant would have a chance to justify its conduct, no matter how pernicious the retaliation. Thus, it would be better to preserve the original provision – 'direct victimisation' – with the suggested amendments,[149] accompanied by guidance, similar to that provided for direct discrimination in the DDA 1995,[150] confining it to where the unfavourable treatment was in response to the protected act, rather than a manifestation of it. A technical concern here is that it is hard to imagine a case like this that does not amount also to a case of direct discrimination. For instance, an employer who singles out for victimisation a worker who complains of racial discrimination is acting *on the ground of race*, even where that worker complained on behalf of a colleague. This implies that a *direct victimisation* provision would be redundant. However, this coincidence will be less common in cases where direct discrimination must on the ground of the *complainant's* sex, or gender reassignment, or age. For example, an employer may deny a pay rise to a male worker for giving evidence in support of female colleague's sexual harassment complaint. The victimisation was not on the ground of the witnesses' sex and so could not amount to direct sex discrimination under the present definition. Thus, a direct victimisation provision should be preserved for these grounds at least, and to avoid any undreamt-of cases escaping liability, it would be better to preserve it in all the statutes.

Recommendations

1 Reframe the existing victimisation definition, with the qualification that it applies only to 'direct' victimisation. Guidance on this should be provided in a similar way to that provided for direct discrimination under the DDA 1995.[151] The comparative element should be repealed as planned, but replaced with *treats unfavourably*, rather than the proposed *cause a detriment.*

149 That is, replace the comparative element with *treats unfavourably* and *any other detriment* with *other employment-related treatment*, see text to n 125.

150 Explanatory Notes to *the pre-consultation draft* Regulations (now Disability Discrimination Act (Amendment) Regulations 2003 SI 2003/1673), § 32.

151 Ibid.

2 Enact an additional cause of action: *victimisation by proxy*, with a general justification defence based on the *Bilka* model, but with some defences specified as lawful or unlawful.
3 The purpose of the provisions should be expressed in the legislation, which is to ensure that workers can enforce the discrimination legislation without fear of deterrents. These workers include complainants, those who support them, and third parties who could be deterred from making or supporting complaints in the future. For example, where other workers could be deterred by the employer's action, it is not necessary for the claimant to suffer tangible harm for liability.[152] This will enable a tribunal to order that the employer cease the challenged practice, and provide costs for the claimant.
4 Replace the phrase *any other detriment* in the employment sections with *other employment-related treatment.*
5 Consider reversing the time-bar rule in *Robinson v Post Office*,[153] and enact a rule that time begins to run in the normal way after the grievance process has been exhausted.[154]

Conclusion

The two scenarios, and the variations discussed, are representative of the victimisation dilemma. At present, the statutory formula provides no leeway for the employer's position. Yet courts sympathetic to employers have dictated policy and provided them a benign motive defence, under a variety of guises: the covert use of the *Kirby* comparator, the distinction between the bringing and existence of proceedings, the requirement for a tangible detriment, the honest and reasonable conduct 'defence' and the notion such conduct causes no harm. This has produced an incoherent and technically flawed body of case law.

The fault does not lie entirely with the courts. They have been compelled to squeeze a broad range of cases into a single constrained statutory formula, which does not envisage the more subtle facts represented by the two scenarios. Thus, at the heart of the problem is the statutory formula and absence of policy expressed by Parliament.

Victimisation requires redefining to recognise different classes of victimisation and provide leeway for employers to defend litigation, but under a predictable and controlled regime. The predictability would benefit employers and claimants alike.

This chapter poses more policy questions than it solves. But these questions require solutions. It would be better for Parliament to do this than the courts to carry on ad hoc under the present statutory definition with the inevitability of

152 Of course, a claimant will need to do this to claim damages.
153 [2000] IRLR 804, [29]–[31].
154 Recommended by Browne-Wilkinson J: *Bodha v Hampshire AHA* [1982] ICR 200, 205F–G (EAT).

creating this fuzzy border between the respective rights of defendant and claimant. Parliament can decide more precisely where the line should be drawn between the conflicting interests. It can research and single out particular scenarios and designate particular responses as lawful or unlawful. However, the overriding principle in this exercise must be the purpose of this law, which is to ensure that workers can enforce the discrimination legislation without fear of deterrents. The tension between this principle and an employer's right to defend litigation is not *fully* resolvable. But a new regime would at least ease the tension somewhat by defining policy and providing clearer and predictable boundaries.

Index

Note: locators followed by "n" refer foot notes.

For Product Safety Concerns and Information please contact our EU representative GPSR@taylorandfrancis.com
Taylor & Francis Verlag GmbH, Kaufingerstraße 24, 80331 München, Germany

www.ingramcontent.com/pod-product-compliance
Lightning Source LLC
LaVergne TN
LVHW021124300926
849160LV00010B/846
* 9 7 8 1 0 3 2 0 3 4 8 6 7 *